# DI...
# IN T...

An Excursion Into
## The American Museum
## of Natural History
### DOUGLAS J. PRESTON

"A delightful book filled with fascinating stories,
anecdotes, and personalities. Highly recommended."

*Library Journal*

"*Dinosaurs in the Attic* is much more than its title claims.
It celebrates natural history museums as testimonials to
Man's heroism and curiosity. Preston has captured with
wit, charm, and sensitivity the pulse of an institution.
. . . Not just chronicle, nor even history—it is literature,
and a damn good read!"

Dr. Charles R. Crumly
Museum of Comparative Zoology,
Harvard University

"Conveys the feeling of excitement and unflagging
curiosity of those working behind the scenes to add to
mankind's knowledge of the natural world . . . Readable
and informative."

Lorin Nevling, Jr.
Director Emeritus,
Field Museum of Natural History, Chicago

# DINOSAURS IN THE ATTIC

## An Excursion Into The American Museum of Natural History

### DOUGLAS J. PRESTON

BALLANTINE BOOKS • NEW YORK

*Grateful acknowledgment is made for permission to quote from the following:*

On pages 276ff, copyright © 1928 Saturday Evening Post. Used with permission.
On page 78, *The Fossil Feud* by Elizabeth Noble Shor, published by Exposition Press, 1974. Used with permission.

The photographs are all reproduced courtesy of the American Museum of Natural History.

Library of Congress Catalog Card Number: 86-13478

ISBN 0-345-34732-3

This edition published by arrangement with St. Martin's Press, Inc.

Manufactured in the United States of America

First Ballantine Books Edition: January 1988

Cover photos: Negative No. 315109 (Tyrannosaurus Rex)
     Transparency No. 13056 (Photo by R. Sheridan)
     Courtesy of The Department of Library Services,
     American Museum of Natural History

*For Mom and Dad*
*and*
*The Magic School*

# Contents

# Acknowledgments

I would like to thank a number of people for their assistance. Alan Ternes, Editor of *Natural History*, and Kate Bennett-Mendez had the dubious wisdom to hire me; Alan compounded the error by giving me a column in the magazine, from which this book sprang. Dr. Thomas D. Nicholson, Director of the Museum, was a great supporter and inspiration. Although a discussion of his dynamic and highly effective tenure is beyond the scope of this book, I would in any case like to acknowledge my debt to him here. I would like to express my deep appreciation to my aunt and uncle, Anna and Bob Taggart, for luring me to New York City many years ago and buying the suit for my first job interviews, without which I would undoubtedly still be buttering toast at the Newton-Wellesley Nursing Home. Finally, I must thank Lincoln Child, my editor at St. Martin's Press, for proposing this book in the first place and for his peerless editorial guidance. I have had many editors and, without question, he has been the best.

There are many others who deserve mention here. David R. Ryus III, former Vice-President of the Museum and a close friend, deserves special thanks. Marshall Schwartzmann read first drafts of chapters and offered excellent editorial advice, saving me from embarrassment at my publisher. I also thank Ann Metcalfe, Chairwoman for Development and Public Affairs at the Museum, for reading the entire manuscript and offering suggestions. I thank Lelia Wardwell, Elisa Rothstein, and others who assisted with research. The Museum Library and its able staff under the superb direction of Nina Root were terribly patient with me during my labors, and most helpful. I acknowledge the Wang VS-80 computer for its help, although I did not appreciate its erasing seventy-five pages of my manuscript late one night. I thank the following scientists for allowing me interviews and/or reading sections of the manuscript: Dr. Jerome G. Rozen, Jr.; Dr. Malcolm McKenna; Dr. Stanley Freed (who was exceptionally helpful); Dr. Harry Shapiro; Dr. Charles Myers; Dr. David Hurst Thomas; Dr. Guy Musser; Dr. Lee Herman; Dr. Martin Prinz; Dr. George Harlow; Mr. Joe Peters; Dr. Betty Faber; Miss Alice Gray; Mrs. Barbara Conklin; Dr. Pedro Wygodzinsky; Mr. Helmut Sommer; Mr. Bill Coull; Mr. Paul Beelitz; Mr. Anibal Rodriguez; Ms. Peggy Cooper; and many others. In addition, I'd like to thank Herb Kurz for advice (and for his future efforts publicizing the book); I wish to express my appreciation to Ernestine Weindorf for being a classy dame; I thank my former associates at *Natural History*, including Tom Page for being such a great guy and Florence Edelstein for trying to teach me to not split infinitives; Colleen Mehegan for carrying the torch; Bob DeAngelis and Marc Breslav for keeping things going during my leave of absence; and Lillian Berger for her honest and forceful opinion of my dreadful handwriting. I acknowledge Peggy Nicoll because she'll kill me if I don't. I thank my brothers Dick and David for leaving me with an intact cerebrum after all our childhood brawls; I thank Michelle Preston for translating the Latin on page 223, which was too obscene to include; and Dr. Charles R. Crumly for explaining cladistics, among other things. I also express my deep thanks to my grandparents for passing on such excellent genes. And last but not least, I acknowledge J. G. Studholme, Chairman and Managing Director of Editions Alecto

Ltd. (simply because I thought it prudent to mention the man who is currently paying my salary).

I alone must take responsibility for any errors and faults in this book.

# Preface

*Dinosaurs in the Attic* is divided into two parts. The first focuses on the explorers, scientists, and collectors who accumulated the Museum's vast collections. It tells the stories of some of the Museum's famous expeditions—as well as some of its more obscure. (Considering that there were over one thousand expeditions to choose from, I have of necessity been highly selective.)

The second part is something of a walking tour of the Museum, the most discursive armchair ramble imaginable; we will talk with curators, explore vaults and storage rooms, take sudden and unexpected leaps in space and time, choose strange or unusual objects and tell their histories. I have been unashamedly guided by whim and prejudice. I am sure cries will be raised in the Museum about my blatant omission of one thing or another. There is nothing here about Margaret Mead, for example, perhaps the most famous curator in the Museum's history. Nor is there much about the science of ichthyology, one of the important disciplines studied in the Museum. The chapter on birds is very short and does not do justice to the Museum's seminal research in ornithology. On the other hand, I have devoted copious passages to insects, which I happen to find extremely interesting. Terribly important people in the Museum's history, such as Theodore Roosevelt, have been neglected, while I have written pages about some of the most obscure characters imaginable—people like the free-lance dinosaur hunter Charles Sternberg, whom almost no one has ever heard of.

At first the reader may see here not a book, but a strange and wild collection of stories, histories, and anecdotes. This cannot be helped. Often the first-time visitor to the Museum sees only a confusing welter of objects. It is my great hope, however, that the reader will find this book —and this Museum—to be not so much a mass of objects and specimens, but rather a complex web of science and history, of human passions, of grand accomplishments and failures, of half-cocked ideas and brilliant insights.

The Museum is physically compact. All of its buildings sit on a sixteen-acre parcel of ground. This is, of course, deceptive. The Museum, in its largest sense, is a diffuse, sprawling, complex and ineffable thing, whose real boundaries extend to the farthest corners of the earth. It is not, by any means, a single entity. While looking back in time may give us the impression of planned and rational growth, in truth the Museum grew in an irregular fashion, driven along by the diverse loves and passions of its myriad explorers, scientists, administrators, and benefactors, all of whom had different ideas of what the Museum was and should be. A straightforward, chronological history of the Museum could capture neither its true nature nor its spirit. Besides, it would have made a boring book. We will instead explore the Museum through many different eyes, and rummage about in its fascinating past.

This book is not so much about "collections," perhaps, as about the people and passions behind them. You will not learn much about the Widmanstätten structure of iron meteorites from reading this book, or much about dinosaur evolution or universal classification. You will learn, instead, about the man who collected more dinosaurs than any other person who ever lived, and the explorer who risked his life to discover the largest meteorite in the world, and the beach bum who stole a priceless sapphire. You will read about a young explorer who became unhinged and killed his guide, and another who gave his life for his work. You will read about a British baron who lost his beloved collection of birds because of a blackmailer. If you look behind and beyond the glass display cases of the famous halls, you will learn more about human passions than about birds and butterflies and mummies.

That is what this book is all about.

Any attempt at enumeration of the items in the collections quickly becomes absurd. Butterflies? The Museum has 2 million of them (in addition to its 1.6 million beetles, 800,000 flies, 1 million spiders, and 5.5 million wasps). Bones? The Museum stores roughly 50 million of them, including 330,000 fossil vertebrates, 100 complete elephants, and the largest skeletal collection of Manhattan aborigines, among others.

It also has one million birds, 600,000 fishes in jars of alcohol, one thirty-ton meteorite, eight million anthropological artifacts, one balding tarantula named Blondie, two skulls of *Tyrannosaurus rex*, several dozen dinosaur eggs, 4,000 Asian shadow puppets, 264,000 amphibians and reptiles, a stuffed gray parrot that once belonged to Houdini, the skeleton of Jumbo the elephant, 120,000 rocks and minerals, the Star of India sapphire, a grasshopper found on the observation deck of the eighty-eighth floor of the Empire State Building, 8.5 million invertebrates, one Copper Man, 250,000 mammals, and one dodo bird.

There are also, I am told, 17 elevators, 35,000 electrical outlets, 800 air conditioners, 400,000 square feet of glass, 25 acres of floor space, 200 scientists and technicians, 600 employees, 1,000 volunteers, and in excess of 650 rooms. Although the Museum's exhibits cover 700,000 square feet of floor space, only about one or two percent of the collection is on display. The rest is carefully organized, preserved, and squirreled away in hundreds of vaults, storerooms, and attics throughout the Museum's twenty-three interconnected buildings.

The Museum defies reasonable description and enumeration. It possesses the most spiders, the most beetles, the most dinosaur bones, the most fossil mammals, the most whales, the most plant bugs, and the most birds of any museum in the world. It has the largest hippo on record (Caliph, who died in a zoo in 1908 of acute indigestion); the largest collection of skunks in formaldehyde, the largest collection of non-Western smoking pipes; the largest crab (twelve feet from tip to tip); Raffles, a starling that spoke more languages than any other bird; the longest elephant tusks; a hermaphroditic moth (left side male, right side female); the longest single piece of Peruvian cloth (about 4,500 years old and replete with ancient mummified lice); the most slowly cooled meteorite known (the Emery, found by sex researcher Alfred Kinsey); the largest collection of gall wasps (5.5 million, also collected by Kinsey); the finest collection of birds of paradise; the finest uncut emerald; the largest piece of polished jade; the largest azurite specimen (the Singing Stone, weighing 4.5 tons); the only red topaz; the largest cut gemstone (the Brazilian Princess); the only two *Pachycephalosaurus* skulls in existence; and the best fossil horse collection.

Far from being a gigantic attic of seldom-seen curiosities, these collections are the lifeblood of the research that is being done at the Museum and, indeed, in the worldwide scientific community. The Museum loans out thousands of specimens a year to scientists all over the world, and hundreds of scientists come to study the collections in New York.

Over the last several decades, the Museum has come to realize that the collections are not only more fragile than previously thought, but also far more valuable. Specimens preserved in fluids, artifacts of wood, leather, metal, feathers, and textiles, require constant care and are very expensive to stabilize and store. Furthermore, large sections of the Museum's collections have become absolutely priceless from a scientific point of view, since they could never be replaced or duplicated. The final compounding problem is that much of these collections, once considered worthless monetarily, have become highly sought after by private collectors and dealers who pay hundreds of thousands of dollars for even mediocre artifacts—adding additional security requirements in a museum not designed for high-security storage.

Over the last fifteen years alone, to conserve and stabilize the collection and provide secure, well-organized storage, the Museum has spent in excess of $39 million, and over the next ten years an additional *$57 million* is expected to be spent before the stabilization is complete. Even when finished, additional millions will be required to maintain the collection.

Just as Sherlock Holmes reconstructed a crime by examining the clues, so a scientist can reconstruct evolution or figure out how a species fits into the staggeringly complex pattern of life on earth by looking at collections. These collections are the *corpus delicti* of natural science, but they are more than just courtroom evidence; many have great beauty or rarity, or represent nature in its most extravagant forms. And the anthropological artifacts are a record of what many peoples created and believed before their cultures were destroyed or changed by the modern world.

Was all this material collected for the sake of science? Of course. But the urge to collect goes deeper than this. It is a part of our very nature as human beings. When dinosaur eggs were first discovered by Roy Chapman Andrews in Outer Mongolia in 1922, the world was astonished. But Andrews wasn't the first to make this discovery. Twenty thousand years earlier, humans in the area had collected dinosaur eggs, fashioned them into little squares, and placed them in graves. Our almost atavistic urge to collect, as Kenneth Clark said, is "a biological function not unrelated to our physical appetites."

So, let us take a look at the myriad ghosts in residence at the greatest *collection* of all—in the American Museum of Natural History. And, if you're prepared to get a little fossil dust on your clothes, the tour is leaving right away.

A map of the Bone Cabin Quarry, c. 1904. This great concentration of dinosaur skeletons originated in an ancient Jurassic river bar. The Diplodocus limb shown in photograph 14, which was the first cut made into the quarry, is taken from a section of the map to the south of this reproduction.

# Part One

# THE HISTORY

As I write this, I am in New York City, sitting in a deck chair on the roof of a building physically larger than the Empire State Building. It is sunset. Central Park stretches before me, a cold expanse of leafless trees, winding paths, and dark ponds; just the tips of the bare branches catch the autumn light. Beyond the park is a row of buildings along Fifth Avenue, their windows flashing gold, reflecting the setting sun. To my left I can see West 81st Street, with its row of elegant old apartment buildings, and behind me stretches a patchwork of Upper West Side rooftops. Beyond the rooftops, straight down 79th Street, lies the Hudson River, heaving slowly along like the gray back of some ancient, sluggish reptile.

I am on the roof of the largest private museum in the world—the American Museum of Natural History. Below me lies a fantastic complex of intersecting rooflines, greenhouses, Gothic arches, and towers festooned with

3

granite eagles and copper globes. Far below are hidden courtyards, tiny parking lots, dumpsters, and low roofs. I can see people working behind hundreds of windows grayed with Manhattan soot: hunched over desks, typing on computer terminals, or fussing with animals in aquaria.

Beneath me, somewhere in this vast maze of buildings —the largest repository of scientific collections in the world—is a beetle. This beetle is no bigger than a grain of sand; to the naked eye it is merely a brown dot, the size of the period at the end of this sentence. Sandwiched between glass on a slide, it can be identified only with the aid of a microscope.

I have chosen this fellow—perversely, you might think —as the starting point for our exploration of this gigantic and unclassifiable storehouse of nature. I have chosen it because it is the meanest, tiniest, and ugliest specimen I could find in the Museum. Indeed, the beetle seems to lack any redeeming quality whatsoever; aside from being small and insignificant, it is also boring.

This creature is a common insect known to science as *Bambara intricata*. It belongs to the family of "feather-wing" beetles, so called because they possess long feathery hairs on their wings. These hairs enable them to drift on the wind, much like dandelion seeds. This particular specimen is locked up with moth flakes in a clean white cabinet along with tens of thousands of other insects. Like all the Museum's specimens, it is carefully preserved to last for an eternity—or at least for as long as modern technology can afford.

This species spends its three-week life span buried in the decaying litter of the forest floor, feeding mostly on fungus spores. It is a peaceful insect, neither an annoying pest nor a crop destroyer. Although it is extremely common (literally billions can be found in most continents of the world), its existence is unknown to all humanity save for a dozen or so entomologists; and of these, only two or three have any *real* interest in the bug. As I sit on the roof of this Museum and consider that here, beneath me, are some of the most beautiful, rare, and extravagant creations of nature and man, I wonder what could possibly be important enough about this little beetle to warrant its inclusion in the Museum's collections.

To answer this question, we must look back thirty or so years to the discovery of *Bambara intricata*. This particular bug hails from the Bimini islands, a low, windswept string of cays in the Bahamas, not far from Florida. In 1947 the Museum established a research station on North Bimini (now closed) named the Lerner Marine Laboratory. Before then, the area had seen little scientific exploration, and only two insects had been reported from the island: the mosquito (whose presence was immediately and unpleasantly apparent to the visitor) and a pretty species of butterfly. Thus, one of the first priorities was to do an insect "inventory" of the islands to collect and record the species that lived there. In 1951 a group of Museum entomologists went to Bimini and spent four months luring and trapping as many insects as they could, using nets, funnels, ultraviolet lights, and white sheets. When they were finished they had collected 109,718 insects and 27,839 arachnids, including thousands of featherwing beetles. (To capture the featherwings, they used an ingenious contraption called a Berlese funnel, which drives tiny insects out of decaying leaves, bark, and soil.) They caught so many tiny featherwings that the beetles "formed a black cloud" when the collecting vials of alcohol were shaken.

Among these thousands of specimens, the Museum scientists found that six species of feathering beetle were present on the island. Eventually the vials of alcohol were transferred to the main entomology storage area in New York City, where for fifteen years they rested in a dark cabinet.

In the mid-sixties, someone finally took an interest in the insects. A curator at the Field Museum of Natural History in Chicago, Henry Dybas, borrowed a number of the vials containing the featherwings for a research project on a strange phenomenon known as parthenogenesis—the reproduction of an animal without fertilization by the male. Dybas had evidence that many species of the featherwing beetle exist in all-female populations, reproducing without the aid of males. He wanted to examine a large number of specimens collected at the same time to see if indeed they were all female. In doing so, he developed several startling theories.

Through his examination of featherwing beetles, Dybas was able to illuminate the complex workings of a small corner of the natural world. He wondered, for example, why the beetles were so small. He wanted to know why many species or populations seemed to have done away with males. Finally, he had observed that the featherwing beetles from Bimini had no feather wings, even though the same species on the mainland possessed them. After some thought, Dybas came up with an interesting interlocking theory that explained these three questions.

First, he had reason to believe that the beetles had evolved from a larger into a smaller size, primarily because they needed to be light enough to float on the wind, and thus to occupy a niche in which smallness was an advantage. In becoming small, however, the featherwings could carry fewer and fewer eggs, since the eggs could not be "miniaturized" the way the insect could. Thus, the Bimini beetles lost the ability to carry thousands of eggs and produce many offspring at a single time, as most other insects do. Indeed, they became so small that the female was only able to carry one egg at a time. That single egg became much more biologically precious when it was the only one available—and thus the female had to ensure that it was fertilized and hatched. Unfortunately, this stricture made finding a male to fertilize the egg quickly rather important. Indeed, finding a male became such a matter of inconvenience for the female of a species with such limited mobility that the population eventually did away with males entirely. Instead, the egg matures *without* being fertilized, by the process called parthenogenesis. And when the males were bypassed in the reproductive process, they eventually died out.

To corroborate his theory, Dybas looked to see if other extremely small insects had developed parthenogenesis.

Just as he suspected, he found other species that had done away with males.

Next, he addressed the riddle of why 80 percent of the Bimini beetles lacked the feathery wings that were present on the same mainland species. The obvious answer came to him in a sudden flash. On a low, windswept island such as Bimini, beetles dispersed by air currents stood a great chance of being blown out to sea and certain death. (On the mainland, of course, dispersal would be a favorable adaptation, allowing the beetles to spread to new habitats.)

Dybas' research, however, did more than just prove his hypothesis. While researching his theories, Dybas examined one vial of American Museum specimens in detail, all supposedly of the same species. He noticed that a particular internal organ in some of them differed markedly from the same organ in others from the same vial. He realized that one of the groups was a new species, entirely unknown to science.

The science of zoology has established that certain things must be done when a new species is discovered. In the first step, the discoverer must select one organism as the "type" specimen. The type specimen then becomes the physical and legal representative of all of its kind. It will be the actual specimen the scientist uses to describe what the new species looks like, and it is the individual that all others will be compared or contrasted with, and measured against, for the rest of time. Today, most species of animal are represented somewhere by a type specimen, many of which date back several centuries or more.*

Thus, from the hundreds of specimens of the new insect, Dybas selected the most normal, the most *average* individual he could find, and designated it the type. In doing so, he made an utterly insignificant beetle—an almost invisible brown period—a scientifically priceless specimen. Underneath me somewhere is that tiny brown

---

*Homo sapiens* was lacking a type specimen until one waggish zoologist proclaimed his body as the type for the human species and issued directions that his body be preserved after death for the edification of future scientists.

beetle, locked in its cabinet, resting in perpetuity as the official representative of all of its kind.

The Museum is the guardian of thousands of such seemingly insignificant specimens, but as each bone in the mighty *Tyrannosaurus* is just a piece in the puzzle of the whole, each tiny bug is an indispensable link in the chain of knowledge that exists in the collections of the American Museum. Like the beetle, virtually every Museum specimen is invested with significance and a history. (Indeed, specimens without a history are often thrown out.) I opened this book with *B. intricata* because it is an example, in microcosm, of what the Museum is. Most of the Museum's more exciting specimens don't have the kind of calm, rational history that *B. intricata* possesses. Roy Chapman Andrews fought gun battles with Mongolian bandits to protect *his* dinosaur specimens; Carl Akeley lost his life in the Belgian Congo collecting for the Museum's African Hall; Fitzhugh Green lost his mind while searching for a continent that didn't exist. These stories seem superficially very different from the story of *B. intricata*—but they are all links in the vastly complex history of the American Museum.

# ONE

# The Museums That
# Almost Were

Abandoned and forgotten in the southern portion of New York's Central Park, not far from Tavern on the Green, lie buried giant, broken molds of dinosaurs and other prehistoric beasts. These molds are all that remain of an extravagant plan to create a huge Paleozoic Museum and outdoor exhibit in Central Park. Modeled after Sydenham Palace, a large glass building and park outside London, the museum was to have exhibited "specimens of animals of the pre-Adamite period," including dinosaurs, extinct mosasaurs and mastodons, giant sloths, and Irish elk. The foundation for this museum was actually excavated in the southwest corner of the park, opposite 63rd Street. It remains there to this day, covered with earth.

This was just one of many failed attempts to found a natural history museum in New York City. In the mid-nineteenth century, New York was rapidly becoming the financial center of the country, and many New Yorkers were amassing fortunes from railroads, banking, and other businesses during the expansion that followed the Civil War. These *nouveaux riches* were embarrassed by the conspicuous lack of cultural institutions in New York City. Most of the great cities of Europe boasted large natural history museums or "royal cabinets," as did many cities in America. Philadelphia had established the Academy of Natural Sciences in 1812, which was followed by the Smithsonian Institution in Washington, D.C., and the Boston Society of Natural History. Louis Agassiz' Museum of Comparative Zoology at Harvard, founded in 1859, was already renowned as the center of scientific learning in the United States. Men of science in Boston and Philadelphia scornfully dismissed New York as merely a center of crass commercialism, incapable of producing a museum of note.

There probably was some truth to this. During the first half of the nineteenth century, lack of interest killed most efforts to build a natural history museum in New York. Those efforts that did materialize were little more than miscellaneous collections of curiosities.

One of the first museums in New York to be completed was Delacourte's Cabinet of Natural History, founded in 1804. Delacourte's museum was typical of the so-called "cabinets of curiosities" prevalent during the eighteenth and nineteenth centuries. Its published catalog listed the "Natural Productions and Curiosities which Compose the Collections of the Cabinet" (a rather motley assortment, as it turned out). In the catalog, Delacourte complained: "There is scarce a city or town of any importance in Europe that is not possessed of a collection of that kind; but in the United States of America . . . there is scarcely a collection deserving of the name."

In the fashion of the time, Delacourte sought "subscriptions" to support his collecting endeavors—in particular, to finance his search for a mastodon somewhere in North America. Although a number of prominent New Yorkers subscribed token amounts, the largest contribution he received was three dollars. On the verge of bankruptcy, he finally sold his collection to Russia.

A few years later, one of Charles Willson Peale's sons (the elder Peale had founded the first museum in America, in Philadelphia) opened a Museum and Gallery of Fine Arts on lower Broadway. Its several galleries displayed paintings and various odd natural history items. A contemporary described it as having "very superior Cosmorana, several wax figures of good workmanship, fossil shells, minerals and miscellaneous curiosities." Like its fellow, this early museum also perished from lack of interest.

The idea of a natural history museum in New York finally began to attract attention with the opening of the Lyceum of Natural History at its headquarters on lower Broadway in 1836. A number of leading scientists joined the Lyceum, including John James Audubon, Alexander Agassiz, and Asa Gray. They met periodically at the Lyceum and delivered papers. Its collections were more systematically organized, and included such things as mastodon bones found in upstate New York, a sheep from the Rocky Mountains, a "catalogue of the vegetables growing within one hundred miles of New York City," minerals, snakes, fossils, plants, and shells. All this material was stored in sixty-two boxes. Unfortunately, the Lyceum became too dependent on the generosity of one man, John Jay, an amateur scientist and collector of rare books. (His fine collections of shells and natural history books are now at the American Museum of Natural History.) In an effort to broaden its support, the Lyceum sent a circular to a number of prominent New York businessmen, asking for money, but raised only seven hundred dollars in the attempt. The Lyceum and its growing financial problems were abruptly ended on May 21, 1866, when a fire totally destroyed its uninsured collections.

## The Great and Wonderful Paleozoic Museum

By far the most ambitious undertaking was the great Paleozoic Museum planned for Central Park. It was to be based on London's famous Crystal Palace, which had been erected for Queen Victoria's Diamond Jubilee and Great Exhibition of 1851. After the Great Exhibition closed, the Crystal Palace had been dismantled and moved to Sydenham Park, outside London, and a painter and sculptor named Benjamin Waterhouse Hawkins had been hired to make full-scale restorations of extinct creatures to decorate the grounds of the park. Working with Sir Richard Owen, the famous English paleontologist who coined the word *dinosauria*, Hawkins put together an ambitious plan that called for an outdoor park complete with pools, streams, and artificial geological formations populated with life-sized models of dinosaurs. The waters were designed to rise and fall like the tide, partially covering the creatures. Under Owen's guidance, Hawkins built a number of giant models, some weighing as much as thirty tons.

Sydenham Park caused quite a sensation.* News of the London dinosaurs reached the States, and soon caught the attention of the Board of Commissioners of Central Park. In 1868, Andrew Green, the head of the board, decided to build a similar Paleozoic museum in Central Park, which was then under planning and construction. "It gives me great pleasure," he wrote to Hawkins, "to propose to you to undertake the resuscitation of a group of animals of the former periods of the American continent." In 1868 the annual report of the Central Park commissioners waxed eloquent about the proposed project:

> For thousands of years men have dwelt upon the earth without even suspecting that it was a mighty tomb of animated races that once flourished upon it . . . Generations of the most gigantic and extraordinary creatures . . . huge fishes, enormous birds, monstrous reptiles, and ponderous uncouth mammals.

---

* On opening night, a dinner was held for twenty-one people in the belly of one of the iguanodons. The invitations were sent on an artificial pterodactyl wing, and the scientists at the dinner reportedly got so drunk that their boisterous singing could be heard across the entire park.

Green pushed hard for the project, calling it a monument to "the degree of culture and advancement" in the New York community. Not everyone, however, agreed with Green's vision of what constituted science. One less-than-enthusiastic scientist described the plan as a

> gloomy and half subterranean receptacle for restorations, a sort of fossil catacombs wherein the visitor, suppressing his dismay and encouraging his understanding, would wander about through shapes of pre-Adamite existence, and escape again into the light of day like Marcellus and Bernardo, "distilled almost to jelly with the act of fear." New York was spared this unnecessary and theatrical episode.

Actually, the park would have been rather spectacular, an extravagance appropriate for New York. A giant iron framework covered with vines was intended to arch over the Paleozoic Museum, and rows of neoclassic columns would have lined both sides. A menagerie of extinct mammals and dinosaurs was to have populated the Museum, a museum devoted to *American* beasts.

Hawkins arrived in the States and enthusiastically set to work, seeking out American fossils and visiting museums all over the country. At the Academy of Natural Sciences in Philadelphia, he was delighted to find the famous *Hadrosaurus* that had been dug up in Haddonfield, New Jersey, in 1858—the first American dinosaur. The Academy had already created a mold of the animal, and Hawkins acquired it for Central Park. Back in New York, he formulated a dramatic prehistoric tableau. He planned to show the *Hadrosaurus* being attacked by a carnivorous dinosaur, *Laelaps*, while two other *Laelaps* feasted on the corpse of yet another Hadrosaur. Nearby, the marine reptile *Elasmosaurus* would lurk in the shallow water of a pool. Moving farther along the evolutionary ladder, Hawkins had planned for two giant armadillos, mastodons, giant sloths, and a giant elk to round out the picture of "pre-Adamite" existence. At a cost of $30,000, the foundation of the Museum was laid near West 63rd Street in the park.

Then the notorious William "Boss" Tweed came to power. Tweed (who several years later would be convicted of embezzling millions of dollars in city funds) made the Paleozoic Museum the target of a political power-play in 1870. He halted work on the restorations on the pretense that the $300,000 price tag of the new museum was unaffordable. (In fact, Tweed was angry because he could find no way to reap illegal profits and kickbacks from the museum's construction.) He installed his own henchmen as Central Park commissioners, who immediately scotched the project and ordered the Museum's foundations plowed under.

Hawkins was persistent, however, and continued to work on the project, hoping that the Smithsonian Institution would in time take an interest in his work. But Tweed wanted him out of New York entirely. The following year, vandals under orders from the Tweed Ring broke into Hawkins' studio and smashed the dinosaurs with sledgehammers. They later returned and destroyed Hawkins' molds and smaller models. Henry Hilton, one of Tweed's henchmen, told Hawkins that he "should not bother himself about dead animals when there were so many living ones to care for."

The fragments disappeared, rumored to have been buried somewhere in the park. Several years later a magazine reported that some of the fragments had been dug up in a southern section of the park, but were "utterly worthless." Hawkins, deeply shocked by the episode and disgusted with America, became an academic recluse at Princeton and later returned to England.

New York was once again without a museum. But other plans were already under way. A young, highly enthusiastic man from Maine, Albert S. Bickmore, had for several years been canvassing the New York elite with a "sketch plan" for a natural history museum in New York City, attempting to persuade them that here—finally—was a museum project worthy of their support. In 1869, the same year that Hawkins was putting the finishing touches on his doomed *Hadrosaurus* models, the American Museum of Natural History was born.

# TWO

# Professor Bickmore's Museum

$S$tored in an obscure drawer in the Museum's vast photographic archives is an unusual trio of photographs. The first shows a Victorian gentleman with a magnificent white beard, wearing a black frock coat, a starched shirt, a tie tack, and a gold watch chain. The second shows the same stiff man in profile. The third, just as formal as the others, is the rear view of the elderly gentleman; all one can see is the back of his balding pate.

This triptych of photographs is the official portrait of Professor Albert S. Bickmore, founder of the American Museum of Natural History, taken around the turn of the century. He directed that his portrait be taken in this unusual fashion because it was the way nineteenth-century anthropologists traditionally photographed their aboriginal subjects: from the front, side, and back, like a series of mug shots. The Museum's photographic archives contain tens of thousands of such photographic trios—snapshots of Eskimos, Aleuts, Mongolians, Ainus, and many others.

That Bickmore requested such a portrait gives us an insight into his character. At the least, it was an eccentric idea that anticipated by a quarter of a century our modern concepts of cultural relativism. Conventional notions of propriety and personal dignity—usually of such importance to the Victorians—didn't concern Bickmore. His colleagues described him as an extremely optimistic and enthusiastic person, able to excite even the most phlegmatic audience. He had an entrepreneur's personality. Bickmore's goal—to found the country's greatest museum of natural history, and to do it in New York City—was ambitious to the extreme. He had no social connections and no money; his academic credentials were fair but not impeccable; and he was young and inexperienced. But he was the kind of man the rich railroad and banking magnates of New York City would understand. And this talent was to play a crucial role in the founding of the Museum.

Bickmore was born in 1939 in St. George, a small town on the Maine coast opposite Monhegan Island. He was the son of an old New England family of sea captains and shipbuilders. In an unpublished autobiography now housed in the Museum's Rare Book Room, Bickmore tells of spending much of his time roaming the woods and shores of Maine, gathering shells, rocks, and other things of which natural history is made.

Bickmore went to Dartmouth College, at that time considered the poor man's Harvard, and there studied chemistry and geology. Upon graduation, he persuaded one of his professors to give him a letter of introduction to study under the eminent Swiss zoologist Louis Agassiz, who had recently established the Museum of Comparative Zoology at Harvard University. In 1860, letter in hand, Bickmore traveled to the Museum in Cambridge. There he was told that Agassiz could be found in the Museum's basement, working in his vast collection. Bickmore descended to the basement and discovered a pompous little man (who turned out to be Agassiz) working "amid a great array of bottles of alcoholic specimens."

Agassiz gave Bickmore his standard "entrance examination." He would give his prospects a specimen—in Bickmore's case, a sea urchin—and require them to study it, in excruciating detail, for weeks on end. "In six weeks," Agassiz told Bickmore, "you will either become utterly weary of the task, or else you will be so completely fascinated with it as to devote your whole life to the pursuit of our science." Bickmore passed the test and, as one of Agassiz' assistants, was charged with caring for the radiates and mollusks in the Museum's collection.

Bickmore had other things in mind than invertebrates. He was nursing a secret ambition, and an opportunity to put his idea to the test soon arose. In 1861 the Prince of Wales visited the United States with his tutor, Sir Henry Wentworth Acland, founder of the Oxford University Museum (England's counterpart to the Museum of Comparative Zoology). When the royal entourage visited Harvard, Bickmore, who was only twenty-two, buttonholed Dr. Acland in private. "Does it seem strange to you, sir," Bickmore asked him, "that Agassiz, our great teacher, should have located his museum of natural history for future America out here in Cambridge, while in Europe the institutions of this character are placed in the political and monetary capitals of the several empires?"

"Yes, it does seem strange," Acland replied, "but what has suggested such a question to your mind?"

"Now New York," Bickmore continued, "is our city of the greatest wealth and therefore probably the best location for the future museum of natural history for the whole land."

"He simply turned toward me," Bickmore recalled, "and, looking me straight in the eye, said, 'My young friend, that is a grand thought.'

"I at once determined that I would work for nothing else by day and dream of nothing else by night."

The young man's plans were hastened, however unintentionally, by Agassiz himself. A European of the old school, Agassiz ran his operation in a dictatorial fashion. He forbade his students to publish their research until he decided they were ready—which was far too long for Bickmore. When Bickmore and other students tried to find jobs elsewhere without informing Agassiz, the scientist was outraged. The final blow came when Agassiz discovered that Bickmore had been secretly raising money for an expedition to the Far East. In 1863, Agassiz declined to recommend Bickmore to a permanent position as his assistant, which amounted to little more than a *de facto* firing.

Having raised enough money for his expedition, Bickmore set out for the East Indian Archipelago, carrying his two most treasured possessions: his Bible and a sketch plan of his own devising for the new museum.* The primary purpose of the trip was to collect birds and shells from the Spice Islands, Borneo, Java, and the other Malaysian and East Indian islands. During the three-year expedition, Bickmore survived several earthquakes, a fall into a volcanic crater, a landslide, and the shock of seeing part of his rare bird collection appear on his dinner plate.

Bickmore enlisted native help in his collecting efforts, and displayed a shrewdness in bargaining that would later be evident in his negotiations with Boss Tweed about the founding of the Museum. "My mode of trading with these people," he wrote,

> was extremely simple and avoided any unpleasant discussion. A small table was placed on the verandah along the front of the raja's house and I took a seat behind it. The natives then came up separately and placed their shells or lot of shells in a row on the table, and I placed opposite each of them whatever price I was willing to pay and then, pointing first to the money and then to the shells simply said, *"Ini atau itu,"* "This or that," leaving them to make their choice.

Upon his return to the United States in 1867, Bickmore wasted no time in making contact with wealthy New

---

*On his way east, Bickmore stopped in England and showed his plan to Sir Richard Owen, who was at that time planning the British Museum (Natural History). Owen and Bickmore pored over each other's plans and each borrowed ideas from the other.

Yorkers who could help further his plans. He had already met with many of these men before departing on his expedition, and they were impressed with the results he brought back. These men introduced the professor to some of their friends, among them J. Pierpont Morgan, Theodore Roosevelt, Sr., and Morris K. Jesup. Bickmore, who was a mere twenty-eight years old, talked many of these men into making the Museum their chief philanthropic pursuit.

He succeeded largely because of his inexhaustible powers of persuasion. One colleague wrote that if anyone showed the slightest interest in his plan, Bickmore would plunge headlong "into that incessant preoccupation of his mind, the new museum building, its future, its uses, how it should develop, how it would feed school, college, and university... how it would expand commensurately with the new continent's metropolis until it outrivaled... the collective shows of all the world."

This cadre of rich industrialists—who spent half their lives avoiding salesmen, people seeking favors and patronage, and business associates—simply could not escape the persistence of the poor young man from Maine.

Bickmore assembled his group, and together they drafted a letter to the commissioners of Central Park. This letter simply informed the commissioners that the group had long desired to establish a great natural history museum in Central Park, and that they now had the opportunity to acquire a rare collection of mounted animals and skeletons from the widow of Edouard Verreaux of Paris. Would the commissioners be willing to provide for its reception and development? In the second week of 1869—at a time when Hawkins was hard at work on the plans for his own Paleozoic Museum—the Controller of the Park, Andrew Green, replied that they were ready to cooperate. On January 19, the group met again, passed a set of resolutions governing the new museum, and selected a board of trustees.

Bickmore's next task was a good deal more difficult and unpleasant: He was charged with pushing the museum's charter through the state legislature, which at this time was still firmly controlled by Boss Tweed. Indeed, with Tweed anything was possible, but without him they hadn't a chance. There was little reason to believe he would be any more sympathetic to the new museum than he had been to previous plans. It was suggested that Bickmore visit the corrupt state senator in Albany with an arsenal of letters of introduction; it was particularly suggested that he obtain a letter from Samuel J. Tilden.

At last, the day came when Bickmore arrived at Tweed's hotel. Bickmore wrote of Tweed:

> I found him to be a man of portly dimensions and comfortably seated in a large arm chair. I introduced myself and my business by saying: "Senator, I am honored by your friend Samuel J. Tilden, with this letter, and I also have these other letters from leading citizens in New York City."
>
> "Well, well, what can I do for Mr. Tilden?"
>
> "These gentlemen, Senator, whose names are on this paper, have asked me to state to you that they desire to found a Museum of Natural History in New York, and if possible on Central Park, similar to Professor Agassiz' great museum in Cambridge—you know of that institution, Senator?"
>
> "Certainly! Certainly!" was his reply (and now I must confess that for an instant a cruel doubt flashed over my mind, as to whether he had ever really heard its name mentioned before in all his life). . . . "All right, my young friend, I will see your bill safely through," was his reply as he thrust our carefully prepared document into his capacious outside pocket.

Whatever Tilden's letter said, or promised—or threatened—it worked admirably. The bill breezed through the committee and was passed unanimously in the State Senate. Ironically—considering the treatment Hawkins had been subjected to—Tweed saw to it that not a single word was changed.

From an office at the prestigious Wall Street firm of

Brown Brothers, Bickmore embarked upon a fund-raising venture to expand the collections (some of which were being temporarily stored in a vault at the same firm). Theodore Roosevelt, Sr., charged Bickmore with the raising of enough money to expand the Museum's collections, and he gave him a list of prospective philanthropists. A week or so later, Bickmore was back in Roosevelt's office with the list of pledges. "As [Roosevelt] unrolled the document," Bickmore wrote, "there came over his face first an expression of surprise and then of radiant delight." Bickmore's indefatigable solicitations had already raised over $40,000 for the new institution. Roosevelt declared, "Professor, New York wants a natural history museum and it shall have one."

Bickmore next persuaded the Central Park commissioners to let the new Museum occupy part of the Arsenal Building within Central Park. He immediately began supervising the acquisition of various collections. The first annual report listed the earliest collections, which included the bones of the extinct dodo, a book on the fossils of North Carolina, 4,000 shells, and Bickmore's own collections including "alcoholic mollusca [and] four skeletons of the sea otter." Bickmore also purchased 3,000 bird skins from Daniel Giraud Elliot, the entire "cabinet" of Prince Maximilian of Neuwied. Baron R. Osten-Sacken, the Russian consul-general in New York City and an avid insect collector, donated 4,000 beetles he had collected in America. Later donations streamed in. Among them were a mastodon's tooth, presented by a Mr. Root; sixteen specimens of algae and one mummified crocodile from a Mr. Young; and a mounted badger from Syria, donated by a Reverend Dodge. Other strange and exotic donations began filling up the storerooms of the Arsenal Building, until it was fairly bursting with bones, stuffed animals, and various exotica. It was all too evident that a new and larger building would have to be found—and soon.

## The Once and Future Museum

In 1871 the Museum and its sister institution, the Metropolitan Museum of Art, jointly petitioned the state legislature for land and buildings to house and display their collections permanently. The petition, signed by 40,000 New Yorkers, persuaded city politicians to offer the American Museum a sixteen-acre parcel of land known as Manhattan Square, adjacent to Central Park on 79th Street. (Manhattan Square had been planned as a park well before the creation of Central Park, but as of 1871 remained undeveloped.) When the Museum took possession, it was a dismal and positively wild site indeed. As Louis Garatacap, a curator in the young Museum, wrote: "It included a rugged, disconsolate tract of ground, thrown into hillocks where the gneiss ledges protruded their weathered shapes, or depressed in hollows filled with stagnant pools, and bearing throughout an uncompromising, scarcely serviceable appearance."

In that period of the late nineteenth century, it was also a very isolated site. The elevated railway that would soon run along what is now Columbus Avenue had not been extended farther than 59th Street, and the bridge connecting Manhattan Square with Central Park (now called the Naturalists' Gate) had not yet been built. The area around the Museum, now the fashionable Upper West Side, was then undergoing the painful process of development. It was a ramshackle patchwork of rundown farms, tenements, rocky outcrops, foul swamps, and undeveloped tracts clustered with vegetable gardens and the hovels of squatters.

Before building could begin on Manhattan Square, a dozen or more squatters had to be unceremoniously removed from the site, along with their herds of goats and pigs. Then the trustees of the new Museum hired Calvert Vaux, one of the designers of Central Park, to be the architect of the fledgling Museum. Vaux contemplated a Museum of lofty and stupendous dimensions. The edifice was to be a hollow square seven hundred feet along each side, containing two long buildings that crossed in the center, forming four interior courtyards. The center of the structure would be an enormous tower called—appropriately enough—the Hall of the Heavens. (Jacob Wrey Mould, J. C. Cady, and other architects would later add details to and alter the plan.)

On June 2, 1874, President Ulysses S. Grant laid the cornerstone for the new building. He was attended by a flock of important officials, including three cabinet members, the governor, and the mayor (as well as a group of curious squatters who had remained throughout the construction.) The ceremony opened with a rousing prayer by a Reverend Tyng, followed by an address by the president of the commissioners of Central Park, who alluded rather apologetically to the forbidding landscape:

> To the stranger who comes here to-day these rugged foundation walls and these rough surroundings are not well calculated to make a pleasant impression; but to us who have watched the rapid growth northward of this city, and who were familiar with the barren and rocky ground upon which Central Park has been created, it required but little strain of the imagination to conceive of the speedy occupation of all these vacant lots by substantial dwellings, and to picture to ourselves the spot upon which we now stand, known as Manhattan Square, as covered by the proposed Museum of Natural History, costing, ere its final completion, not less than $6,0000,000, and embracing a collection of objects of scientific interest second to none other in the world.

All was silent as Grant troweled the cornerstone and time capsule into place. The trowel, a little silver affair supplied by Tiffany's, was stolen moments later.*

---

*The time capsule consisted of a copper box containing a dozen New York newspapers, and some magazines, coins, reports, and other historical flotsam. As the Museum complex grew over the years, the location of the cornerstone was lost, and the time capsule, due to be opened in the 1920s, remained sealed. It wasn't until the Museum's centennial in 1969 that a diligent search finally turned it up. When the time capsule was opened, it was discovered that water had more or less destroyed its contents.

The first building was opened to the public on December 22, 1877, with President Rutherford B. Hayes presiding. It was an asture Victorian structure that looked out upon a landscape of rubble, undrained ponds, and piles of rock. An early photograph of the Museum, taken from the roof of the Dakota Building,* shows the Museum standing in this wasteland, with a number of shanties, gardens, and various animals still inhabiting the fringes of Manhattan Square.

Grand hopes were sounded in a series of opening speeches, and Bickmore looked forward to the coming weeks, when the Museum would be thronged with crowds of excited visitors. But the following day, Bickmore opened the doors of the Museum to a paltry crowd, and in the following months Bickmore found himself wandering unhappily through virtually deserted exhibition halls. Unexpectedly, so soon after its jubilant opening, the Museum was plunged into a period of crisis that threatened to shut its doors permanently.

## Misery on Manhattan Square

Between the opening of the first building and 1880, the Museum got into serious trouble.

During the first heady years of its life, the Museum had purchased a number of expensive collections. In 1874, for example, it paid $65,000 for a fossil invertebrate collection of Professor James Hall. This was undoubtedly an important purchase, and it kept this significant collection from being sold to a hungry German museum. (Louis Agassiz had once said that "whoever gets this collection gets the geological museum of America.") During a lifetime of meticulous collecting, Hall had amassed tens of thousands of fossils representing over 7,000 species; indeed, the collection was so important that the nomenclature of the geologi-

---

*The building was named after the remote Western state because its uptown location was considered equally remote.

cal structure of North America had been based on Hall's fossils. But it was also a very expensive acquisition—one that the thinly stretched Museum budget could ill afford.

The Museum hoped to pay for the Hall collection with a public subscription. Unfortunately, the public proved to be quite uninterested in an aggregation of gray invertebrate fossils. Very little money came forth. The trustees found themselves in the uncomfortable position of making up the shortfall—not an inconsiderable amount for the time. The Hall collection and other enthusiastic purchases of a similar nature put the Museum seriously in debt.

The location of the new Museum aggravated the cash-flow problem. The exhibition halls were virtually empty; more people visited the "rump" collection of natural history junk left behind in the Arsenal Building than came to the new Museum. The first two Presidents of the Museum, John David Wolfe and Robert L. Stuart, lacked the energy and time to put the Museum on a sound footing. Most of the other trustees were losing interest; fewer and fewer were coming to trustee meetings because the trip uptown was so inconvenient. In an effort to attract public attention, Bickmore would again and again persuade the trustees to advance funds for a new purchase, and again and again he would stage a grand unveiling. But each time, the flurry of visitors would soon drop off, leaving the Museum once again deserted.

Some of the trustees began seriously to question the value of the Museum itself. One wrote that "no matter how fine the exhibits are, if no one saw them what good are they?" By 1880, the Museum was on the brink of extinction. The trustees had by and large clamped down on large purchases, public interest was at a critically low level, and Museum President Robert L. Stuart had said that when he retired, he would recommend closing the Museum if no one could be found to take his place.

The trustees decided that a report on the future needs and direction of the Museum was necessary. They gave the task to Morris K. Jesup, a Museum founder and wealthy railroad magnate and banker. They directed Jesup to devise a plan that would scale down the Museum's aims and goals, reduce expenses, and—most important—curtail the extravagant purchases of Bickmore and several other sympathetic trustees.

Jesup was not particularly interested in or sympathetic to the science of natural history, and his sixth-grade education certainly didn't prepare him for understanding the complexities of the institution. But after spending time with Bickmore, wandering about the halls gazing at the fossils and stuffed animals, and chatting with the two curators taking care of the collections, he underwent a conversion. Rather than winding the place down, he told the trustees that the Museum should be vigorously expanded and provided with an endowment. He shrewdly noted that the exhibitions should cease to focus on boring fossil invertebrates, but instead look to "lions" and other big mammals to arouse the public interest. He argued passionately that the Museum could be "a power of great good" for the people of New York City. The trustees were impressed by his report, and when Robert L. Stuart resigned, they made Jesup the third President of the Museum.

Jesup's presidency lasted more than a quarter-century, and during that time he completely transformed the Museum. In 1881, when he arrived, there were some 54,000 square feet of exhibits; twenty-five years later, there were close to 600,000. In 1881, the Museum employed twelve people; by 1906 the number had grown to 185. In 1881, the endowment was zero; in 1906, it stood at well over a million dollars. Much of this was due to Jesup.

Jesup was one of the nineteenth century's quintessential self-made men. He was a man of great self-control, with an uncompromisingly moralistic view of the world. He was born in 1830 into a strictly religious and quite wealthy family. Theatergoing, cardplaying, and dancing were forbidden as the Devil's amusements. Morris was the fifth of eight brothers and sisters. He was devoted to his mother, to Christian duty and the Presbyterian Church, to charity and honor. His many charities included the New York City Mission and Tract Society (which published Christian tracts and distributed them with zeal to the poorer classes), the Five Points House of Industry (a rehabilitation center for wayward boys), the American Sunday School Union, the Society for the Suppression of Vice, and the Society for the Relief of Half-Orphan and Destitute Children, among others.

His life was uneventful until 1837, when the serious financial panic of that year completely wiped out the family fortune. Almost immediately afterward, the seven-year-old Jesup's father died, leaving Mrs. Jesup a destitute widow with eight children to support (Jesup would later see all his siblings but one die of tuberculosis). His family's financial condition continued to grow worse until, at the age of twelve, Jesup was forced to drop out of school to help support his mother. He landed a job as a messenger boy at the Wall Street firm of Rogers, Ketchum & Grosvenor, run by one of his father's old friends and Jesup's namesake, Morris Ketchum. Rogers, Ketchum & Grosvenor manufactured locomotives and cotton mill machinery, and Jesup began learning the business.

From this pathetic, Horatio Alger–like beginning, Jesup amassed and then gave away one of the great fortunes of the nineteenth century. In 1852, at age twenty-two, Jesup left the firm, and with a bookkeeper named Charles Clark set up Clark & Jesup. This firm did a commission business, buying railroad supplies from manufacturers and reselling them to the railroads. It was a financial success, and several years later Jesup formed a new concern, M.K. Jesup & Company, which in time branched out into the investment banking business, eventually buying entire railroads. Jesup's specialty was to buy a controlling interest in a failing railroad, reorganize it, and sell it at a spectacular profit. When he became one of the original Museum incorporators in 1869, he had only been in business seventeen years and had already built a vast fortune.

Jesup was fifty-one when he was elected to the presidency of the Museum, and at fifty-four he retired from business to devote himself to it full-time. His sixth-grade education never hindered his understanding of science, and may in fact have been an asset. One scientist wrote, "He began his duties untrammelled by tradition. He was the advocate of no established school or method. . . . His oft-repeated remark, 'I am a plain, unscientific man; I want the exhibits to be labelled so I can understand them, and then I shall feel sure that others can understand,' summed up his prime desire."

Perhaps most importantly for the Museum, Jesup recognized that the foundation for good exhibitions was good research and *active collecting*. He launched the Museum into a golden age of exploration—the fifty-year period from 1880 to 1930, when the Museum sent over a thousand expeditions into the field, many to the remotest corners of the earth. By 1930 the Museum had been involved with expeditions that discovered the North Pole; that penetrated unmapped areas of Siberia; that traversed Outer Mongolia and the great Gobi Desert; that penetrated the deepest jungles of the Congo—expeditions that, in fact, were to bring Museum representatives to every continent on the globe.

## THREE

# The First Grand Expedition

It was a golden age for natural science. The world stood poised on the edge of the twentieth century, but an explorer could still come face to face with Stone Age peoples who were entirely unaware of the existence of an outside world. Exploration and collection were still a dangerous business, in which the loss of life was not uncommon. On the other hand, science had matured to the point where people realized that the earth's resources were not infinite. The new science of anthropology, for example, suddenly made people aware that cultures were dying out all over the world, and that an effort had to be made to save what was left. Technology had recently provided the tools to do so—including the camera and the wax-cylinder phonograph.

On the other hand, zoologists and biologists saw an entire globe virtually unexplored scientifically, and accessible in a way that it never had been before. New discoveries in many branches of natural science were following thick and fast: dinosaurs were discovered in the American West, remarkable new species of animals were found in the African jungles, new lands discovered in the Arctic. More than anything, natural scientists of the late nineteenth century believed deeply in the value of *collections*. To them, collections were *facts*. They held secrets about the world; secrets that could be extracted through careful study. Collections would reveal the relationships among all life on the planet, including human beings. They would be a resource for scientists centuries into the future, long after such things no longer existed in the wild. And on a more human level, spectacular collections and brilliant discoveries brought glory and fame to collectors, their institutions, and the benefactors who provided them with funds.

In 1895, President Jesup hired a young man, Franz Boas, to be the assistant curator in the Department of Ethnology. An austere man with a forceful personality, Boas was a meticulous, careful researcher who had unconventional—even radical—ideas about cultural anthropology. Before Boas, anthropologists had ranked human societies on a kind of evolutionary ladder; some races, they believed, were obviously better than others. The best and most advanced of all, of course, was the white Protestant culture of Western Europe and America.

Boas disagreed. He believed that all cultures were intrinsically equal—a view called cultural relativism. If this was so, Boas figured, one could learn as much about humanity by studying a small tribe in British Columbia as by studying a great civilization. But Boas saw many of the small cultures he wanted to study dying out, and he believed that with their death, priceless information would be lost forever. Time was running out, and he felt the urgent need to collect and save everything possible from these cultures for the benefit of future generations. In particular, Boas saw the fragile aboriginal cultures of the North Pacific rim of North America poised at the edge of extinction, and he realized that his might well be the last opportunity anyone would have to study these cultures. In earlier trips to the Northwest Coast, he had already begun to see the beginnings of a decline, stemming from the desire of the Indians to possess Western technology, and from the growing suppression of Northwest Coast culture by the provincial government of British Columbia. In Asia he saw disease and starvation decimating the native populations whenever they came in contact with the West. What was happening in Siberia was a mirror image of what was going on in the Western United States—and Boas knew perfectly well what the final result would be. His overriding desire was to save every possible thing related to these societies for future study and ultimately for the common heritage of humanity.

When he first came to the Museum, Boas may have seen that there was a chance President Jesup would not support a kind of shotgun approach to collecting in the area Boas was studying, the Indians of the Northwest Coast. Jesup was a man who liked definite goals and tangible results. Therefore, Boas presented Jesup with a definite theory that required testing—that the Indians of North America had entered the New World from northeastern Siberia across the Bering Strait.

The origin of Native Americans was in fact one of the great unsettled questions in anthropology at that time. Some scientists identified them with one or another of the tribes of Asia or the South Pacific, while others insisted they were culturally—and perhaps racially—independent of the Old World. Boas argued that the way to prove his theory was to send a major expedition to explore and study the cultures living along the Northwest Coast of North America to the aborigines of eastern Siberia.

Jesup seized upon the problem with great interest. He was growing old (in 1895 he was already sixty-five), and he wanted a major scientific discovery to come out of his presidency. His shrewd financial management of the Museum had left it flush with funds, and whatever money the Museum didn't have for an expedition, Jesup would find within his own pockets. Boas would now be able to accomplish his secret agenda while at the same time pursuing this important anthropological question.

By 1897, Boas had organized the Jesup North Pacific Expedition. In the entire field of anthropology, nothing of comparable size or scope had ever been attempted before. Boas hired over a dozen anthropologists and assistants who fanned out among the tiny aboriginal cultures living along the circum-Pacific: the Ainu of northern Japan, the Tungus and Yakut of southern Siberia, the Yukaghir and Chukchee of northern Siberia and the Koryak of the eastern coast; the Asiatic and Alaskan Eskimo; and the Kwakiutl, Salish, Bella Coola, and Thompson Indians living along the Northwest Coast of Canada.

Boas directed the fieldwork in North America himself, reserving the Kwakiutl and Bella Coola Indians as his own. On earlier expeditions to the area, Boas had made the acquaintance of George Hunt, a part-Kwakiutl man living at Fort Rupert in British Columbia. Boas asked Hunt to join the expedition, and the two men worked together, collecting objects, transcribing myths, and gathering ethnographic material. Whenever Boas went into the field, Hunt accompanied him and acted as advance man, interpreter, and guide. When Boas was not in the field, George Hunt collected and transcribed myths, which he sent to Boas through the mail and for which he received payment of fifty cents per page. He was deeply knowledgeable about Kwakiutl customs and myths, and contributed valuable material for Boas' resulting analyses. Allen Wardwell, in his book *Objects of Bright Pride*, turned up an illuminating piece of correspondence between Boas and Hunt. Just before Boas left New York for British Columbia in 1897, he sent Hunt a letter, which read in part:

> It occurred to me that in laying out our work, it would be a very good plan to have the Indians clearly understand what we are about. For this purpose, I enclose a letter which I have written to the Kwakiutl tribe. . . . I hope you will read this letter to them, translated, of course, into Indian, and in doing so, you better invite them to a feast, for which I will pay when I see you.

In the files of the Museum, Wardwell found part of the following letter, which Boas had enclosed in his letter to Hunt (the last pages of it are lost):

> Friends, I am Mr. Boas who is speaking to you. I am he whom you called Heiltsaqoalis. It is two winters since I have been with you, but I have thought of you often. You were very kind to me when I was with you. . . . It is difficult for you to show the white men in Victoria that your feasts and potlatches are good, and I have tried to show them they are good. . . . I am trying to show them that your ways are not bad ways. . . . I am sorry to see how many of your children do not obey the old laws, how they walk the ways of the white man. The ways of the Indians were made differently from the ways of the white man at the beginning of the world, and it is good that we remember the old ways . . . your young people do not know the history of your people . . . it is not good that these stories are forgotten. . . .

Boas was particularly anxious to preserve the myths of the Northwest Coast Indians. Most artifacts can survive the extinction of a culture; pots, house foundations, knives, stonework, and burials will last for thousands of years. But myths, Boas realized, are the most delicate artifact of a culture, and the first to disappear in the face of cultural change. Boas believed that myths were the key to understanding a culture. Like the majority of artifacts, myths reveal influences, contacts, and ideas from other cultures. They also reveal, Boss believed, the way a culture organizes and makes sense of a complex world. Myths integrate—in one structure—the many traits of a culture.

Despite his grasp of their importance, however, Boas found myth-gathering a tedious business. An entry in one of his journals attests: "I had a miserable day today. The natives held a big potlatch again. I was unable to get hold of anyone and had to snatch at whatever I could get. Late at night I did get something, [a tale] for which I have been searching—'The Birth of the Raven.'" He went on to complain about how much nonsense he was forced to listen to before getting one valuable myth.

The expeditions along the Northwest Coast yielded the largest and most important collection from that area in the world. Besides virtually the entire creation and myth cycle of the Kwakiutl and other Indians, Boas and Hunt brought back magical transformation masks, shamans' dance shirts, huge carved bowls and painted chests, shamans' rattles, exquisite carvings in bone, cedar, and slate, feast dishes, and giant totem poles (for which they paid one dollar per foot).

These items were saved just in time. By 1910 the Northwest Coast Indian culture had been suppressed and the potlatch (the periodic feasts where important chiefs would try to outdo each other in giving away their wealth) outlawed; the Indians had stopped creating their extraordinary art. What Boas feared most had come to pass.

## Expeditions in Asia

Meanwhile, Boas had sent three men to conduct parallel work in Asia. The first two were Russian anthropologists, Waldemar Borgoras and Waldemar Jochelson, both of whom had been exiled to Siberia by the Czar for belonging to revolutionary societies. Once in Siberia, the two were more or less free to travel and research as they pleased, only mildly inconvenienced by the shadow of the Czar's secret police. The third man, Berthold Laufer, a German, was put in charge of research among the tribes living along the Amur River, which runs along the present-day border of China and the Soviet Union.

Laufer, Jochelson, and Borgoras hired their own assistants and traveled separately. At this time, Siberia was still one of the remotest regions on the earth, containing areas that were entirely unexplored. Many of the photographs taken by Jochelson, Borgoras, and Laufer show landscapes and peoples being seen for the first time by Western man.

\* \* \*

The first to arrive in Russia, Laufer landed at Vladivostok in June 1898. From there he traveled by steamer to Sakhalin Island (a large, remote island in the Sea of Okhotsk, northwest of Japan), where he remained for the bitter Siberian winter studying the Gilyak, Tungus, and Ainu tribes. A letter he wrote to Boas on March 4, 1899, reveals a glimpse of the details of his fieldwork:

> I did not succeed in obtaining any anthropometric measurements. The people were afraid they would die at once after submitting to this process. . . . I succeeded in measuring a single individual, a man of imposing stature, who, after the measurements had been taken, fell prostrate on the floor, the picture of despair, groaning, "Now I am going to die tomorrow!" . . .
>
> I took phonographic records of songs, which created the greatest sensation among the Russians as well as among the natives. A young Gilyak woman who sang into the instrument said, "It took me so long to learn this song, and this thing has learned it at once, without making any mistakes. There is surely a man or a spirit in this box which imitates me!" and at the same time she was crying and laughing with excitement.

Jochelson arrived in Siberia a year later than Laufer, to research the tribes that made their home above the Arctic Circle. Both Jochelson and his wife, Dina Brodsky Jochelson, were imposing figures, well suited to the kind of expedition they undertook. They were intrepid explorers, hazarding everything to acquire new knowledge. In 1901, during their second year in Siberia, they attempted the almost unthinkable—a two-month trek across the breadth of Siberia, from Gizhiga Bay on the southern side to Nishe-Kolymsk on the northern side, near the East Siberian Sea. In order to take advantage of the shortest route to these remote tribes, they planned to take packhorses across the extremely remote Stanovoi Mountains, over unexplored territory to a small town on the Korkodon River. There they would build a raft and float north to the Arctic Ocean.

In a letter to Boas, Jochelson wrote about the harrowing journey:

> This journey was the most difficult one that it was ever my fortune to undertake. Bogs, mountain torrents, rocky passes and thick forests combined to hinder our progress. . . . A heavy rain which fell during the first few days of our journey soaked the loads of the pack-horses and caused the provisions to rot. Therefore we had to cut down on our rations from the very beginning. After crossing the passes of the Stanovoi Mountains, we reached the upper course of the Korkodon River. By this time our horses were exhausted, and it was necessary to take a long rest. Meanwhile the cold was increasing day by day, and haste was necessary if we were to reach the Verkhne-Kolymsk before the closing [freezing] of the river.
>
> It took us one day to build a strong raft, and then we began our descent of the river, made dangerous by numerous rapids and short bends, by the rocky banks and by jams of driftwood. Our guides had intimated that we could make the descent in two days, but instead we spent nine days on the raft.

Jochelson did a great deal of research and collecting with the Koryak, a group of small tribes living along the shores of the Sea of Okhotsk. While among the Maritime Koryak, Jochelson and his wife lived most of the time in the tribe's underground dwellings, which could be entered only through a tree-trunk ladder descending through the smokehole. He complained to Boas:

> It is almost impossible to describe the squalor of these dwellings. The smoke, which fills the hut, makes the eyes smart . . . walls, ladder, and household utensils are covered with a greasy soot, so that contact with them leaves shining black spots on hands and clothing. The dim light which falls through the smoke-hole is hardly sufficient for writing and reading. The odor of blubber and of refuse is almost intolerable; and the inmates, intoxicated with fly agaric, add to the discomfort of the

situation. The natives are infested with lice. As long as we remained in these dwellings we could not escape these insects, which we dreaded more than any of the privations of our journey.

The pair continued their trek first to the Arctic coast and then inland again. By 1902 they had crossed the Lena River and reached the town of Yakutsk. During much of this journey, Jochelson was shadowed by secret police, on the orders of the Russian Interior Ministry, who did everything they could to hinder and thwart the success of the expedition, without much success.

Jochelson made extremely rare and valuable collections among the Yukaghir, the Tungus, and the Yakut tribes of eastern Siberia. The material Jochelson gathered remains today one of the most thorough and important collections of Siberian ethnography in the world.

Borgoras was the most daring of the three explorers, traversing areas of Siberia unknown even to the Russians. He left Vladivostok in the early summer of 1900, bound for the remote tribes of the Pacific. He landed at the mouth of the Anadyr River in late July of 1900, at Mariinsky Post, at that time the most remote Russian settlement in eastern Asia—nothing more than a detachment of cossacks, living in barracks next to a native village. He studied and made collections with the Reindeer Chukchee and the Ai'wan tribe, the Asiatic branch of the Alaskan Eskimo. Borgoras then made a large loop, lasting a year, following the Siberian coastline north to Indian Point, one of the extreme eastern points of Asia, then cutting inland, following the Anadyr River south and exploring the northern part of the Kamchatka Peninsula. His extensive collections were hauled by dog sled to Mariinsky Post, loaded on a steamer to Vladivostok, and finally sent to New York via the Suez Canal.

The explorations of eastern Siberia were completed in 1902, and Borgoras and Jochelson traveled to the Museum in New York to edit and publish their results. Boas kept Laufer in Asia, directing him to make collections in China. Jochelson stayed at the Museum until 1908, returning to Russia once to lead another expedition. He then remained in New York until his death in 1937. Borgoras stayed in Russia and was imprisoned after the 1905 Revolution. Eventually he became a leading Soviet citizen, and lived a peaceful life until his death in 1936.

The collections and ethnographic notes brought back by the Asian leg of the Jesup North Pacific Expedition are a priceless record of the fragile tribes of the area. Boas made it clear that he wanted the explorers to collect everything they could lay their hands on. A letter from Borgoras listing the various results of one expedition gives a clue to the sheer scale of the work. Borgoras shipped back to New York volumes of ethnographic notes; 5,000 objects; 33 plaster casts of faces; 75 skulls; 300 myths, tales, and legends; 150 texts transcribed in the Chukchee, Koryak, Kamchadel, and Asiatic Eskimo languages; 95 wax-cylinder phonographic records; anthropometric measurements of 860 individuals; and hundreds of photographs.

Since Boas hoped to show a physical affinity between the American Indians and the north Asiatic peoples, physical anthropology—especially the study of racial features and types—was an important part of the expeditions. The anthropometric measurements referred to above (such measurements as the distance between the eyes, the shape of the skull, and arm lengths and leg lengths combined in various ratios) were a way of quantifying similarities and differences in appearance to determine how two groups might be related. Measured individuals were usually photographed from the front, side, and back (remember Albert S. Bickmore), resulting in a series of photographs that looked like mug shots.

The Museum had gone to Asia just in time.

Wherever they went, all three men had observed one grim fact: mass starvation and disease were decimating these tiny tribes. American whaling had driven away sea mammals vital to the maritime tribes' survival. Various

Russian fur traders and missionaries had brought measles, smallpox, and venereal disease. Periodic epidemics swept through villages, killing one-third or more of the inhabitants. World War I, the Russian Revolution, and the general spread of Western culture and technology contributed to the rapid and total extinction of some of these tribes, and the utter transformation of the rest.

When the Museum built the Hall of Asian Peoples in 1980, much of the Siberian material was removed from storage and placed on display. A group of visiting Soviet anthropologists, viewing the partially completed hall, were astonished at what the Museum had. According to one anthropologist, the Museum's collection was the greatest aggregation of northeast Asian ethnography in the world, unsurpassed even in the Soviet Union.

## The End of the Expedition

The Jesup North Pacific Expedition ended in 1903, when Jesup, impatient to see results, and feeling that the question of the origin of the American Indian—from migrations of Asiatic nomads across the Bering Strait—had been amply solved, cut off funds. Boas, an extremely cautious scholar as well as an abrasive person, felt that years more work and study were needed for the definitive answer. By nature, Jesup simply couldn't understand Boas' attitude. Additional problems arose when the Museum hired a new Director, Hermon C. Bumpus, to manage much of the administration details of the Museum. After 1903, the Museum administration began to grow increasingly skeptical about Boas' activities, and especially about the work of the one man who continued to work in Asia after the Jesup expedition ended.

That man was Berthold Laufer, who had moved from Siberia to China. Typically, Boas had asked him to get every possible thing he could find on daily Chinese life, especially objects illustrating the life of the common man in China. Laufer was a painstaking collector, and a flood of material poured into the Museum—more than 20,000 specimens of every conceivable kind of thing.*

Laufer was working during this time under extremely difficult conditions. The Boxer Rebellion of 1900, a Chinese uprising against foreigners, had been heavily squelched, and resentment against Westerners ran high. In addition, there were the usual collecting difficulties. As one of Laufer's letters to Boas, defending his failure to procure an industrial collection, attests: "Please do not think that making collections in this country merely means going shopping; it is an awful hard task which requires a great deal of good nerves, the self-control of a god and an angel's patience; sometimes it even wearies me to death and makes me tired of life."

Boas constantly wrote to Laufer, telling him what to collect and what to save for later, and the two sometimes became involved in unpleasant disagreements. But despite haggling, the final result of Laufer's work was summed up by a present-day anthropologist as "one of the finest records of the material culture of a civilization ever assembled."

Meanwhile, Boas' troubles at the Museum were deepening. As Jesup grew older, he became more insistent that Boas publish the definitive work of the expedition—the proof that America was peopled by tribes from northeastern Asia. Boas also quarreled with Hermon C. Bumpus about the Northwest Coast exhibition. Boas, the strict scientist, wasn't able to understand what a popular museum should be, and detested seeing his work simplified for the general public. Bumpus meanwhile was alarmed at the seemingly endless flow of artifacts coming from China and filling up valuable Museum storage space, and he tried to curtail Asian collecting. The end result of all this internecine strife was that in 1905 Boas resigned in anger and took a teaching position at Columbia University. Ironic though it is that Boas never published his *magnum opus*

---

*Laufer even tried to obtain the heads of executed criminals to aid the research of physical anthropologists at the Museum.

proving the migration of early man across the Bering Strait, most anthropologists generally agree that the expedition proved the question beyond a reasonable doubt.

At Columbia, Boas continued to work with anthropologists and collections at the Museum, even though he held no official position. Among his students were Ruth Benedict and Margaret Mead, who spent over fifty years at the Museum. Boas' influence on American anthropology, both through his own work and through his students, shaped the course of American anthropology in a profound way. Even today, many of our contemporary ideas about culture, race, and society originated with Boas and his students.

# FOUR

# Exploration at the Top
# of the World

A map of the world, circa 1890, reveals few unexplored areas. Africa had been penetrated and mapped, the Amazon traced to its source, the vast Sahara crossed and recrossed. The map shows, however, two vast blank areas, surrounded by dotted lines, each one straddling a geographic Pole. At that time the northern blank spot covered an area of over one million square miles on the top of the globe, overlapping parts of both North America and Greenland.

No one knew what would be found at the North Pole. Conservative scientists speculated a wasteland of ice, or perhaps an unknown landmass. Still others predicted an "Arctic Atlantis," a lost continent heated by hot springs and populated with wild game. Some even advanced wild theories about a maelstrom or a tropical sea at the Pole.

Curiosity about the Pole grew out of the centuries-long quest for a Northwest Passage—the hypothetical and economically important sea route between the Atlantic and Pacific oceans, and thus between the rich markets of Europe and the Orient. The search for the Northwest Passage, begun in America's infancy, soon metamorphosed into a search for new lands and peoples. As Greenland and the Northwest Territories were gradually explored and mapped, the search finally focused on the North Pole itself. Polar exploration excited the public as no exploration had before, and an explorer returning alive from the far north could expect a tumultuous welcome as well as certain wealth in the form of book royalties and lecture fees.

While most people saw polar exploration and the discovery of the Pole as ends in themselves, President Jesup and the Museum seized upon this opportunity to acquire collections of animals and artifacts from within the unknown regions. The Museum helped finance a number of polar expeditions, in return for receiving the resulting scientific collections. Jesup cared little for the flags, sledges, and souvenirs that other institutions such as the National Geographic Society wanted; the Museum was much more interested in the zoological specimens, Eskimo artifacts, and geological data accumulated along the way.

Jesup's interest brought the Museum into association with a young naval lieutenant, Robert E. Peary, who had been exploring Greenland and the far north with the ultimate goal of getting to the Pole. Jesup first learned of Peary when the explorer's wife asked him to contribute a thousand dollars to a "Peary Relief Expedition," organized to rescue her husband, who was stranded in northern Greenland at the time. Jesup struck a sort of deal with Peary: He would help finance the explorer's work and pull strings to keep him on leave from the navy if Peary would make collections in the Arctic for the Museum.

The ethnological work dovetailed neatly with the work of the Jesup North Pacific Expedition. In 1897, the same year Boas left New York for British Columbia, Jesup obtained leave from the navy for Peary by writing to President McKinley. His letter told the President of Peary's potential value in helping to make the Arctic collections at the Museum "second to none in magnitude and completeness." Jesup was influential enough to obtain almost ten years of cumulative leave for Peary. He also paid for some of his ships and equipment, and formed the Peary Arctic Club—a group of his wealthy friends, who poured money into Peary's efforts.

Jesup's investment was soon to pay handsome dividends in collections. Among the zoological and ethnographic material that eventually found its way back to New York were numerous birds, Arctic hares and foxes, polar bears, marine mammals, Eskimo artifacts—and several huge meteorites.

## Peary's Iron Mountain

In the spring of 1894, after one of many unsuccessful attempts to reach the Pole, Peary found himself waiting out the Arctic spring with nothing to do. Like many Arctic explorers before him, Peary had heard stories about an "iron mountain" somewhere in northwestern Greenland. Now, with so much time on his hands, Peary decided to locate the fabled mountain once and for all.

The story of the iron mountain dated back to 1818, when an English explorer, Sir John Ross, sailed north to the head of Baffin Bay in an effort to locate the Northwest Passage. On the western shores of Greenland he discovered an unknown tribe of Eskimos—among the most northerly peoples in the world. He was astonished to find that these Stone Age peoples, without the knowledge of smelting, somehow possessed knives and spearheads made of iron. The Eskimos refused to reveal the source of the metal, saying only that it came from a mountain of iron, or *saviksoah*,* and had been their source of metal since time im-

---

*Throughout this chapter and those that follow, I have mostly used the explorers' phonetic spellings of Eskimo names, instead of their Greenlandic spellings, to avoid confusing the reader when those names appear in diary and article extracts. For this same reason, I have commonly made use throughout the book of place names contemporaneous with the periods involved, as opposed to the names by which they are known today.

memorial. Ross returned to England with some of the tools, which were analyzed and found to have a high nickel content—much higher than in any naturally occurring alloys on earth. The mountain of iron, English scientists decided, was a gigantic meteorite. A number of explorers following in Ross's footsteps tried to locate the iron, to no avail.

Peary had several advantages over the earlier explorers who had searched without success for the meteorite. By now the Eskimos were trading iron knives, spearheads, and even guns with the white men and no longer had need of the *saviksoah*. More important, the Eskimos liked and trusted the young lieutenant. Peary found an Eskimo who agreed to lead him to the mountain of iron in return for a gun. On May 16, 1894, the Eskimo, Peary, and expedition member Hugh Lee started on their journey with a sledge and ten dogs.

The Eskimo led them south along the Greenland coast, toward Cape York and Melville Bay. They sledged along the frozen bays rather than attempting the sheer cliffs and headlands of the fjords. May is possibly the worst month to travel in the Arctic. Warmer weather breaks up the ice pack, making sea travel difficult. Blizzards are frequent and fearsome events. As it happened, soft ice and a powerful blizzard immediately beset the party, and after two days the Eskimo guide refused to proceed further, sledding off into the whirling snow. Peary and Lee doggedly pushed on to a nearby Eskimo village and found another guide, a man named Tallakoteah. Tallakoteah spoke of three irons, which he called "the Woman," "the Dog," and "the Tent." During the next week, Tallakoteah led the party through some of the severest conditions Peary had yet experienced in the Arctic. The sea ice began to disintegrate, and they sometimes found themselves balancing across cakes of floating ice and wading through waist-high slush. At night, freezing winds piled up huge drifts, covering their igloo and dogs. Finally, when the sea ice became impassable, the party had to haul its dogs and sledges up to the top of a thousand-foot plateau to avoid open water. On May 27, near the shore of Melville Bay, Tallakoteah halted on a large, level snowfield and planted his sawknife in the hard-pack. He announced they had reached the Woman. From a hill, Tallakoteah pointed out the location of the other two meteorites. Peary was skeptical; all that was visible was a bit of "blue traprock" poking out of a drift. Nevertheless, the Eskimo deftly cut through the snow with his knife, exposing a smooth brown surface. Soon he had enlarged the hole to a pit three feet deep and five feet across. In the middle sat an ugly, squat lump of brown iron. "The brown mass," Peary wrote in his book, *Northward Over the Great Ice*, "rudely awakened from its winter's sleep, found for the first time in its cycles of existence the eyes of a white man gazing upon it." The explorer leaned into the hole and claimed the object by scratching his initial *P* into its malle-able skin.* Surrounding it were hundreds of broken stones, with which the Eskimos had been hammering off flakes of iron for centuries. (The meteorite itself reveals a dented surface, completely covered with hammer marks.)

Tallakoteah then told Peary the legend of the three irons. According to the local myth, they had once been a sewing woman and her dog who lived in a tent in the sky. An evil spirit hurled the woman, the dog, and the tent from heaven and they landed on earth as lumps of iron. Al-though Peary took this as proof that the Eskimos had wit-nessed the fall of the meteorites, today scientists feel that the three meteorites—all part of the same shower—fell thousands of years before the coming of the Eskimo to Greenland.† It is more likely the Eskimo made up the story, knowing Peary thought (absurd white man!) that the irons had fallen from the sky. A common problem that anthropologists face is the less-than-truthful informant.

*I have been unable to find his initial on the meteorite, which is now on display in the Museum's Hall of Meteorites.

†Scientists know that all three came from the same shower because they possess identical chemical composition and crystalline properties. The three irons originated as a single mass that struck the earth's upper atmosphere and exploded, sending the pieces slamming into an ice sheet. As the sheet retreated, it deposited the pieces on the ground. Since Peary's day, smaller pieces from the same shower have also been found.

They left the meteorites in place, taking careful note of their locations, then headed back to camp. Although equally harrowing, the return trip was without major catastrophe.

That August, Peary returned to Melville Bay with his ship, the *Falcon*, to collect the meteorites, but the ship was driven back by drifting pack ice. The following year, 1895, he returned with a steamer, the *Kite*, during Greenland's three-week "summer," anchoring in Melville Bay. He was received by a large group of Eskimos, who had gathered to witness the foolhardy white man's attempt to take their *saviksoah*. The Eskimos, who no longer needed the irons, didn't object to Peary taking them away. Besides, they believed the venture would end in an entertaining disaster.

Working in haste before the winter ice would lock them in, Peary hauled the 900-pound Dog meteorite down to the water and floated it to the ship. The 2 3/4-ton Woman was next. They rolled and dragged it to the shore, placed it on a large ice flow overlaid with planks, and secured it with tackle. Just as the floating cake reached the boat it began to break up—much to the merriment and satisfaction of the Eskimos—but the tackle held and the Woman was hauled aboard. Peary wisely left the Tent behind, which, at thirty tons, was at least ten times larger than both other meteorites combined. It rested on an island about six miles from the others.

Peary returned to Melville Bay in 1896 with a new ship, the *Hope*, several heavy hydraulic jacks, and a mass of chains, ropes, railroad rails, and heavy timbers. With the *Hope* anchored in Melville Bay, Peary and his crew dug around the meteorite, and soon could maneuver the hydraulic jacks under the giant iron. In *Northward Over the Great Ice*, Peary wrote:

> The first thing to be done was to tear the heavenly visitor from its frozen bed of centuries, and as it rose slowly inch by inch under the resistless life of the hydraulic jacks, gradually displaying its ponderous sides,

it grew upon us as Niagara grows upon the observer, and there was not one of us unimpressed by the enormousness of this lump of metal.

They had good reason to be impressed; it was the largest meteorite ever discovered. After much discussion they decided to roll it down the steep hill to the ship, using the hydraulic jacks to turn it over.

It was interesting, though irritating, to watch the stubbornness of the monster as it sulked and hung back to the last inch. Urged by the jacks, the huge brown mass would slowly and stubbornly rise on its side, and be forced into a position of unstable equilibrium. . . . A few more pulls . . . and the top of the meteorite would move almost imperceptibly forward, the stones under the edge of revolution would begin to splinter and crumble, then amidst the shouts of the natives and our own suppressed breathing, the "Iron Mountain" would roll over. When it struck the ground the hard rocks would elicit streams of sparks from its brown surface before they crumbled, the softer ones would dissolve into dust and smoke, and the giant would bury itself half its depth in the earth with a slow, resistless motion.

The sheer weight of the meteorite began to wear out all three jacks, and the weather worsened. A gale broke the ice barrier holding the sea ice out of Melville Bay, and winds drove it toward the ship, threatening to trap the vessel for the winter. Peary and his crew worked feverishly through the night,

a night of such savage wildness as is possible only in the Arctic regions. The wild gale was howling out of the depth of Melville Bay through the *Hope*'s rigging, and the snow was driving in horizontal lines. . . . Towering above the human figures about it, and standing out black and uncompromising, was the *raison d'être* of it all.

The next morning they abandoned the meteorite on shore and fled from the bay just before the ice pack closed in behind them.

Peary wouldn't give up. He returned again with the *Hope* and still heavier equipment in the summer of 1897. The meteorite still stood on a low bluff at the shore of the island, and this time Peary brought the large ship right into a stretch of deep water next to the bluff, thereby putting the boat in an extremely dangerous position. Any storm or shifting currents could have nudged the ship against the shore, sending it straight to the bottom. Working fast, Peary's crew laid steel rails across the narrow stretch of water between the bluff and the deck. As the "monster" was inched along the rails, which had been greased with soap tallow, the ship groaned and lurched, causing an uproar among the Eskimos, who felt that heaven was finally going to punish Peary for his audacity. But the meteorite was at last brought on board, where it literally sank into the complaining timbers of the ship's deck. Peary's four-year-old daughter was aboard, and she broke a bottle of wine over it and uttered a string of nonsense syllables, "ah-ni-ghi-to," which immediately became the meteorite's name. (Officially, this meteorite has three names: the Tent [its Eskimo name], Ahnighito [its popular name], and Cape York [its scientific name, in keeping with the nomenclature of meteorites, which are usually named after the nearest landmark]. The scientific name of the Woman and Dog is also Cape York.)

"Never," wrote Peary later, "have I had the terrific majesty of the force of gravity and the meaning of the words 'momentum' and 'inertia' so powerfully brought home to me as in handling this mountain of iron." When the meteorite was safely aboard, the ship's navigator found his compass needles locked in the direction of the iron mass.

The *Hope* arrived at the Brooklyn Navy Yard, where the Ahnighito was unloaded by a 100-ton floating crane (it had previously broken a fifty-ton crane) and stored under a tarpaulin. There it sat in obscurity while Jesup and Mrs. Peary, acting as her husband's agent while he was trying to reach the Pole, haggled amicably over a price. Mrs. Peary wanted $60,000, but Jesup felt the price was too high, especially considering the Museum's large financial support of Peary.

Mrs. Peary felt that these meteorites, gained at such effort, were worth a payment from the Museum above and beyond the normal support. She wrote a somewhat facetious letter to Jesup, in which she pleaded,

> The meteorites are all I have and I feel that I should make an effort to turn them into money and invest it so that my children will have something with which they may be educated to earn a living. . . . Mrs. Jesup would scold me but what can I do? . . . I have come to the conclusion that it is easier to go to the Arctic and do the thing you are interested in and want to do than it is to stay at home, bring up the children, fight your husband's battles and look out for the bread and butter for the family. I think hereafter I will do the exploring and let Mr. Peary take care of the home life.

The Museum, anticipating ownership, had by this time already taken possession of the meteorites. While everyone generally agreed that Peary was due an extra payment for the irons, the amount of the payment was yet to be resolved. The Ahnighito caused a sensation when it was moved from Brooklyn to the Museum. First floated up the East River on a barge, it was unloaded at the East 50th Street Pier and placed on a massive, custom-built cart. A block-long line of twenty-eight horses in fourteen teams hauled it to the Museum. The trip drew flocks of whooping street urchins and clerks in derby hats, who noisily followed its progress through the streets.

Twelve years after the Ahnighito's arrival in New York— five years after its delivery to the Museum—Mrs. Morris K. Jesup sent Mrs. Peary a check for $40,000, and the meteorites became the official property of the Museum.*

---

*Although the Ahnighito is still the largest meteorite ever recovered, a larger one does exist in the deserts of South Africa. Called the Hoba, it has never been fully excavated and is estimated to weigh nearly twice as much as the Ahnighito.

By most accounts, the Polar Eskimos enjoyed the rare visits of white explorers to their land, and it is not surprising that on two occasions, at the Eskimos' request, Peary brought them back on his ship to show them his own country. Unfortunately, the change from Greenland to New York was as much, if not more, of a shock to the Eskimos than the change from New York to Greenland was for the explorers. When Peary returned to New York in 1897 with the great Ahnighito meteorite, his ship, the *Hope*, also carried six Polar Eskimos from Smith Sound in Greenland. The Eskimos planned to spend the winter in New York City and then to go back north in the spring. (In 1894 the explorer's wife, Josephine, had returned to New York with an Eskimo girl from Smith Sound. The girl, whom the Pearys called "Miss Bill," lived with Mrs. Peary for a year and reportedly enjoyed herself immensely; the following year, Peary took her back to her family in Greenland.)

Exactly why Peary brought six Eskimos back with him in 1897 is unclear. According to an account by the Museum's Director at the time, Hermon C. Bumpus, Peary told him that the Eskimos had asked to be taken to New York for the winter. A Museum anthropologist, the late Junius Bird, believed that Peary brought them back "that they might see how others lived," a common practice among eighteenth- and nineteenth-century explorers.

It was not long before ill effects resulted from the radical change in climate. Soon after their arrival in New York, the Eskimos were observed to have slight colds, and in four of the Eskimos the colds developed into influenza, bronchitis, and then tuberculosis, one of many diseases to which it was later realized that the Eskimo have a poorly developed immunity. By the spring of 1898, the four had succumbed.

Two Eskimos survived: an adult named Uisâkavsak and a little boy of about eight to ten years, named Mene, the son of one of the dead Eskimos. That spring, Peary offered to carry them back to Greenland on his ship, the *Windward*. The adult accepted, but Mene said he wanted to stay in America and was adopted by a Museum employee, William Wallace. Mene grew up in the Wallace home and later returned to Greenland, where he joined an American Museum of Natural History expedition to seek out a large, unknown continent thought to exist northwest of Ellesmere Island. Hired by the expedition's leader, Donald MacMillan, Mene was one of seven Eskimos and five Americans who set out from Smith Sound in March 1914. On the first leg of the expedition, the explorers endured a grueling trip across Smith Sound and up the eastern side of Ellesmere. When they reached the foot of the massive Beitstadt Glacier and were faced with a climb up a nearly vertical wall of ice, Mene announced he wanted to return to Smith Sound, and MacMillan let him go. A second Eskimo, Tau-ching-wa, deserted only a few hours later. (Another Eskimo told MacMillan that Mene had decided to return to Greenland to enjoy the company of Tau-ching-wa's wife. This other Eskimo had alerted Tau-ching-wa, who decided that the expedition came second to his wife's virtue.)

A year later, however, Mene rejoined the expedition, "very repentant over his failure of the year before," according to MacMillan. In the end, he proved himself an able explorer.

There is an interesting story attached to the other Eskimo, Uisâkavsak, who survived his trip to New York. He returned to Greenland in 1898 aboard the *Windward*, and as far as we know, he was the first adult Polar Eskimo to visit the white man's land and return to tell about it. (Miss Bill had been too young to understand much of what went on around her.) A Danish explorer, Knud Rasmussen, was in Greenland around the time of Uisâkavsak's homecoming, and he described the Eskimo's return (quoted by Rolf Gilberg in his excellent monograph *The Big Liar*, translation from the Danish by Gilberg):

> When Uisâkavsak returned, he gathered around him a large audience to tell them of the marvels he had seen. "The ships," he said, "sailed in and out there, like eiders on the brooding cliffs when their young begin to

swim. There weren't many free drops of water in the
harbor itself; it was filled with ships. You'd risk your
life if you tried to go out there in a kayak, you'd simply
not be noticed, and you'd be run down unmercifully.
People live up in the air like auks on a bird cliff. The
houses are as big as icebergs on a glacial bank, and they
stretch inland as far as you can see, like a steep chain of
mountains with innumerable canyons that serve as
roads.

"And the people. Yes, there are so many of them that
when smoke rises from the chimneys and the women
are about to make breakfast, clouds fill the sky and the
sun is eclipsed. . . ."

Rasmussen went on to report that Uisâkavsak was "in-
toxicated by his listeners' amazed expressions" and that
"he could not stop talking." He told them about "streetcars,
big as houses, with masses of glass windows as transparent
as freshwater ice. They raced on without dogs to haul
them, without smoke, full of smiling people who had no
fear of their fate. And all this because a man pulled on a
cord." Rasmussen reported that "Uisâkavsak's listeners
began to doubt him seriously, but he gave them no time to
think, and went on to tell them about the 'distance
shrinker' (the telephone). He, Uisâkavsak, had stood and
talked to Peary, who was visiting another village. Without
shouting to one another, they had talked together through a
funnel, along a cord."

At this point, Rasmussen said, the tribe's respected
leader stood up and shouted angrily, "Uisâkavsak, go tell
your big lies to the women!"

Eskimos consider lying to be a gravely serious matter,
and Uisâkavsak, who had hitherto held a position of esteem
among the Polar Eskimos, lost a great deal of respect and
was relegated to an inferior position in the society. He was
given the name "The Big Liar."

"Rasmussen," Gilberg writes, "tried to restore Uisâkavsak's honor by confirming what was said, but one of the
influential Polar Eskimos discreetly advised him against
this, for it might hurt [Rasmussen] personally."

Uisâkavsak very sensibly stopped talking about his experiences in America, and he later moved south, away from the tribe, and discovered a rich hunting land unknown to them. Here was a place, he may have thought, where he could restore his honor and reputation. He later returned to his tribe's area loaded with wealth, and was accepted as a powerful hunter. Unfortunately, his wife died, and as there was a shortage of women in the tribe, he stole the wife of another Eskimo. This Eskimo, who had been with Peary on his trip to the North Pole in 1909, didn't take this lightly and later, with an accomplice, lured him out on the Inglefield Fjord. There they shot and killed Uisâkavsak, "The Big Liar."

# FIVE

# The Search for the Arctic Atlantis

The American Museum of Natural History has over the years been unusually lucky; almost all of its expeditions have returned with valuable results and collections. The Museum's success with polar expeditions, however, came to an abrupt end with the Crocker Land Expedition—perhaps the greatest scientific failure in the Museum's history.

In June of 1906, nine years after successfully recovering the Ahnighito meteorite, Peary stood on the summit of Cape Colgate in the extreme northwestern part of North America—only nine degrees from the Pole—and carefully scanned the northern horizon with his binoculars. He was the first explorer to have reached this headland, and before him lay a vast, uncharted area covering over a million square miles. Later he recorded what he saw: "North stretched the well-known ragged surface of the polar pack, and northwest it was with a thrill that my glasses revealed the white summits of a distant land."

Several days later he stopped at Cape Thomas Hubbard,

closer to the northwestern edge of the unknown land. It was a splendid, crystal-clear day, and Peary again trained his glasses to the northwest. He wrote:

> The clear day greatly favored my work in taking a round of angles, and with the glass I could make out apparently a little more distinctly the snow-clad summits of the distant land to the northwest, above the ice horizon. My heart leaped the intervening miles of ice as I looked longingly at this land, and in fancy I trod its shores and climbed its summits, even though I knew that the pleasure could be only for another in another season.

He estimated that the unknown land lay about 120 miles offshore, and he christened it Crocker Land, in honor of one of his financial backers.

In 1913 the Museum set out on its most ambitious polar expedition to date—to discover, explore, and map Crocker Land. The Crocker Land Expedition lasted from 1913 to 1917. It was to be the first time in the Museum's history that an expedition became a spectacular failure.

By 1910 much of northern Greenland, Ellesmere Land, and the area around the North Magnetic Pole had been explored, and Peary himself had finally taken the geographic Pole in 1909. The discovery and mapping of Crocker Land thus became a top priority of Arctic exploration. While some geologists and geographers questioned whether Crocker Land actually existed, most others felt that the question was settled and began instead debating its size and extent. In 1911 a tidal expert with the U.S. Coast and Geodetic Survey studied Arctic currents and concluded that a great landmass or island archipelago stretched from northwestern North America across to eastern Siberia. This was confirmed by several reports that mountain peaks had been seen from northern Alaska over the ice horizon of the Polar Sea.

Now that the North Pole had been exposed as an icy wasteland, Crocker Land became the object of extensive scientific speculation. Some believed that Crocker Land would turn out to be, in the words of Peary, "an isolated island continent, an Arctic Atlantis, with a flora and fauna of its own." "Volcanic ashes have fallen on Greenland," wrote explorer Fitzhugh Green. "The Aleutians are buried furnaces. If there be an ice-cooled desert, why not a steamed-heated paradise?" The Eskimos themselves talked about a distant land, a sort of Shangri-la, dotted with herds of game and warmed by the sun. According to the Eskimos, all who came across this land chose not to return.

The Museum had supported Peary on his expedition to the North Pole and other Arctic explorations, and so it seemed natural that the Museum should organize an expedition to Crocker Land. The discovery of a new landmass would not only bring the Museum fame and glory, but it would open up a whole new area for zoological research and collecting. Perhaps even a new tribe of northern peoples would be discovered. Crocker Land was a tempting scientific plum indeed. The American Geographical Society, the Peary Arctic Club, and various American and British philanthropists backed the expedition as well.

The Museum chose Donald B. MacMillan to lead the expedition. MacMillan had accompanied Peary on his last polar expedition, and knew the ways of the north. (The Museum's original choice for the expedition's leader, George Borup, drowned in a tragic accident while plans for the expedition were being finalized.) Elmer Ekblaw and Ensign Fitzhugh Green assisted MacMillan; Ekblaw to work on geological and botanical studies and Green to handle the cartographic, meteorological, and seismological studies. (Peary himself had retired from Arctic exploration after his polar conquest.) Neither Ekblaw nor Green knew much about survival in the north, but the Museum noted confidently that Green came from "old Colonial stock" and that his experience in the navy "has already taught him how to command as well as obey."

The Museum laid grand plans for the study of Crocker Land. First the expedition would make scientific observations in the far north. Then, as they headed across the Polar Sea toward Crocker Land, they would take soundings and make tidal and meteorological observations. They were to spend two months mapping Crocker Land itself and collecting specimens, then the expedition was to return to Greenland to make a first ascent to the summit of its ice cap.

The expedition set sail in July 1913, on the *Diana*, carrying stoves, food, clothes, sledges, and scientific equipment. In Boston they picked up eleven tons of pemmican (a nutritious mixture of dried beef and suet, with raisins thrown in to help prevent constipation) and eleven tons of army hardtack. In Nova Scotia they took aboard seventeen tons of Spratt's Dog Biscuit. Then the *Diana*'s drunken captain ran his ship aground off the coast of Labrador, and a new ship had to be chartered, at a cost of $15,000. This ship, the *Erik*, took the expedition north through Baffin Bay along the western flank of Greenland, to Smith Sound. This was a narrow sound at the head of Baffin Bay, separating Greenland and Ellesmere Land. The captain unloaded the expedition at Etah, a Polar Eskimo settlement that was at that time the most northerly human settlement in the world. It was now August and the party settled in for the winter, planning to begin the search for Crocker Land just before the Arctic dawn in February, when the ice pack would be hard and smooth.

Peary had learned one great lesson in the north: to survive, one had to live, eat, and travel like the Eskimo. MacMillan, who had been with Peary in Greenland, introduced his companions to the ways of the Eskimo, who taught them about Arctic survival—skills such as building igloos (tents were useless), driving dogs, hunting game, wearing native clothing, and caring for the feet.* They planned to travel by dogsled and subsist on pemmican and on what walrus, musk-oxen, polar bear, and caribou they could get. Green later wrote that by learning the Eskimo way of life, they "bought their lives."

As February drew near, MacMillan divided the expedi-

---

*The Eskimo, MacMillan wrote, were "mortally afraid of having their feet frostbitten, nursing them as tenderly as a mother would her youngest child."

tion—nineteen Eskimos (including Mene Wallace), the
three explorers, a surgeon named Hunt, and a zoologist
named Tanquary—into four parties. On February 7, 1914,
the first party, led by Fitzhugh Green, departed into the
Arctic night over the ice of Smith Sound. Tanquary left the
next day, Ekblaw on February 9, Hunt on February 10, and
MacMillan on February 13.

MacMillan had mapped out their route. They planned to
cross Smith Sound to Ellesmere Land, cross the glaciated
heights of Ellesmere, and descend to Eureka Sound on the
far side. From there they would follow Eureka Sound
northwest to Cape Thomas Hubbard, from which Peary
had sighted the mountains of Crocker Land eight years before.

On February 13, MacMillan and his party crossed Smith
Sound in bitter cold, following in the footsteps of the three
advance parties. While following north along the coastline
of Ellesmere, he came across two dead dogs on the trail.
On the night of February 14, they couldn't find hard-
packed snow to build an igloo and were forced to sleep
unprotected. In an effort to keep warm, MacMillan built a
fire out of his biscuit boxes and accidentally set his sleeping bag on fire. ("I was warm at last," he joked in his
journal.) The next day he joined up with the advance parties camped on the ice of Hayes Sound, and discovered that
several of the Eskimos had caught the mumps. They all
agreed the expedition had to return to its base camp. Back
in Etah, MacMillan decided to prune the size of the group
to "eliminate the chicken-hearted," and to try again in
March.

So on March 11, MacMillan, Green, and Ekblaw started
out again, this time with just seven Eskimos and one
hundred dogs. They traversed Smith Sound in a record six
hours, and in five days had worked northward along Ellesmere to their crossing point at the Beitstadt Glacier, a
nearly vertical wall of ice plunging into the frozen Beitstadt
Fjord. The glacier stretched across the breadth of Ellesmere and, once it had been ascended, the crossing would

be relatively easy. The Eskimo leader, Pee-a-wah-to, who had been one of Peary's most trusted companions on his polar attempts, chose a route up the glacier and began cutting steps in the ice with his hatchet. In a grueling day's work they managed to haul the sledges up the glacial wall. (By this point, Mene Wallace had left for home, ostensibly in search of an immoral conquest.)

Several days of hard sledging brought them to the crest of the Ellesmere ice cap, almost a mile high. Here they commanded a spectacular view of Axel Heiberg Land, with its towering peaks and winding glaciers. Far below and to the west lay Eureka Sound, dimly visible through the Arctic haze. The team descended toward Bay Fjord, and reached the face of the glacier in one sixteen-hour march. (A "march," in Arctic parlance, is a day's journey by dogsled.) Again they faced a sheer wall of ice, but this time a long search failed to reveal a route down. Finally, Pee-a-wah-to discovered an ice ravine down the face of the glacier cut by meltwater, and the group descended to the head of Bay Fjord on the western flank of Ellesmere.

Unfortunately, Ekblaw's feet had been badly frostbitten during the crossing, and he had to return to Etah immediately. MacMillan asked Green and four Eskimos to accompany Ekblaw back to the base camp, with the understanding that Green and his Eskimos would come back along the route and rendezvous with MacMillan at Cape Thomas Hubbard, their launching point for Crocker Land.

MacMillan drove his dogsleds to Eureka Sound, where he found the ice scoured smooth by strong northerly winds —perfect for sledding. By March 30, MacMillan and the Eskimos had reached Schei Island, in the middle of Eureka Sound, where they found plenty of game, including muskoxen, blue foxes, and Arctic hares. They were even rushed by a large pack of white wolves that had apparently mistaken them for musk-oxen; when the wolves discovered their mistake, they fled in terror. With such plentiful game, MacMillan decided to wait for Green on Schei Island. "Our four days at Schei Island," he wrote later, "stand out as one of the bright spots of our trip—a large, well-warmed, and well-lighted igloo, plenty of food, and a wealth of fresh meat for the dogs."

After waiting five days without sight of Green, Mac-Millan left a cache of meat for Green's dogs and pushed north along Nansen Sound to Cape Thomas Hubbard. On April 11 he reached what he thought must be the cape, but violent winds and heavy drifts forced him upon arrival to dig out a shelter underneath a cliff. The next morning, above the howling of the wind, he heard crunching ice; Green and two Eskimos had arrived with loaded sledges, ready for the dash across the Polar Sea to Crocker Land. They holed up in the dugout and waited for the storm to pass.

April 13 dawned sunny and brilliantly clear, and Green and MacMillan went off in search of the cairn that Peary had left at the spot from which he sighted the new land. At the summit of the cape they failed to find any trace of Peary's cairn, or of the mountains and glaciers that Peary had sighted "over the ice horizon."

Undaunted, the next day they headed northwest over the rolling blue ice of the Polar Sea, in the direction of Crocker Land. As they drew away from the shore, they sighted Cape Thomas Hubbard to the north of where they had been camped, and were pleased that they had only missed it by a few miles.

A day's journey on the ice brought them to a series of transverse pressure ridges—areas where tidal currents had compressed the polar ice into huge, broken ridges. After making camp at the bottom of the first ridge, MacMillan and Pee-a-wah-to climbed up it to get a view of what lay ahead. When they reached the top, no one spoke. Ahead of them stretched the bane of Arctic exploration—lanes of open water, or "leads," which had been opened by high tides generated by the full moon on April 10. To cross a lead, one must either go around it (which is often impossible, since a lead can be dozens of miles long), or wait for it to freeze over or close up.

The following day the party hit the first lead, which was over a hundred yards wide, with no sign of any imminent closing up. They built their igloos and decided to take their first sounding. With an ice axe as a weight, Green began unreeling the sounding wire through a hole in the ice. Two hundred fathoms were passed, then five hundred, then a thousand, and finally two thousand before they gave up. They concluded that since they were only seventeen miles from land, a coastal current was carrying the light pick along at an angle. For five hours they slowly reeled in the line, when suddenly it snapped and the axe was lost. Mac-Millan searched through their belongings for another weight, but the only possibility was their last ice axe, which they didn't dare risk. MacMillan wrote angrily: "To think that my dogs had pulled that reel . . . weighing about forty pounds, for nearly five hundred miles, only to have it thrown away without a single sounding!" He dumped the useless wire on the ice and they retired for the night.

The next morning the first man up looked through the peephole of the igloo and shouted that the lead had frozen up. The men and dogs edged out over the rubbery saltwater ice; several dogs broke through but were retrieved, and they reached the other side safely. Twelve miles later they hit a second lead, which suddenly closed up into a grinding mass of ice, allowing them only a few harrowing moments to cross. Toward the end of the day they hit a third lead, where they made camp. Again, a cold night froze the lead and they were able to cross the following morning.

Leads continued to plague the expedition. On April 19, MacMillan wrote in his diary:

It has been a succession of leads throughout the day . . . at 12:30, at 2:45, at 3:30, and at 4. We found them all covered with the same dangerous thin ice, which bends and buckles like rubber.

As we crossed the last it came together and rose beneath our feet, lifting dogs, sledges and men with such a grinding, crushing noise that I could not hear the Eskimos yelling their instructions.

They made it, however, and by the end of that day, they figured by dead reckoning that they were fifty-two miles offshore. ("Dead reckoning" is an estimate of position based on a guess of how many miles have been traveled in a given direction from a known point. It is the most unreliable form of navigation.) The peaks of Ellesmere to the east finally slipped below the horizon, but mist had obscured their view to the west. MacMillan waited impatiently for a clear day.

April 21 was such a day. Green rose early and MacMillan heard him cry, "We have it!" "Following Green," MacMillan recorded, "we ran to the top of the highest mound. There could be no doubt about it. Great heavens! What a land! Hills, valleys, snow-capped peaks extending through at least one hundred and twenty degrees of the horizon." Pee-a-wah-to, however, displayed a singular lack of enthusiasm. When quizzed, he "astounded" MacMillan by replying that he thought Crocker Land was *poo-jok*, or mist. The other Eskimos were evasive and noncommittal. While still sure they had seen land, Green and MacMillan were nevertheless taken aback by the Eskimos, and they thought it might be a ploy to deceive them into turning back. But as the sun swung across the sky, the land changed its appearance. At sunset, it disappeared entirely.

On April 22, MacMillan figured they were one hundred miles from shore by dead reckoning. The men's eyes were constantly turned west: "On this day," MacMillan recorded, "there was the same appearance of land in the west but it gradually faded away toward evening as the sun worked around in front of us."

By April 23 the Eskimos were becoming restless and dissatisfied. MacMillan took out his map showing the location of Crocker Land in brown, and emphatically told the depressed Eskimos that they were going to the brown spot on the map. At noon the next day, Green stopped to take the first careful sighting of their actual position (rather than relying on dead reckoning), while MacMillan continued on. (Green hadn't taken a sighting of their position earlier because it required remaining in one spot while the sun changed position in the sky. They had been in too much of a hurry.) When Green caught up with MacMillan at the end of the day, he explained that his sightings showed they were considerably ahead of their dead reckoning. In fact, they were actually *150 miles* due northwest from Cape Thomas Hubbard. MacMillan was stunned. "We had not only reached the brown spot on the map," he wrote, "but were thirty miles 'inland'!"

They climbed to the top of the highest pressure ridge and scanned every foot of the horizon. Not a thing was in sight. Ice stretched away on all sides, as far as the eye could see. Beyond that was clear blue sky.

MacMillan and Green discussed their problem. They had food for two days' farther advance. To the west, however, the sea ice presented a new spectacle—a "perfect chaos" of pressure ridges crisscrossing in every direction. "Two days work through the ice would net possibly eight or ten miles . . . It was late in the year; we had more than thirty leads behind us; a full moon was due on May 9; we had more than covered our distance." They could see no land fifty miles to the west; thus any land, if there, had to be at least two hundred miles offshore. It was physically impossible, therefore, that Peary had sighted land. *He had merely recorded an Arctic mirage.* "We were convinced we were in pursuit of a will-o'-the-wisp, ever receding, ever changing, ever beckoning. . . ."

Bitterly disappointed, they headed back over the Polar Sea. Whenever they looked back, MacMillan wrote, "the mirage of the sea ice resembling in every particular an immense land, seemed to be mocking us. It seemed so near and so easily attainable if we would only turn back." On the return leg the weather was splendid and the leads frozen. In just four days they had traversed the 150 miles back to Cape Thomas Hubbard, where they could see outlined against the sky the cairn that Peary had built in 1906 on the spot where he sighted Crocker Land. MacMillan and Green wearily ascended the cape, where they found a bit of silk flag and a note inside a cocoa tin in Peary's hand, recording the date and sighting. "Standing beside this cairn,"

MacMillan wrote, "Peary saw and reported Crocker Land to lie 120 miles due northwest. We looked toward the distant horizon. Glasses were not necessary. There was land everywhere! Had we not just come from far over the horizon we would have returned to our country and reported land as Peary did."

MacMillan ordered that he and Green should return to Etah by different routes. While he, MacMillan, would continue north to Cape Colgate to secure a written note (called a "record") left by the explorer Sverdrup, Green and Pee-a-wah-to would explore part of the western coast of Axel Heiberg Land—two marches down and one march back.

The morning they parted dawned gray and ominous. Leaden clouds covered the sky, and a hard wind was starting to pile up heavy drifts. As MacMillan headed from the camp he called good-bye to Green and Pee-a-wah-to; he wrote, "above the sound of the drifting snow I heard his faint reply in broken English and saw him run toward the south."

An hour after leaving Green, MacMillan realized that the storm was going to be even worse than he thought. Soon the swirling snow was driving so hard they had to fight for breath. MacMillan searched in the gale for one of their earlier igloos just south of the cape. The wind was so violent that at times the dogs couldn't move, but at last the igloo was reached.

The next morning the gale was still gusting at full force. "The wind," MacMillan wrote, "dropped down upon us with the force of an avalanche. The flying snow eddied and whirled and wrapped us in a white mantle, until dogs and men seemed as white specters." As they struggled forward, a white wolf came bounding out of a gale and lurked around them for ten miles until they reached the dugout where MacMillan had holed up in April while waiting for Green. He knew it would be impossible to reach Cape Colgate, so he abandoned his plan and dug himself in to await Green's return.

Strong winds and shifting shows continued for several more days, and MacMillan became increasingly concerned about Green. Six days had elapsed, but Green and Pee-a-wah-to had only left with three days' food. MacMillan knew Green was still not fully seasoned to the north, but he also knew that Pee-a-wah-to was one of the finest Eskimo guides in Greenland. "Where could they be and what could have happened?" MacMillan wrote. "So constantly did I watch that point to the north throughout the day [May 4] that the picture is still in my mind—the broken ice, the sloping shore, the high bluff, the white hill."

Toward late afternoon, MacMillan finally saw a black dot with a sledge appear on the horizon. As the sledge got closer, he recognized it as Pee-a-wah-to's. An eerie meeting then took place.

"I ran along the ice foot," wrote MacMillan, "to meet the sledge. Yes, those were Pee-a-wah-to's dogs. As the question, 'Where's Green?' was about to burst from my lips, the driver, whose eyes were covered with large metal glasses, seemed to turn suddenly into a strange likeness of Green. He looked as if he had risen from the grave.

"This is all that is left of your southern division," he said.

"What do you mean—Pee-a-wah-to dead? Your dogs and sledge gone?" I inquired.

"Yes, Pee-a-wah-to is dead; my dogs were buried alive; my sledge is under the snow forty miles away."

As the two men talked, MacMillan learned the whole story of what had happened during those days on the ice. After consideration, they decided it would be best to deceive the Eskimos into thinking that Pee-a-wah-to had been killed in an avalanche of snow. The truth would probably have provoked the killing of Green and possibly other members of the expedition. When they finally reached Etah in early June, the Eskimos apparently did accept their explanation, and the expedition proceeded without interruption. Even the Museum was kept in the dark for over a year as to what had really happened.

Despite the great failure to find Crocker Land, the expedition still had other work to accomplish. In 1914 and 1915, the men explored unknown areas of Ellesmere and attained the summit of the Greenland ice cap. In 1915 the ship *Cluett* arrived to return the expedition to New York, but was crushed in the ice, leaving the expedition members and crew stranded in Parker Snow Bay with provisions for only three months. As a result, the expedition members returned north to the Eskimo settlement at Etah to bring food and skins back to the stranded crew of the *Cluett*. While there, Green and two others outfitted a sledge party to reach South Greenland in hope of getting help. After sledging a thousand miles southward Green and two other expedition members reached a small Danish port on the coast, only to discover that World War I and German attacks on shipping had made any sort of rescue impossible for the time being.

Finally, in July 1916, the *Danmark* arrived at the Greenland coast, and Green arranged for its charter to rescue the rest of the expedition. Green himself took another ship to Copenhagen and anxiously awaited news. In August the *Danmark* disappeared somewhere in the north without having reached Etah, and yet another year passed, the expedition hearing nothing and seeing no ship. (They would later learn the fate of the *Danmark*; it had caught fast in the ice, and over the winter its crew had mutinied.) In July of 1917, Green chartered yet another ship, the *Neptune*, a staunch Newfoundland sealer, to rescue his stranded friends. The *Neptune* made it. Finally, on July 29, 1917—five years after the start of the Crocker Land expedition—the ship steamed into Etah and carried the stranded party back to New York.

They brought back to the Museum thousands of photographs, Eskimo artifacts, and a wealth of new geographical and meteorological information about the Arctic. They also came back to a rather chilly reception at the Museum.

Henry Fairfield Osborn, then the Museum's president, was furious at the cost of the expedition. The Museum had originally committed "up to $6,000"; instead, the length of the expedition—and especially the chartering of no less than six ships—had cost the Museum a small fortune. The other financial backers of the expedition—the American Geographical Society and the University of Illinois—had pulled out of their original financial commitments, leaving the Museum with a staggering bill of well over $100,000, just when wartime inflation was eroding the institution's capital. Furthermore, Osborn was not a little displeased with the scientific results of the expedition. MacMillan and Osborn quarreled over the book and film rights to the expedition, and when Osborn learned that MacMillan had been bad-mouthing the Museum to the National Geographic Society, he became infuriated. He called MacMillan into his office and demanded a written apology. Instead, MacMillan sent him a long letter highly critical of the Museum, full of grievances and alleged wrongs the Museum had committed against the expedition, of which he sent copies to several prominent institutions. And then a most unwelcome letter arrived from the U.S. Secretary of State, inquiring about an alleged murder of an Eskimo by expedition member Fitzhugh Green.

Green's journal is stored in the Rare Book Room of the Museum, and it tells a chilling story indeed. On April 30, 1914, according to the journal, Green and Pee-a-wah-to left MacMillan and rounded Cape Thomas Hubbard. Around the corner of the cape they were struck by violent winds and a rapidly building storm. Pee-a-wah-to went on ahead and Green followed in his tracks, but he had trouble getting his dogs to move, "no matter how I beat them" (Green wrote in his journal). Green finally caught up with the Eskimo, who had built a small igloo near a ridge of ice. The snow drifted so heavily over the igloo that soon they couldn't keep their air hole open, and as a result their stove wouldn't burn. Finally, when they were in danger of suffocating under the snow they cut a hole in the roof. "P. went out," Green recorded, "telling me to stay inside."

Pee-a-wah-to then built a second igloo directly on top of the first. Green wrote, "He said my dogs were O.K. but didn't tell me he had changed his own [i.e., dug up and moved them]."*

Green continued in his journal:

When we finally got out in a lull in the storm I found my team had been buried under about 15 ft. of snow. We dug in vain.... [Green's dogs and sledge were too deeply buried and had died.] The storm came on again. P. and I were both made sick by the fumes [of the stove] in the illy ventilated igloo.

*Friday, May 1, 1914.* We tried twice before we got away. A lull in the storm was always followed by more wind and snow as before.

P. refused to go south or stay here [i.e., he wanted to return to the base camp instead of continuing on in the face of the storm]. I was forced to follow as I had no dogs or sledge.

We got away finally at seven A.M. In a little while it was as bad as ever. I could not ride as my feet were very wet and several toes seemed to be frosted.

We were both going over the glare ice and P. kept whipping up his dogs. I told him I could not keep up and he advised me to follow his trail. This was impossible. I then snatched the rifle from the load and warned him to keep behind me. A few minutes later I turned and saw him whipping up the dogs away from me.

I shot once in the air. He did not stop. I then killed him with a shot through the shoulder and another through the head.

I had trouble finding the igloo at the Cape.

*Saturday, May 2, 1914.* The storm abated considerably and I went over to Peary's cairn. I photographed it after removing record. I left a copy of Peary's record and the following of my own. [Green's record, which he copied in his journal, merely repeats why he shot the Eskimo.]

---

*In the Arctic, Eskimo dogs allow themselves to be buried by drifting snow during a storm, which collects about them and provides insulation. If the snow gets too deep, however, the dogs will suffocate.

Green later published an account of the killing in the United States Naval Institute Proceedings. "A moment before I had faced the end of everything," Green wrote. "He that had loomed hostile and a deceit between me and safety lay now crumpled and inert in the unheeding snow.

"For once fate was balked . . . I had baffled misfortune. The feeling sent red gladness to my anaemic humor . . . the present was perfect, ecstatic. To prolong the moment was my impulse. I laughed, not fiendishly, but because I was glad."

He lashed the body to the sledge and carried it through the storm to an abandoned igloo closer to his rendezvous point with MacMillan. He dragged the dead body into the igloo, and fell into an exhausted sleep, which was suddenly interrupted by a nightmare. When he awoke in a cold sweat, he found himself looking at the dead Eskimo. "A horrible sight met my eyes," he wrote. "His eyes were open, glaring and malignant, fixed upon me."

Green leaped up and dragged the body outside behind an ice hummock. "Perhaps the wolves and foxes did not find it for several days," he wrote. "Made little difference . . . I do not write to boast morbid delight in a truly sorrowful experience. . . . Let the right combination of circumstances, edged by the pitiless elements, cut a man to the quick and he will turn savage by the very logic he once boasted was his certificate of culture." It took Green two more days of horror battling the storm to return to the dugout camp where MacMillan was waiting for him.

MacMillan has revealed little of his feelings about his assistant's killing the Eskimo. He repeatedly stated that since Green felt it was necessary to take the life of his Eskimo companion, it was not up to MacMillan to pass judgment. In *Four Years in the White North*, MacMillan touches on the killing and does present a veiled criticism of his companion. He wrote:

Green, inexperienced in the handling of Eskimos, and failing to understand their motives and temperament, had felt it necessary to shoot his companion. Pee-a-wah-to was a faithful assistant of Peary for more than two years, his last trip as one of the famous starvation party to the world's record of 87°6'. He had been my traveling companion from the first, and one of the best.

In 1921 the Danish explorer Knud Rasmussen learned the truth about the killing of Pee-a-wah-to. He wrote a long letter that made its way to a Danish Minister and from there to the U.S. Secretary of State. In turn, the Secretary of State sent it to Osborn, asking for an explanation. Rasmussen, himself part Eskimo, was a close friend of Pee-a-wah-to's. When Rasmussen had arrived in Etah in 1916, he heard about his friend's death and asked MacMillan for an account of it. MacMillan merely told him their prepared story about an avalanche. But the story seemed suspicious to Rasmussen, and when he ran into Green in South Greenland he posed him the same question. According to Rasmussen, "Green's face suddenly changed color, and in evident confusion he replied that this was a matter which Mr. McMillan [sic] had told the members of the expedition not to speak about." Rasmussen added, "I only regarded [this explanation] as evidence of Mr. Green's mental condition, for I knew that during the winters in the northernmost Greenland his nerves had become absolutely ruined."

But then, several years later, Rasmussen picked up MacMillan's newly published *Four Years in the White North* and read the passage quoted above. He was enraged. He was especially incensed at the callous way MacMillan had described the shooting, "just as if there was only a question of a dog." In his letter he demanded that MacMillan provide a full account of the Eskimo's death, and that the Museum take care of Pee-a-wah-to's widow and children. He added that there was no need to prosecute Green for his crime: "Green was most certainly a nervous wreck," he wrote, "who cannot be regarded as responsible for his act." The nature of exploration in those times brought explorers into extreme circumstances, and it was clear to everyone that Green really felt he was defending his life when he shot the Eskimo.

The Museum replied that Green had helped Pee-a-wah-to's family while he was in Etah, that Pee-a-wah-to's widow had remarried, and that all of his children were either married or independent, except for one. An acrimonious exchange of letters took place. The Danes put the matter before a committee, which concluded in a report sent to the U.S. Secretary of State that Green had misunderstood Pee-a-wah-to's motives. The Eskimo, it reported, merely meant to exhort Green to keep going, thinking the white man meant to give up, and that he was only trying to escape from the deranged Green after Green fired the warning shot. It said, "Green, in a condition of despair and excitement, killed a well-meaning traveling companion." But the report noted that Pee-a-wah-to's widow had died and the children grown up, so that the claim for compensation was being dropped. The matter, having been brought up and dealt with by the proper authorities, was concluded.

The Crocker Land Expedition was the last to explore the Arctic using dogs and sledges; indeed, it was one of the last expeditions to explore the unknown without motorized travel and modern equipment. A decade later the airplane would prove conclusively that Crocker Land, the "Arctic Atlantis," was just a vast, frozen sea, broken and heaved into masses of ice, covering the pole and stretching from western North America to Siberia and beyond.

# The Great Dinosaur "Gold Rush"

During the first ten years of Jesup's tenure at the Museum, a dinosaur "gold rush" was in full swing in the American West. This gold rush was fueled primarily by two wealthy men—Othniel C. Marsh and Edward Drinker Cope—who were engaged in a pitched scientific battle to see who could discover and name the most dinosaurs. The two men hated each other bitterly, vilified each other in public and private, and poured their personal fortunes into searching for and digging up dinosaurs—Marsh for the Peabody Museum at Yale and the U.S. Geologic Survey, and Cope for the Academy of Natural Sciences in Philadelphia and his own private collection.

The extraordinary rivalry between these two eminent paleontologists began sometime in the late 1860s or early 1870s. While the exact moment of the break is in question (the two men had originally been friends), it probably came in a dispute over the fossil beds of Haddonfield, New Jersey, where the first American dinosaur had been discovered in 1858. At the time, Cope was living in Haddonfield and collecting specimens in the area. In the spring of 1868, Cope showed Marsh around the various quarries. Not long afterwards, Cope later alleged, Marsh paid off the quarry owners, and Cope suddenly found the quarries closed to him and open to Marsh. The rivalry intensified, although still on a professional level, when Cope reconstructed an *Elasmosaurus* skeleton and erroneously placed the skull on the end of the tail.* Marsh lost no time rushing a correction into print, in which he jokingly said that Cope should have named the animal *Streptosaurus*, meaning "twisted reptile." The article must surely have embarrassed and galled Cope.

In 1871, however, Cope turned the tables, and began digging in one of Marsh's fossil localities in Kansas (after hiring away one of his assistants). Similar incidents followed, with both Marsh and Cope luring each other's collectors away with more money; often, these collectors came with proprietary secrets about the location and extent of fossil beds. (Marsh and Cope did little of the actual collecting themselves. Instead, they hired and directed collecting parties.) In 1872 and 1873, in a nasty exchange of letters, Cope and Marsh accused each other of stealing specimens. Marsh also accused Cope of fudging the dates of publication of certain scientific articles, thus stealing credit for new discoveries away from Marsh. This question of dates was no trivial matter. The actual excavation of a new species meant little; it was the publication date of the *report* on the find that established to the scientific community who would get credit for the discovery. Often Cope and Marsh were making the same new discoveries, and thus the object of the race was to get into print first. Indeed, Cope even spent a large portion of his fortune buying a controlling interest in the journal *American Naturalist*, in order to rush his discoveries into print faster. Their scien-

---

*Elasmosaurus* was a long-necked, long-tailed marine reptile, and the specimen Cope was using was incomplete. The mistake was not as egregious as it may sound.

tific papers increasingly contained *ad hominem* attacks on each other, thinly disguised as "scientific criticism." "It is plain," Cope wrote in one paper, "that most of Prof. Marsh's criticisms are misrepresentations, his systematic innovations are untenable, and his statements as to the dates of my papers are either criminally ambiguous or untrue."

Before 1877, only scattered dinosaur remains had been found in England, western Europe, and America. But within a six-month period in 1877, three large dinosaur finds—culminating with the spectacular discovery of the vast fossil fields of Como Bluff, Wyoming—intensified the rivalry between Cope and Marsh, and greatly increased the scientific stakes. The find also served to popularize dinosaurs, and indirectly led the American Museum of Natural History into the arena of dinosaur collecting.

Marsh learned of this first major dinosaur find when he received a letter from Colorado schoolmaster and geologist, Arthur Lakes, who wrote him of "some enormous bones...of some gigantic saurian." Lakes enclosed a sketch.

At first, oddly enough, Marsh showed little interest in this letter and other letters that followed, some of which he didn't even bother to answer. But when Marsh learned that Lakes had then written to Cope, he immediately instructed his chief collector, Samuel Williston, to investigate the locality.

Coincidentally, at about that same time, Cope had received a letter from another Colorado resident, informing him of a find of large bones in a different spot. When Marsh learned of *this*, he again sent Williston out to investigate. Williston soon reported that Cope's men were indeed excavating and shipping large dinosaurs back to Philadelphia.

The third and most significant discovery came in a letter to Marsh from two men calling themselves Harlow and Edwards. Harlow and Edwards, whose real names were Carlin and Reed (and which they kept secret in an effort to protect their discovery), worked for the Union Pacific

Railroad, and they told Marsh they had discovered dinosaur fossils in Como Bluff, Wyoming Territory. In another letter, they warned Marsh that there were others in the area "looking for such things" (i.e., dinosaurs), and that they were operating in strict secrecy.

Marsh again dispatched Williston to reconnoiter. After a delay due to ill health, Williston arrived at Como Bluff on November 14, 1877. Williston had been there only hours when he fired off a letter to Marsh, which read in part, "I have seen a lot of bones that they have ready to ship and they tell me the bones extend for *seven* miles and are by the ton. . . ." Several days later, Marsh received another letter from Williston, confirming the extent of the deposit and warning him that "there will be great danger from competition next summer." Marsh knew, of course, exactly what kind of competition Williston was referring to.

Marsh's men worked feverishly at Como Bluff through the winter and spring, but despite their efforts at secrecy, word of the finds leaked out to the local newspaper. Shortly thereafter, Williston reported some disturbing news to Marsh: "One of Cope's men was here. He first purported to be selling groceries!! Gave his name as '*Haines*,' thick heavy set sullen portly man of about forty, shaven except mustache and whiskers." Later that day, Williston elaborated in a second letter. "I have been talking further with Carlin about this man 'Haines.' There is no doubt he is direct from Cope. . . . He gained *no definite* information from Carlin or my brother. He went up into the hill and returning said that he had found no fossils,—*of course* he lied."

Soon Cope's collectors had opened a quarry not more than three hundred yards from one of Marsh's, and once again their rivalry heated up. At Como Bluff, the two collectors resorted to such schemes as destroying minor or incomplete fossils in their own quarries to prevent the rival party from collecting them, and filling up abandoned quarries with stones and dirt. On at least one occasion, rival parties nearly came to blows over sites, and one of Marsh's collectors felt it necessary to have several "strong men" with him whenever he was in the field.

For a while this battle was known only within embarrassed scientific circles. But all that changed on January 12, 1890, when the *New York Herald* announced in a headline on its front page, "Scientists Wage Bitter Warfare." Elizabeth Noble Shor, author of *The Fossil Feud*, wrote about the reaction of the scientific world:

> Most scientists of the day recoiled in horror—and read on with interest, to find that Cope's feud with Marsh had at last become front-page news. Those closest to the scientific fields under discussion, geology and vertebrate paleontology, certainly winced, particularly as they found themselves quoted, mentioned, or misspelled. The feud was not news to them, for it had lurked at their scientific meetings for two decades. Most of them had already taken sides.*

The series of *Herald* articles, which were shamelessly slanted against Marsh, continued for several weeks. Cope and Marsh, unable to restrain themselves, made many rash and eminently quotable statements. Cope, for example, was quoted as saying such things as:

> Professor Marsh has shown that he never was competent to do work of this kind. Unable to properly classify and name the fossils his explorers secured, he employed American and foreign assistants who did the work for him. . . . His paper on the mammals of the Laramie formation . . . is the most remarkable collection of errors and ignorance . . . ever displayed. . . . To cause the government to father the most monumental ignorance and pretension and plagiarism in quarto volumes.

Marsh was quoted in a subsequent article:

> Professor Cope's mental and moral characteristics unfit him for any position of trust and responsibility. In addi-

---

*Henry Fairfield Osborn, who was then a vertebrate paleontologist at the Museum, sided with Cope, which of course made him an enemy of Marsh.

tion to his great vanity, which leads him into vicious
species work, he is inordinately jealous and suspicious
of every other worker, and these two traits combined
give him that hysterical temper and gift of voluble de-
nunciation rarely found in persons of his sex.

It goes without saying that, even without the aid of this
scientific feud, dinosaurs had riveted the public's attention.
From being obscure and almost unknown in the 1860s and
early 1870s, dinosaurs had now become big business. The
end results of Cope and Marsh's rivalry were streams of
extraordinary fossils of huge dinosaurs and other prehistoric creatures flowing eastward and being assembled and
mounted in such cities as Philadelphia and New Haven.

At the American Museum of Natural History, President
Jesup saw the commotion in both scientific and popular
circles over dinosaurs and other prehistoric life, and
quickly realized that the Museum would be left behind if it
didn't get into fossil collecting with all haste. Jesup first
approached Marsh and tried to woo him (and his fossils)
away from the Peabody Museum at Yale. Marsh was not to
be budged. Then, in 1891, the president of Columbia University proposed to Jesup that Columbia and the Museum
hire a young paleontologist, Henry Fairfield Osborn, to
take a joint appointment at the two institutions. Jesup liked
the articulate, tall, brilliant, and very rich young man, and
Osborn was hired in June of that year to start the Museum's
Department of Paleontology.

Osborn gradually began to gather about him a group of
fossil hunters and paleontologists who would put the Museum on the paleontological map, turning it into the center
of vertebrate paleontology research in the United States.
Osborn would stay at the Museum until 1933, eventually
succeeding Jesup as President. Jesup had given the Museum its life, but Osborn would develop it into one of the
three foremost museums of natural history in the world.

Osborn had been called, with justification, "the father of
American paleontology." While Cope and Marsh were perhaps perceived as erratic scientists and collectors who em-

barrassed their colleagues in England and Europe, Osborn was the supreme scientist. His academic credentials were impeccable, his publications voluminous and important, his memberships in the most prestigious scientific societies outstanding. By all accounts he was also an egotist of the first rank—a man who could (and did) destroy the scientific reputations of those who opposed him. He presided over the Museum during its zenith of fame and influence.

It was Osborn who brought dinosaurs to the Museum. Osborn's star dinosaur hunter was a man named Barnum Brown, who, by the end of his life, would dig up more dinosaurs than any other man who ever lived.

## Barnum Brown's Bones

When Barnum Brown arrived at the American Museum in 1897 at the age of twenty-three, the Museum possessed not a single dinosaur. When he died in 1963, just one week shy of his ninetieth birthday, it was chock-full of them, the largest and best collection in the world. Many of the Museum's finest specimens—including the superb *Tyrannosaurus rex*—were discovered by Brown during his sixty-six-year career. He worked in every major geographical area of the world except Japan, Australia, Madagascar, and the South Sea Islands. To get to and from those places with his picks and whisk brooms, he once said he had used every available form of transportation except the submarine. Of the two dinosaur halls in the Museum, one, the Hall of Late Dinosaurs, is a virtual monument to Barnum Brown, as he collected most of its skeletons.

Like Marsh and Cope, Brown found most of his dinosaurs in Western North American, and he became something of a celebrity. Wherever he went, he was fêted by the local populace, who came in droves to meet his train, and who would vie for the honor of having him in their carriage. Called "Mr. Bones" by both press and public, Brown's ability to locate dinosaurs became legendary. A scientist wrote that he could "smell fossils, even though they had been buried 200 million years."

A paleontologist locates fossils in much the same way a sophisticated prospector locates minerals. The fossil hunter begins with an extensive knowledge of geology and a deep study of the geological landscape of the area to be searched. Usually the hunter will try to follow sedimentary beds known to contain fossils across intervening strata to an unexplored outcrop. Like the prospector, the fossil hunter tends to rely on intuition and even hunches to locate fossils, as well as such hearsay evidence as idle bar conversation, chats with ranchers, oilmen, and prospectors, and so forth.

But like the prospector, the fossil hunter combines this with his knowledge of geology to make a strike. For example, an upfold of strata (called an anticline) is often an excellent formation in which to find fossils. Usually the top of the anticline is eroded away. If fossils have been found on one side of the anticline, where a particular layer of rock has been exposed, one can usually find similar fossils on the other side. However, the other side may be many miles away, with complex terrain in between. The great fossil hunter can map out the intervening terrain and pinpoint where that particular fossiliferous layer will reappear on the far side.

Brown was a complex man. A photograph in the Museum's archives, taken at a remote site in the desolate badlands of Wyoming, shows him in a magnificent and costly fur coat, gravely examining a fossil through his gold-rimmed pince-nez. He usually dressed impeccably for the field, and one of his crew members who had worked with him as a youth said, "Woe to the boy who spilled plaster of paris on his shiny boots." One colleague reported that he was an accomplished ballroom dancer, in great demand among the ladies. Another said that Brown's "grave, sometimes melancholy countenance" suggested the mien of a Presbyterian minister. Like many great explorers, he was an indifferent scientist. He cared little about publishing his finds, and his colleagues often gently upbraided him for it.

Barnum Brown was born in Carbondale, Kansas, in

1873. His parents had moved to Kansas by wagon train before the Civil War and had built a pioneer cabin, which later grew into a rather prosperous farm with side businesses. His parents named him, somewhat prophetically, after the great showman P.T. Barnum, because, as Brown explained later, it added alliterative interest to his dull surname. As a boy he would follow farmers' plows through the fields of Carbondale, picking up the hundreds of fossil shells turned up by the blades. His collection eventually filled the laundry building on the family farm. At the University of Kansas he met Professor Samuel Williston, Marsh's former head dinosaur hunter, who initiated him into that arcane profession. In 1896 he came to the Museum to work part-time on a fossil prospecting party, and the following year the Museum brought him on staff.

Henry Fairfield Osborn had plans to make the American Museum the foremost repository for vertebrate fossils and, indeed, the center of fossil vertebrate research in the world. In many ways Osborn was to vertebrate paleontology what Boas was to anthropology; just as Boas is called the father of American anthropology, Osborn was named the father of American vertebrate paleontology. He was mainly interested in fossil mammals; but he knew that it was the mounted skeletons of dinosaurs, more than mammals, that would attract attention, publicity, and money to the Museum. In the summer of 1897, Osborn sent Brown and a collecting party to Como Bluff, Wyoming, to explore the Upper Jurassic beds where Othniel C. Marsh had earlier made spectacular discoveries. (Marsh was none too pleased by this "raid" on one of his quarries, and he and Osborn became lifelong opponents as a result of this and of Osborn's support of Cope.) After spending most of the summer excavating barren rock, Brown concluded that Marsh had pretty well exhausted the quarry's fossils.

Perseverance, however, paid off in the end. Later that summer Osborn himself arrived to inspect the site, and he and Brown explored a nearby bluff. Brown noticed some bones weathering out of an outcrop, and the two men examined them with mounting excitement. The bones were undoubtedly saurian—the Museum's first dinosaur. Brown and another member of the expedition traced these fossil-bearing beds to an unexplored outcrop known as the Medicine Bow Anticline—and here they struck pay dirt. A photograph in the Museum's archives showing the unexcavated spot gives an idea of just how rich this area was. It reveals a hillside strewn with hundreds of dinosaur bones —more common than the surrounding rocks. The bones lay about in such profusion that, years before, a sheepherder had built an entire cabin out of them. Naturally, the locality became known as Bone Cabin Quarry.

This site yielded some of the most impressive dinosaurs yet discovered. In 1898 the Museum party cut into the hillside and surrounding strata, and over the next six years they uncovered dinosaur after dinosaur. In the fall of 1898 alone they shipped thirty tons of bones in boxcars to New York; in 1899, another twenty tons; in 1900, ten tons; and in the last year of excavation, when everyone had begun to complain that the quarry was petering out, they brought back a mere five tons.

During the excavations, some of the paleontologists took side trips to outcrops of the same formations, hoping for another mother lode of fossils. In 1898, some five miles south of Bone Cabin Quarry, at a place known as Nine Mile Crossing of Little Medicine Creek, Walter Granger, one of Osborn's paleontologists, discovered a promising site where some bones had weathered out of the rock. The succeeding summer they established a separate camp and started removing the fossil—a magnificent *Brontosaurus*.

It was an exceedingly difficult excavation because of the size and weight of the specimen (the right thigh bone alone weighed 570 pounds). Enormous blocks of matrix (the stone in which a fossil is embedded) were quarried out of the bank and shipped to the Museum, where it took another two years to chip away the matrix, piece together the brittle, shattered bone, cement it, and restore areas of missing bone. Another three years passed while the skeleton was being mounted, and when at last it went on display in the

Museum, it was the largest fossil skeleton ever mounted anywhere.

As with most mounted dinosaurs, missing bones were either replaced with fossils from other finds or modeled in plaster. Even though the *Brontosaurus* was unusually complete, it required bones from Como Bluff and vertebrae and toe bones from Bone Cabin Quarry to fill in the gaps; various other bones were modeled in plaster after specimens in the Yale Museum.

Unfortunately, an exhaustive search failed to turn up a skull for the *Brontosaurus*. This was not the first time such a thing had happened. Marsh, the original discoverer of the *Brontosaurus* (now correctly termed *Apatosaurus*), had first described the animal from a headless skeleton found in 1879. But in his haste to beat Cope, he had crowned the creature with a restoration made from two fragmentary skulls found miles from the site. Osborn accepted Marsh's restoration, and topped his *Brontosaurus* with a cast of the Marsh skull. In 1915, however, Earl Douglass, a paleontologist from the Carnegie Museum of Natural History in Pittsburgh, discovered a *Brontosaurus* skeleton with a completely different skull right underneath it. Douglass suggested in a paper that Marsh might have given his *Brontosaurus* the wrong skull. Perhaps because this challenged the Museum's reconstruction, of which Osborn was so proud, Osborn, "in a bantering mood" (Douglass said), dared the Carnegie paleontologist to mount the new skull. Apparently, Douglass was disinclined to pick a scientific fight with the great and powerful Osborn, and he never did mount his skull—or *any* skull. The Carnegie *Brontosaurus* went headless until Douglass' death in 1932, when a copy of the old Marsh head was finally mounted.

Not until 1975 did anyone step forward to challenge the Marsh skull. Finally, two paleontologists (one at Carnegie) published a paper maintaining that the Marsh skull was entirely incorrect, and should be replaced by the Douglass skull. The evidence they presented was overwhelmingly persuasive. In 1979 the Carnegie Museum decapitated their *Brontosaurus* and crowned it with the much more graceful

Douglass skull. Other museums followed suit. The American Museum has intended to replace *its* wrong skull and obtained a copy from the Carnegie Museum. Unfortunately, an examination of the Museum's *Brontosaurus* mount revealed that any head-switching would be risky unless the entire skeleton was restored. So—for the time being, at least—the old skull is still in place, topping the great *Brontosaurus* in the Museum's Hall of Early Dinosaurs.

Getting back to Barnum Brown: Brown continued to scour the West, working quarries and prospecting. While Jurassic dinosaurs were being pulled out of Bone Cabin Quarry, Brown struck fossil gold in another location—Hell Creek, Montana. These were Upper Cretaceous beds, dating from the apex of the Age of the Dinosaurs, and in 1902 Brown organized a Museum expedition to the Hell Creek formation. His nose proved unerring. Buried in the sandstone matrix he discovered the skeleton of a huge carnivorous dinosaur, previously unknown to science. The sandstone was exceptionally hard, and the fossil had to be dynamited out of its tomb. Tons of sandstone blocks containing the rare fossil were hauled from the site by horse-drawn wagon 130 miles to the nearest railroad. When finally assembled, this grim meat-eater was christened *Tyrannosaurus rex*, "King of the Tyrant Lizards."

Five years later at Hell Creek, Brown found another *Tyrannosaurus* in superb condition. The Museum kept both tyrannosaurs, which were the only two reasonably complete skeletons of this dinosaur that had ever been found, and were considered a national treasure. During World War II, when it was feared that the Germans might bomb New York, the Museum donated the first *Tyrannosaurus* to the Carnegie Museum in Pittsburgh, where it remains to this day.

By the end of 1908, Brown had more or less cleaned out the Hell Creek beds, and he started casting about for a third locale. Again, his luck held out. One day a talkative visitor from Canada showed up in his office. The man owned a large ranch along the Red Deer River in Alberta, and he mentioned that he had picked up bones along the banks of the Red Deer just like the bones on display in the Museum. Although Brown was somewhat skeptical, he nevertheless paid a visit to the ranch in 1909. One visit was all Brown needed. The rancher had collected a mass of bones, and most were saurian.

Brown immediately organized an expedition, which arrived at the valley of the Red Deer River in the early summer of 1910. Getting to the fossils—and getting them out—proved a difficult problem. The fossils were eroding out of the steep canyons along the river, and were thus inaccessible from the top. The only option available, Brown decided, was to float down the river on a barge big enough to carry his crew and all the fossils they would collect. They constructed a twelve-by-thirty-foot flatboat topped with a large canvas tent. The barge included such amenities as a cook stove (with chimney), and a rowboat for shore landings. The entire thing was controlled with two large oarlike "sweeps," used for steering the boat through rapid water.

The party started downriver from Red Deer, scanning the canyon walls for signs of fossils. At first they found only scattered mammalian remains, but at a bend in the river near Content, Alberta, the walls began yielding dinosaurs in increasing numbers. As they lazily floated along, Brown would scan the canyon walls with his binoculars, and the crew would then land at promising sites. The dinosaurs kept rolling in. "Box after box," Brown wrote, "was added to the collection till scarcely a cubit's space remained unoccupied on board our fossil ark."

After the Canadian expedition, the next two decades were quiet ones for Brown. He diversified his collecting activities and traveled the world, finding everything from mummified musk-ox to fossil turtles. Then came the 1930s, and with them the discovery for which Brown is perhaps best remembered—the gigantic dinosaur graveyard at Howe Ranch. In 1931, Brown had led prospecting parties to the Lower Cretaceous beds of Montana, following the fossil-bearing rock southward to Greybull, Wyoming. Here he ran into a Mrs. Austin, herself a fossil enthusiast, who told him about some large bones she had seen on the Howe Ranch, at the base of the Bighorn Mountains. Two years later, Brown and several companions reconnoitered the ranch, and were guided to the big bones by a crusty eighty-two-year-old rancher named Barker. They were hard to miss; the bones were weathering out of a horizontal strata of rock adjacent to the ranch buildings. During the next week, Barker looked on while Brown painstakingly chipped away at the bones with his crooked awl to get a sense of what was there. A week of this was almost too much for Barker. Disgusted by the slowness of the work, he had to be physically restrained from hacking out the bones with a pickaxe. Brown realized that at least two large sauropod skeletons were embedded in the rock, but his limited team and financial resources made excavation impossible.

Large sums of money would be needed to recover the skeletons, and Brown turned to an old supporter, the Sinclair Oil Company, whose logo is, of course, a dinosaur. Readers may remember the dinosaur booklets and stickers that the Sinclair Oil Company gave out to motorists during the 1930s and 1940s. Brown wrote the booklets, while Sinclair bankrolled many of his expeditions.

In 1934, a much bigger expedition led by Brown returned to the Howe Ranch, and on June 1 they began uncovering the quarry to bedrock. Brown wrote:

> It soon became apparent that . . . there was a veritable herd of dinosaurs, their skeletal remains crossed, crisscrossed, and interlocked in a confused and almost inextricable manner. . . . Through the warping of the strata incident to the nearby mountain uplift, the bones had been checked and fractured to a high degree, so all had to be thoroughly shellacked as soon as uncovered. Never have I see such a thirsty lot of dinosaurs.

After the length and breadth of the bone deposit was determined, the area was gridded into three-foot squares. The bones were in such a tangle that all had to be drawn *in situ* first, and the relationships of the body sections mapped out before anything could be removed. To accomplish this, a man was hoisted in an old barrel about thirty feet above the quarry, from which photographs could be taken straight down on the tangle of bones.

Fortunately the bones were embedded in soft clay, and work progressed quickly. Finally, on November 17, the last crate of fossils was loaded into a boxcar bound for New York City. Packed into the car were 4,000 bones in 144 cases weighing 35 tons. At least twenty, and probably more, dinosaurs were represented by individual bones and entire skeletons. Most of the dinosaurs were the swamp-dwelling kind—the large-bodied, long-necked sauropods.

The Howe Quarry presented a mystery. Never had such a concentration of dinosaur bones been discovered before. The bones were not water-worn or abraded, as would be expected if the Howe Quarry had been an eddy in an ancient stream bed.* Nor had the bones been separated or scattered by scavengers. The bones were extensively interlocked, indicating that a single event may have killed them all at approximately the same time.

Even the distribution of bones was odd. Around the edges of the quarry were scattered single bones from smaller species; but in the center, a dozen limbs of large species were found standing upright on articulated feet. Surrounding the bones was a very fine silt of the kind deposited only in standing, muddy water.

Brown studied the quarry and drew his own conclusion, which is more notable for the image it conjured up than for its accuracy. The following passage, published in *Natural History* in 1935, did much to shape our conception of the last days of the dinosaurs:

---

*Many rich fossil beds were once areas where rivers or flash floods washed bones into a bank or eddy. Large numbers of bones could collect in such spots over many years before they were finally buried in silt and fossilized. Such spots are easily recognized; they usually occur in ancient, crossbedded channel sands. The bones themselves often show abrasion from being swept downstream, and few articulated bones are found in such localities.

The climate was tropical, and we see a flat land rich in vegetation, dotted by countless shallow lakes and marshes. Cycads, palms, and palmettos cover the lowlands, with pines on the uplands. Countless ferns, thick grass, and rushes form a rank vegetation over the marshy, hummocked shores.... [The dinosaurs] congregate by thousands, huddling close together as reptiles do, and filling every lagoon as far as the eye can see.

Now Mother Earth changes the stage setting. The impulse that finally was expressed by the nearby mountains elevated these lowlands. The large lakes were drained and the swamps vanished. The dinosaurs became more and more concentrated in the remaining pools as they were pushed together in huge herds....

As the water receded, the smaller, weaker dinosaurs were trampled and their bones scattered on the borders of the pool; the larger ones huddled closer and closer together as they made their last futile stand against fate.

Brown's description is somewhat off the mark. The quarry probably represents the remains of a herd of dinosaurs that perished in a drying lake. However, it was a local phenomenon, not a worldwide extinction, since these were Jurassic dinosaurs, which lived relatively early in the Age of Dinosaurs. The event that caused the drying of the lake was probably nothing more than a severe drought, not the uplifting of the land, which usually takes millions of years.

Brown retired from the Museum in 1942, but continued to work until the week before his death in 1963. In his later years, as he conducted visitors through the fossil halls of the Museum, he would murmur, "Here's another one of my children." While he was planning a trip to the Isle of Wight to dig dinosaurs out of its 800-foot cliffs (and while the Museum was planning his ninetieth birthday bash), Barnum Brown died.

His "children" can still be seen—the ponderous *Brontosaurus*, the *Tyrannosaurus*, and dozens of others, their huge, shellacked skeletons a memorial to the greatest dinosaur collector of them all.

## Sternberg and the Dinosaur Mummy

In addition to the dinosaur-collecting efforts of Barnum Brown and others on the Museum staff, Osborn also enlisted the services of various free-lance fossil collectors. A rare breed of man was the free-lance collector. Often wealthy (but not always, as we shall see), the free-lancer hunted dinosaurs for sheer pleasure, with a passion similar to that of prospectors for gold or uranium. Some of the rich collectors kept their collections themselves and donated specimens to various museums; others were hired by museums to collect a particular species missing from their vaults.

Charles Hazelius Sternberg and his sons were a family of such free-lancers, collecting on a fee basis for museums all over the world. Osborn was hungry for spectacular fossils, and the Museum had the money to buy them. He followed Sternberg's progress closely, ready to pounce when anything spectacular came to light. He was certainly not disappointed. One of the rarest fossils of all time—and certainly one of the strangest dinosaur specimens on display—was discovered by Sternberg and acquired by Osborn just before it was to be sold to the British Museum.

It is worth taking a close look at Sternberg. Science requires the activities of two very different kinds of people —the brilliant thinkers and synthesizers, and the hardworking but unimaginative compilers of data. A great deal has been written about the former but virtually nothing about the latter. Sternberg was a member of this group, and is today almost forgotten despite his significant contribution to vertebrate paleontology. He never served on the staff of an institution and never claimed to be more than a fossil collector, although he did publish descriptive papers on his finds. His scientific ideas tended toward the bizarre. Often, greedier and more ambitious scientists would publish Sternberg's discoveries without giving him proper credit. Sternberg was an eccentric in the classic tradition of professional fossil collectors. He was a wizened man with a game leg, a stone-deaf ear, and a propensity to quote the Bible.

The son of a Lutheran minister, Sternberg was born in upstate New York in 1850 but grew up on a small farm outside of Ellsworth, Kansas, which was still very much a frontier town. He learned early how to shoot buffalo and fight Indians, and in his autobiography he describes how the "dead cart" would pass through the town most mornings to pick up those who had been killed in saloons the night before. Sternberg himself was once shot in the head during a robbery, but it wasn't a serious wound.

It was in this environment that Sternberg somehow stumbled across a copy of Darwin's *Origin of Species*, which "thrilled" him and explained for the first time the fossil shells he had collected as a little boy. Sternberg and his brother had gathered a large collection of fossil leaves from sandstone outcroppings, and Sternberg vowed to devote his life to "collecting facts from the Crust of the Earth"—a plan vigorously opposed by his father, who felt that there was no money in a life of fossil hunting. But Sternberg approached his chosen profession in a businesslike manner. He financed his collecting by selling his fossils to museums in America, Germany, England, and France.

Over his father's objections, he enrolled in the Kansas State Agricultural College, where he studied paleontology. After graduating, he wrote a letter to Edward Drinker Cope and audaciously asked for three hundred dollars to outfit an expedition to the chalk beds of western Kansas. The wealthy Cope, hoping that Sternberg might be able to add to his growing fossil collection, sent the money, and Sternberg was off.

Later in the season Cope himself joined Sternberg's party, and they moved the expedition to Montana to look for Cretaceous dinosaurs. The area was barren and lacking decent water, and the nights were freezing. Cope had physically pushed himself almost too far, and was so weak at times that he "reeled from side to side as he walked." Sternberg described in his memoirs how the excitement and danger of their work "seemed to make us reckless of life." At night Cope suffered from hideous nightmares that kept the camp awake. "When we went to bed," Sternberg recalled, "the Professor would soon have a severe attack of nightmare. Every animal of which we had found traces during the day played with him at night, tossing him into the air, kicking him, trampling upon him.

"When I waked him, he would thank me cordially and lie down to another attack. Sometimes he would lose half the night in this exhausting slumber. . . ."

Sternberg never became rich hunting fossils, and indeed was often desperately poor, but he boasted proudly that he had made more money than if he had "utterly wasted" his life as a farmer or businessman. Like Brown, much of his success was due to his uncanny ability to turn up fossils in localities that had already been thoroughly combed by others. (He once claimed that rich fossil beds were revealed to him in dreams.) Sternberg usually collected alone or, later in his life, with his three sons, Charles Jr., George, and Levi, who went on to become notable fossil collectors themselves.

Sternberg was a deeply religious man who wrote devotional poetry in his spare time, and he felt that God had particularly called him to the life of a fossil hunter. He published a wretched poem in quatrains entitled "The Story of the Past: Or, the Romance of Science."

At one point in the poem, Sternberg described what it was like to discover a fossil—in this case a mosasaur (a huge, carnivorous marine reptile) which he had found in the chalk beds of Kansas:

> A grinning skull first comes in sight,
> Armed with strong teeth, all shining bright.
> The spinal column follows fast,
> On either side great paddles cast,
> While a long tail of swimming form,
> Like a screw propeller it is borne.
> The mended bones show us the place,
> Where he was injured in the chase. . . .

Among his other accomplishments, Sternberg discovered one of the Museum's greatest fossils. The story begins in 1908, when Sternberg wrote to the British Museum of Natural History. He knew the British Museum lacked a good *Triceratops* skull, and he offered his services. The British Museum wrote back and agreed to purchase a specimen if one was found, but would not commit itself to funding the expedition. Sternberg gave the British Museum first refusal on any other specimens as well. There was good reason to be skeptical, since the area where Sternberg claimed he could find the fossil, Converse County, Wyoming, had been thoroughly searched by the American Museum of Natural History some years before.

Sternberg was accompanied on this expedition by his three sons, who had at this point never collected a dinosaur before. They were highly enthusiastic and spent weeks scouring the remote desert without success. When their food began to run out (their diet was almost exclusively boiled potatoes), Sternberg reluctantly saddled up his horse and cart for the five-day round trip for provisions. Just before he left, his son George had found some bones sticking out of a sandstone outcropping. Sternberg gave George and Levi instructions for uncovering the fossil while he and his son Charles Jr. went into town. In his memoirs, George Sternberg wrote about the discovery:

> Finally by the evening of the third day, I had traced the skeleton to the breast bone, for it lay on its back with the ends of its ribs sticking up. There was nothing unusual about that. But when I removed a rather large piece of sandstone rock from over the breast I found, must to my surprise, a perfect cast of the skin impression beautifully preserved . . . traces of skin were to be seen everywhere.

When his father returned to camp, George told him about the discovery, and the father insisted on visiting the site immediately. The two arrived at the site in the gathering dusk. "One glance," George wrote, "was enough for my father to realize what I had found and what it meant to science. Will I ever forget his first remark as we stood there in the fast approaching twilight? It thrills me now as I repeat it. 'George, this is a finer fossil than I have ever found.'"

What George had found was no mere dinosaur skeleton. It was a fossilized *mummy* of a dinosaur, a kind popularly called a "duck-billed" dinosaur because of its large bill-like mouth. Skin, tendons, and shreds of flesh—all fossilized—clung to the dinosaur's gaping ribcage. The animal's head was twisted grotesquely behind its back.* Sternberg, in his *Life of a Fossil Hunter*, also wrote about the discovery:

> Shall I ever experience such joy as when I stood in the quarry for the first time, and beheld lying in state the most complete skeleton of an extinct animal I have ever seen, after forty years of experience as a collector! The crowning specimen of my life's work!...It lay there with expanded ribs as in life, wrapped in the impressions of skin whose beautiful patterns of octagonal plates marked the fine sandstone above the bones.... Even the flesh was replaced by sandstone....How wonderful are the works of an Almighty hand!

Osborn had previously written to Sternberg expressing his doubt that the area would yield anything of value, but he had been keeping a wary eye on his activities anyway. When news of the find reached Osborn, he immediately dispatched a man to Converse County to secure the specimen, despite the fact that the British Museum, according to paleontological etiquette, had a prior claim to it. The Museum's agent appealed to Sternberg's patriotic principles with the promise that the specimen would remain in the country on display. A substantial (but unknown) cash payment sealed the deal. The duck-billed dinosaur mummy was encased in plaster and shipped to New York, where

*Dinosaurs were sometimes found with their necks arched and contorted, which paleontologists believe is caused by the drying and shrinking of powerful tendons.

Osborn installed it in a glass case labeled "Mummy Dinosaur." It can still be seen in the Museum's Hall of Late Dinosaurs, lying in a glass case on its back, looking so much like the partially decomposed carcass it once was that one can almost smell it. Its grinning skull, partially clothed in flesh, still arcs behind the body, and traces of fossilized flesh and pebbled skin are everywhere.

Sternberg collected other specimens for the Museum, but the duck-billed mummy was certainly the finest. For the first time, paleontologists were able to study the skin of a dinosaur and other details not detectable from a skeleton. In his final years, Sternberg would visit the Museum's dinosaur halls, admiring his finds. After one such visit to the dinosaur mummy, he was inspired to write, "My own body will crumble in dust, my soul return to the God who gave it, but the works of His hands, those animals of other days, will give joy and pleasure to generations yet unborn."

# SEVEN

# In Deepest Africa

*The Belgian Congo, high on the slopes of Mount Mikeno. Tuesday and Wednesday, November 16 and 17, 1926:*

Mr. Akeley, in effect, is growing worse and worse [the Belgian zoologist J. M. Derscheid wrote in his field journal], and I was overwhelmed by the change in his appearance. We try with every means at our disposal to keep him warm and sustain him. He has had one hemorrhage after another today, and is dreadfully weak and pale. In the last hemorrhage he lost more than a quart of blood. . . . He breathes with great difficulty and groans unceasingly. . . . During the evening he has been delerious several times, and speaks of Museum, of electrical projects, etc., etc. . . ."

*[That night]:* We take turns in watching over him. Outside, the snow-covered Karisimbi glitters in the moonlight.

At eight o'clock [A.M.] I found the pulse practically

imperceptible. I asked Mr. Akeley if we might give him a hypodermic injection; he consented and I gave him a dose of caffeine. At about nine o'clock the pulse had become strong again, but the respiration remained abrupt, short and noisy. He groaned unceasingly and was entirely unconscious. I frictioned him. About eleven o'clock the heart action fell again. I gave him another injection of caffeine, but this time without result. About 11:35 there was no pulse or respiration perceptible. I had the impression he was dead. I held his hand in both of mine, watching for any sign of life. The mouth was wide open, the muscles stiffened, the eyes open in a fixed stare. As it was quite cold outside (the frost had not yet melted), I had the little tent kept very warm. I made two more injections of caffeine, but in vain. The head and the hands were growing cold, and the complexion was becoming a dull white, but it was not until about four-thirty that Mr. Raddatz and I were able to convince ourselves of the reality.

The Gorilla Group in the Akeley Hall of African Mammals depicts an actual place located less than a mile from the camp where Carl Akeley, the African explorer, died in 1926. The spot is located in the Kivu Volcanoes of the Belgian Congo, two miles high in the rain-forested slopes of Mount Mikeno (now in the Virunga National Park in Zaire, just over the border from Rwanda and Uganda). It lies just south of the Equator, in the center of the African continent. In the foreground of the diorama, a family of mountain gorillas forages for food, while the dominant male stands erect in a classic pose, beating its chest. An infant and several other gorillas sit nearby, munching on wild celery leaves. A massive tree trunk, sheathed in moss, lies rotting in the center of the scene. Framing the gorillas is a tangle of vines and ancient cusso trees, their heavy limbs hanging with moss, ferns, bearded lichen, and pendant bedstraw. Brilliant flowers and Ruwenzori blackberries grow in abundance. Behind the gorillas, the rain forest falls away into a steep declivity, dropping four thousand feet to sun-dappled plains and forests. Two giant volcanoes, Mount Nyiragongo and Mount Nyamlagira, smoke lazily in the distance, their clouds catching the amber light of late afternoon. Below and to the south lies the shining expanse of Lake Kivu. Almost invisible in the haze, at least a hundred miles away, can be seen another great mountain range on the far side of the lake. To the right rise the precipitous ramparts of Mount Mikeno itself, thickly covered with jungle foliage displaying an almost infinite range of greens and yellows. It is a scene of breathtaking beauty.

At the time of his death, Akeley was leading a small expedition to this wild and remote area of the Belgian Congo to collect plants and animals, take photographs, and paint background studies for the gorilla diorama. It was the culmination of nearly seventeen years of work on the Museum's African Hall. Accompanying Akeley were his wife, Mary L. Jobe Akeley—a well-known explorer in her own right—and three other scientists. Although Carl was sixty-two, he had recently married Mary, and this was their first trip to Africa together—a honeymoon of sorts. Carl especially wanted to bring his wife to see "the most beautiful spot in all the world"—the break in the trees that he had chosen for the gorilla diorama setting and background.

During the long trip into the African interior, Carl experienced a relapse of the fever and dysentery that had stricken him on an earlier expedition in Tanganyika, yet he insisted on pushing on. As they at last approached their destination, a camp on a high ridge between volcanoes, commanding a spectacular vista across one hundred miles of the western Congo, Akeley had to be carried much of the time in a hammock. The following day he died.

Akeley's long journey to the rain-drenched jungles of Mount Mikeno began when he was a young boy. At an early age he had developed an interest in stuffing animals, and at sixteen he felt competent enough in this profession to print up business cards that read, "Carl E. Akeley—Artistic Taxidermy in All Its Branches." At nineteen he landed a job at Ward's Natural Science Establishment in Rochester, New York, at a wage of $3.50 per day. Ward's was one of the leading taxidermy studios in the country, and it often did work for major American museums. The establishment specialized in stuffing animals and mounting skeletons, and Carl was placed in the taxidermy section. He soon tired of his work and was about to quit when news came that Jumbo, P. T. Barnum's famous elephant, had been killed by a speeding freight train in Canada. Barnum chose the Rochester studio to stuff the skin and mount the shattered bones. Akeley was charged with the task, and he did a brilliant job.

Shortly thereafter, Akeley took a job at the Field Museum in Chicago, where he worked for many years. He began collecting and mounting animals for the Field, and gradually he perfected a revolutionary new method of taxidermy (more on this later). In 1905 he mounted an impressive pair of elephants for the Field, and the American Museum sent him to Africa in 1909 to get a bigger and better group for New York.

Such collecting was not without its hazards. While Akeley was stalking an old bull elephant on the slopes of Mt. Kenya, the elephant unexpectedly charged him. Akeley's gun jammed, and in a matter of seconds the old bull was on top of him. Akeley, having mentally rehearsed just such an emergency, grabbed each tusk in his hands and swung down on the ground between them. The elephant sank his tusks into the earth, pressed his curled-up trunk against Akeley's chest, and then whipped the trunk across his face, slicing open Akeley's cheek and breaking his nose. Akeley lost consciousness as the elephant continued to drive its tusks into the earth. (Had the tusks not struck an underground obstruction, Akeley would have been crushed.) The Africans fled from Akeley, thinking he was dead, and he lay unconscious for four or five hours. He finally revived, and spent three months in the bush (there was no nearby hospital) recuperating from punctured lungs and broken ribs. (On another occasion Akeley was attacked by a leopard, which he killed barehanded.)

During this long period, Akeley started thinking about the rapid changes he had seen since his first trip to Africa.

The game was disappearing as civilization spread increasingly to the hinterlands, bringing with it farms and cattle. The cry was raised that the wildlife of Africa must make way for agriculture. Akeley realized that the Africa he had come to know would not last much longer. While brooding over this question, he conceived an idea.

Upon his recovery and return from Africa with the elephants, Akeley proposed his idea to the Museum. He wanted to preserve Africa in its unspoiled state in a great Hall of Africa at the American Museum of Natural History. The hall would include examples of African mammals in their original habitats, and no expense would be spared to make the exhibits achieve a realism that was beyond anything ever done before. Akeley told a friend of his, "Everything that has been done in the American Museum of Natural History in the way of African exhibits must be thrown out and completely discarded; we must start over again."

The idea of the habitat group—the showing of animals and plants in their native habitat against a realistically painted background—had originated at the Museum around ten years earlier. The concept was first tried out with the Museum's Hall of North American Birds, which drew tremendous popular acclaim. By 1909 the techniques of duplicating plants, flowers, rocks, trees, and backgrounds had been perfected. Akeley, however, wanted to take the habitat group a step further. Some habitat groups still appeared static and unreal, even though they were technically almost perfect. Akeley wanted to create habitat groups on a huge scale, and he wanted them to be bursting with vitality and spontaneity, to be esthetically beautiful as well as scientifically accurate. In short, he wanted his habitat groups to be works of art. For Akeley, this meant going back to Africa and starting from scratch—from collecting the animals and plants to photographing the landscapes and hiring and training new artists.

The Museum needed little persuasion. Akeley impressed the Museum with the need for the hall and the short time left to create it. The Museum began making plans to start work on the hall in 1914. All the collecting plans, however, were interrupted by World War I, and Akeley spent the war sketching plans and sculpting scale models.

Museum President Osborn put Akeley in charge of raising money for the African expeditions to collect for the new hall. Before raising money, Akeley felt he had first to return to Africa himself to crystallize many of the ideas he had been turning over in his head. So in 1921, Akeley went to Africa accompanied by a wealthy couple, the Bradleys, who wanted to hunt exotic animals. They hired Akeley as a "white hunter," with the understanding that the Museum got first choice of any animals they shot. On this trip, Akeley penetrated the high rain forest of the Belgian Congo for the first time and was captivated by its surreal beauty. In fact, he was so impressed by the area that he eventually persuaded King Albert of Belgium to declare a large section of the Kivu a national park and gorilla sanctuary—thereby helping to save the rare mountain gorilla from extinction.

This small area encompasses remarkable ecological extremes. The Kivu volcanoes rise from a sweltering lava plain where temperatures reach 120 degrees. At a higher altitude the flora becomes first a bushy scrub and then a thick bamboo forest. The higher slopes of the Kivu are covered with true jungle, although the weather resembles northern England more than equatorial Africa. Due to the high altitude, the volcanic slopes are soaked daily with cold rains and bone-chilling fog; hailstorms and nightly frosts are common. Higher up, the rain forest gives way to dwarf trees and subalpine conditions. Finally, at the summit, the volcanic craters themselves are barren and usually covered with snow.

Here, shy mountain gorillas live in a narrow band along the steep—almost vertical—mountain slopes, in the upper regions of the bamboo and the lower regions of the rain forest. On the 1921 safari, Akeley and Bradley shot several gorillas in this area—enough for Akeley's planned gorilla group in the hall. (On one hunt, Akeley had to lash himself and his dead gorilla to a tree in order to skin it on the steep slope.) During this trip, Akeley also took the first motion-picture footage of a gorilla in its native habitat.

It seems strange to us today that Akeley would find no contradiction in shooting rare animals for inclusion in a hall, whose purpose was to *preserve* African wildlife for future generations. In truth, Akeley saw hundreds of rare animals being slaughtered by professional hunters and their wealthy clients. In addition, thousands of square miles of wilderness were being cleared and fenced for farmland and grazing. What could be wrong, he reasoned, with taking a few more for the noble purpose of the Museum's African Hall, which would preserve the Africa he loved for future generations? Akeley himself, however, took little joy in killing, and on several occasions was unable to bring himself to shoot an animal he needed for a habitat group.

After his return from the 1921 safari, Akeley realized he needed to raise large sums of money if his hall was to be done properly. A wealthy friend, Daniel Pomeroy, suggested that George Eastman (of the Eastman-Kodak Company) might be able to help. Akeley seized upon the suggestion with such enthusiasm that Pomeroy was taken aback. He asked Akeley—somewhat nervously—how much he was going to ask Eastman to contribute. Akeley replied, "I'd like to see Mr. Eastman give us a million dollars." Pomeroy was horrified and tried to "tone Carl down," but Akeley was too excited.

On the night train to Rochester, Akeley kept Pomeroy up all night talking about the hall. "African Hall," Pomeroy later wrote, "had grown as important to him as life itself." As Pomeroy tried to sleep, Akeley remained in his seat, puffing furiously on his old corncob pipe. Periodically he burst out, "By heaven, Dan! If Mr. Eastman only can see how important, how necessary this is—" And then he would break off, too excited to continue.

When they met Eastman the next day, Akeley launched into a heated description of the hall. He told Eastman that he had a chance to create the "greatest exhibit in the world." "Even though I warned him," Pomeroy wrote, "about killing the goose that laid the golden egg, he could not refrain from naming a high figure." Without letting Eastman catch his breath, Akeley asked him point-blank for a million dollars.

The rotund, genial Eastman nearly fell out of his chair. But Akeley's enthusiasm had done the job, and Eastman promised an initial gift of $100,000, which would cover the cost of three or four dioramas.* Pomeroy himself chipped in $25,000, and others followed suit. Each contributor of a diorama got, in turn, the chance to hunt for that particular group in the upcoming expedition, under the guidance of Akeley and other Museum explorers, and to have their names engraved in the hall. It was an attractive deal for anyone with a loose $25,000, and it allowed the Museum to control exactly how many and what animals were shot. The expedition was named the Eastman-Pomeroy-Akeley African Expedition.†

Akeley himself decided to collect several groups. Most importantly, he wanted to do all the work for the Gorilla Group, which he envisioned as the finest in the hall. (Indeed, he hoped to make it the greatest diorama ever created.) Although he had collected the gorillas themselves on the 1921 expedition, he needed to return to the Kivu Volcanoes to gather material and take photographs for the foreground and background.

The expedition arrived in Africa early in 1926, and divided into small parties collecting in various areas of Africa. Before embarking for the Belgian Congo, Akeley went south to Tanganyika (now Tanzania) to obtain several specimens for another group. While there, he became ill with a fever and had to return to Nairobi to recuperate. But what Akeley had seen in East Africa in 1926 shocked him

---

*The cost of creating the African Hall dioramas was staggering. Akeley had budgeted $25,000 for each small group, and $50,000 for each large one—costs that did not include securing the specimens in Africa. Today, even if one could create these extraordinary habitat groups, the costs would be somewhere in the vicinity of a half-million dollars each.

†It was later renamed the Akeley-Eastman-Pomeroy African Expedition by Akeley's wife.

deeply. The destruction of wildlife was occurring at a much more rapid pace than he had previously thought possible. "I have not appreciated," he wrote to the Museum's Director during his convalescence, "the absolute necessity of carrying on the African Hall, if it is ever to be done, as I do now after this painful revelation. *The old conditions, the story of which we want to tell, are now gone, and in another decade the men who knew them will all be gone.*" (Akeley's emphasis.)

Shortly, Akeley declared himself fully recovered. His wife and the others tried to dissuade him from the planned Congo expedition, as they felt his health was still poor, but Akeley insisted on carrying out the remaining duties of collecting for his favorite habitat group. He selected William R. Leigh, a brilliant young landscape painter, to accompany him and make the background paintings and studies. He chose a Museum preparator and expert taxidermist, R. C. Raddatz, to collect and prepare all the necessary specimens and materials for the foreground. Finally, a Belgian conservationist and cartographer named J. M. Derscheid accompanied them to map the unexplored Kivu Volcanoes and make zoological studies. Their plan was to approach the Congo from the east, through Kenya and Uganda.

On October 14, 1926, they started out along Kenyan roads in three trucks and a car. As they traversed the great plains of the Rift Valley, Akeley pointed out fenced-in farm areas that had once been covered with game. The government had set a bounty on crop-destroying animals such as zebra, and a wholesale slaughter was going on. The group ran into one old Boer farmer who told them, while pounding violently on their tea table, "Deeze zebra only vermin. I made good kill of two hundred myself only. . . . All farmers glad when all zebra are shot. We must raise crops."

In Uganda they camped near the domain of a Ugandan king, who welcomed them with lavish hospitality, presenting them with milk, chickens, eggs, dry wood for their fires, and bananas. The king promised that on their return he would call his 7,000 subjects from his 2,500 square miles of territory so that they could be photographed by Carl. They continued along an old caravan route from Mombasa to the Nile, where the elephant grass grew twenty feet high, punctuated every so often with papyrus swamps and groves of ancient rubber trees (standing untapped because the going wage of a laborer—four cents per day—was too expensive).

At Kabale, in the far western corner of Uganda, next to the Belgian Congo border, the motor road came to an end. From this point on, all transportation would be over jungle trails by porter. Akeley hired two hundred porters "of magnificent physique," at the standard rate of five cents per fifty pounds per seven miles. At Lake Bunyoni, the first round of porters loaded up a flotilla of dugout canoes with their bundles and returned to Kabale. On the far side of the lake, beating drums summoned a new group of two hundred porters to continue the expedition up into the foothills of southwestern Uganda.

At the border of the Congo, they rested on a high ridge and gazed west into the geographical heart of Africa. Spread out before them they could see the sweeping plains, winding rivers, and smoking volcanoes of the Kivu in the pale, hazy atmosphere. High up on the green, forested slopes of the volcanoes, Akeley knew he would find his gorillas.

Carl always outdistanced his wife on the trail, but shortly after passing the Congo border, Mary came across her husband resting in the shade. He told Raddatz that they had to stop because he felt very "strange and dizzy." But by the next morning, after a frightful thunderstorm, Carl felt better and they continued on to the town of Rutshuru, the government post for the Eastern Kivu. From Rutshuru, the expedition trekked southwest over the foothills of the Kivu Mountains. Along the way, Mary herself came down with a touch of fever and had to be dosed with quinine.

Soon, they attained the lower slopes of the volcanoes. As they gained altitude, the dry scrub and unbearable heat was overtaken by an eerie bamboo forest, so thick that the group was enveloped in a strange twilight even at midday.

Heavy fog and rain had turned the trail into a morass of sticky mud, and the forest floor spouted a profusion of brilliant orchids and fuschias. As their porters sliced through the bamboo with machetes, they ascended the slope, finding abundant signs of elephant, buffalo, and other big game. Finally, at about 7,000 feet, they came across a patch of uprooted bamboos, where a band of gorillas had taken its morning meal of tender shoots.

They continued upward, climbing a steep ridge running up the flank of Mount Mikeno, bordered by two precipitous cliffs, toward the Rweru (sometimes spelled "Rueru") camp that Carl had established in 1921. The camp lay nearly two miles high, at the transition zone between the bamboo and the true rain forest. Upon arrival, they found it almost returned to wilderness in the five years since Akeley had left it. "A few sodden bamboo and grass huts stood about in straggling disorder," Mary later wrote in her book *Carl Akeley's Africa*. "Everywhere was a close tangle of vegetation."

Heavy clouds had moved in during the day, and that night the drenching fog became so thick that visibility dropped to a few feet. Mary wrote:

> The voices of the naked porters echoed and reechoed as if amplified by the fog which enveloped us. Invisible jungle fowl, disturbed in their roosting places, squawked incessantly as darkness fell. . . . But the weirdest sounds of all were the cries of the tree hyrax, indescribable, like nothing else I have ever heard. At midnight someone went out of his tent with a lantern. It evidently startled the tree hyrax for they set up a most appalling racket in which frogs and crickets joined until the whole world seemed quavering with the noise. . . . It was all too strange for sleep.

In the morning, following a rain, the clouds broke through, revealing a glimpse of the snow-capped volcanic peaks of Mikeno and Karisimbi. Almost a mile below them lay the blue sheet of Lake Kivu, blending imperceptibly into the sky. During the few fleeting moments of sun, Carl had taken his cameras down to the rim of the canyon to get a photograph of Nyamlagira, but missed the shot as the fog had once again descended by the time he arrived. He sent back his assistant with a note to Mary, asking her to join him to see the spectacular view when next the clouds broke. Mary and Carl waited together for over two hours without success, while the fog condensed and dripped off the hanging vines. Finally Carl gave up and told Mary that they could return tomorrow. There would be plenty of time, he said, to enjoy the loveliest view on earth. But Mary would not see this vista while Carl was alive. This would be their last moment alone together; the next day at the Rweru camp, Carl became sick with the violent dysentery that would later kill him.

Mary L. Jobe Akeley was a remarkable woman, in some ways even more remarkable than her husband. To understand Mary's role during the rest of the expedition, let us step back in time a moment to look at her earlier life. In Mary Akeley's old house in Mystic, Connecticut, is a box of photographic portraits, taken of her before she married Carl Akeley. One photograph shows a tall, rather stout woman with a big hat, wearing an outfit of oversized bloomers, leading a group of girls in a vigorous round of calisthenics. Another depicts her in a similar pair of bloomers and high-button boots, walking stick in hand, ascending the slopes of a mountain in the Canadian Rockies. A third shows her on horseback, on a mountain trail, with the Selkirks of British Columbia in the background. There are photographs of her in blizzards, standing on mountain peaks, and struggling through roaring torrents. By the time she married Carl Akeley, she was already a famous explorer in her own right, and she never allowed her fame to be overshadowed by Akeley's. (Indeed, when she died in the early 1960s, many newspapers erroneously reported that the Museum's African Hall had been named after *her*, not her husband.)

Mary Jobe came out of the Midwest and attended Bryn Mawr and Columbia. While there, she accompanied a botanical expedition to British Columbia, and shortly afterward Mary herself led an expedition to map the headwaters of the Fraser River. On this expedition she climbed a previously unexplored peak in the northernmost Canadian Rockies, later named Mount Sir Alexander. She attempted a first ascent, but was driven back by avalanches and a blizzard. During the next several years she led seven expeditions to Canada, and the Canadian government christened a high peak in the Rockies "Mount Jobe" in her honor.

In 1916, believing that young girls needed strenuous physical exercise, she founded Camp Mystic for Girls, in Mystic, Connecticut. She ran the camp like a Marine drill sergeant, teaching her campers outdoor survival and the value of physical fitness, sports, and exercise.

In 1920 she was introduced to Carl Akeley, who was then married to Delia, his wife of seventeen years. Carl and Delia underwent an acrimonious divorce in 1923, and Carl and Mary married in 1924. He was sixty years old and she was thirty-eight.

After her husband's death in the Belgian Congo, Mary continued to explore and to write books about Carl and herself (one of which prompted Delia to threaten a libel suit). As she grew older she became a rather crabby and suspicious recluse, living on top of a hill in Mystic in a rambling house stuffed with elephant-foot wastebaskets, leopard skins, African carvings, stuffed animals, decorated gourds and pots, and other bric-a-brac. In 1966, at the age of eighty, she died in a convalescent home, with few close friends and no close family.

In 1977 the executors of her estate sent the Museum a couple of bulging cardboard boxes filled with yellowing folders, crumbling newspaper clippings, hand-tinted glass lantern slides, books, and a half-dozen journals tied in a bundle with a red silk ribbon. These were her field journals, recording in a dense, almost illegible hand the progress of her various expeditions.

The first of the journals date from about 1915. The last one of the batch contains a hasty scrawl on the inside cover: "*Kivu* High Camp on slopes of Mt. Mikeno—Nov. 14, 1926 et seq." This rare and extraordinary journal—whose existence was previously unsuspected—begins with their arrival at Rweru Camp on Mount Mikeno, where Carl tried to show Mary the view of Nyamlagira from the canyon rim. Entries continue through her husband's death and after. It is a remarkable narrative, a detailed account in which Mary recorded with dispassionate accuracy her husband's illness and death.

The volcano, Mary wrote, "we could see plainly almost every night as its fiery furnace of boiling lava illuminated the clouds & sky or as flame occasionally shot into the heavens. . . .

"Often," Mary continued, "when looking out of my tent, it seemed as if I were standing on the brink of a gulf, the clouds were so dense—& as if the whole world were falling away from me. At such times I could hear the song of the thrush."

On November 11, Mary tells us, Carl had his first serious attack of nausea, which prevented their going to the canyon rim to photograph Nyamlagira. On the twelfth he felt better, but they decided to postpone moving up to their next camp until the weather cleared. He had another attack on the thirteenth, but felt somewhat better the following day. Carl was terribly anxious to reach the next camp, which lay on the saddle between the Karisimbi and Mikeno volcanoes, and so, on November 14, he ordered the expedition to break camp. Mary wrote:

He was only weak when he got dressed, but walked up the hill at a quick pace. There he got in the hammock. I walked first behind him & we often remarked about the beautiful forest. Once, he made the boys stop to show me a beautiful tiny nest of the sun-bird hung in a great banner of gray-beard moss. Again when we came to the big trees with the platforms of fern-hung green moss, he said, "Mary, do you see now where the fairies dance?"

Finally, when we got into the deepest, most beautiful forest, he said, "Now I am on my old trail. . . ."

They continued up the trail—Carl carried in the hammock, Mary walking beside him—until they were about a quarter-mile from the Saddle Camp, when Carl said he was cold and would walk. The forest was dark and dismal, and the graybeard moss was dripping with water from the fog. At the camp, Carl sat down under the fly of the cook tent, ordered a charcoal brazier lit, and had a cup of tea. "He talked energetically to Derscheid about the gorillas there," Mary recorded.

That night, Mary didn't undress and visited Carl often in the night "when he was quiet." The next morning Carl was still feeling sick and couldn't keep down any food or drink.

I got Raddatz to sorting supplies & Leigh & Derscheid went up to look for the place where Bradley killed his gorilla. There was a heavy hailstorm. I kept Carl warm & gave him hot water which was all he could take. I said to him in the A.M., "Well, I have got them all at work, if that is any consolation." He said, "It doesn't seem to matter now. But it will in the long run, I know." I asked him when the hailstorm came down if he wanted me to stay with him, if "he was afraid." He laughed a little laugh and said "No, honey, I'm not afraid. You go keep warm in your tent." That night Bill and I staid up. He seemed to sleep considerably & was quiet.

When Raddatz asked him how he felt the morning of the seventeenth he said, "Quite comfortable." But soon after he had three intestinal hemorrhages in quick succession. When I tried to give him nourishment he was unable to take it but suggested chlorodyne to stop the hemorrhage, which I gave him. He said, "I've never taken it myself but I have used it with good results." So I gave it to him according to directions & at 9 it apparently made him feel better. He said, "If I had some means for intestinal feeding it might do some good." Then after the last hemorrhage he said "I can stand about one more."

But from 9 to 11:30 he seemed quite comfortable tho very weak. Derscheid who felt his pulse suggested caffeine hypodermic. I said to him, "Dear, can the doctor give you a little tonic hypodermically" and he said "Yes." We gave it to him & he seemed to rest afterwards. Finally at 12:30 his bowels began to move again. Bill heard him stir, trying to get up. He put him back in bed. "I fixed a cloth for him."

After a little while another hemorrhage came. I took care of him, washing him & putting a pad of soft cotton & a soft [illegible] and said "If anymore comes you are all taken care of." He had looked to see what had passed from him & then he lay back on his pillows. "I can't lie on my left side or back anymore," he said. In a few minutes he turned on his back and began to breathe spasmodically. I propped him up on extra pillows & put pillows under each arm. His eyes seemed looking far up to Karasimbi [illegible]. In about half an hour his heavy breathing stopped & he seemed to breathe quietly and turned over on his right side. I could still feel his pulse, faintly in his wrist but more pronounced in his neck. Derscheid gave him some more caffeine believing he was only in a stupor. But as he never reacted to it, his soul must have passed in those moments of rest following his heavy breathing. It was not, however, until 2:30 that we could believe that he had gone.

Carl Akeley was dead. They kept his body in the camp until November 21, while several dozen of the porters, working in twelve-hour shifts around the clock, excavated a tomb in the soft lava rock on a high point above their tents. Raddatz embalmed the body, and told Mary that there was scarcely any blood left in Akeley's veins. He also made a coffin of heavy native mahogany, which they lined with tin cut from galvanized containers. Mary quilted the inside with the soft gray blanket that Carl had bought her for their wedding trip. Inside the coffin she placed her wedding ring, engraved, "Mary and Carl, October 28, 1924," along with his glasses, his soft eiderdown pillows, "and the warm Jaeger blanket we had so often slept in."

Surrounding the burial plot they built an eight-foot-high stockade topped with sharpened spikes to keep out scavengers. On the right-hand side of the plot, Mary directed that a space be left for her ashes. "I want to be cremated," she wrote, "and have my ashes repose beside his loved body. There is a space left on his right side for me. . . ." (Her wish, for some reason, was never fulfilled, and she is buried in Ohio.) Before the coffin was lowered, they gave a short reading and a simple service. "I staid with him," Mary wrote, "for a few moments after the others had gone." As they carried him to the tomb, the sun broke through the clouds, "revealing what he had always said was the 'most beautiful spot in the whole world.' He had often said 'I want to die in harness and I want to be buried in Africa.'"

Finally the question had to be faced: what should be done with the expedition? Mary stated that it would continue, with her as leader. She told the party—most emphatically—that Carl would have expected her to complete the work for his Gorilla Group. She felt that the diorama would be a kind of memorial to her husband, and that it would be made as perfect and as beautiful as possible. The other expedition members, who had been ready to head straight down the mountain and out of the jungle, came around to her point of view. They asked her what they should now do. First, Mary decided, they had to locate the spot that Carl had chosen as the background of the Gorilla Group, the spot where Bradley had shot a large gorilla in 1921 (the male gorilla beating its chest in the diorama). The place was a spectacular break in the forest just above a massive, centuries-old cusso tree about a mile from the camp. With the help of a photograph Carl had given her, Mary located it without difficulty, and they set to work. Leigh began work, painting studies for the spectacular background that visitors can see today in the diorama. Mary and Raddatz began making the detailed collections and studies necessary for Museum preparators back in New York to duplicate the site in exact detail. They catalogued every variety of plant growing at the spot—over fifty species. From these they selected the thirty or so dominant ones, collected at least one fine specimen of each, and preserved them in jars of formalin. Since plants become soft in formalin, Raddatz also took more than two hundred plaster casts of leaves and stems to help the Museum preparators make identical copies.

Mary took hundreds of detailed photographs, including stereoscopic shots of each plant and panoramic shots using a special camera. She selected two large trees that were to be replicated in the diorama, and photographed them from every angle. (Such photography necessitated cutting large swaths in the forest in order to obtain the right angle at a reasonable distance.) Raddatz stripped bark and moss off trees, and gathered everything he could find at the site, including dirt samples, broken twigs, dead moss, and leaves from the forest floor. The weather was bitterly cold and they were drenched daily by freezing rain, sleet, and hail. At night the temperatures would drop to freezing, and gale winds would sweep up the mountains, bellying out their tents.

All members of the expedition were pushed to their limits during these six weeks. Many of the porters became ill and had to return to Rutshuru, and replacements could not be found. Provisions ran low. Everything was wet. There was the constant danger that the African bearers would desert in the middle of the night, as they were clearly unhappy with the entire situation. Mary worked feverishly, trying to complete the work before things fell apart.

At last, on December 19, work was finished, and the group make its weary way down the mountain and back to the comparative civilization of Kenya.

In 1936—ten years after Akeley's death—the Akeley Hall of African Mammals opened in the Museum. Museum preparators created the habitat groups using Akeley's revolutionary new method of taxidermy. Instead of stuffing animal skins with straw or excelsior—which resulted in a lumpy, insect-infested animal—Akeley had invented a different approach. First he mounted the skeleton in the desired pose. Then, using the bones as a guide, he laid on each muscle and tendon in clay, until the body of the animal appeared as it would if it had no skin. Finally—when every muscle, tendon, and engorged vein was in its proper place—Akeley would fit the skin over a cast of the sculpture, molding it to the details of the animal's musculature. Details such as saliva around the animal's mouth or a glass eye were added last. This method of Akeley's revolutionized the science of taxidermy. While in the past taxidermy had required little knowledge, now the taxidermist had to be an expert anatomist and sculptor.

The foregrounds were built up using a combination of artificial and real elements. Twigs, thin branches, mosses, and tree bark were actually collected at the site and used in the diorama. Preparators modeled the more perishable things—flowers, leaves, fleshy plants, and berries—in wax or paper. The dirt was often real, having been carried thousands of miles from the actual site. Boulders, tree trunks, and other heavy items were replicated, often using molds taken of their originals.

The background paintings and lighting required consummate skill. To achieve the illusion of space, the backgrounds were painted on a double-curved surface. Such a surface invariably created complex problems in perspective for the painter. In addition, the backgrounds and foregrounds had to merge so seamlessly that the viewer would find it difficult to tell just where the painted background began.

Most delicate of all was the task of duplicating the marvelous *light* of Africa. Each diorama was different. One depicted the broad grasslands at high noon; another, a deep jungle dripping with rain; a third, the harsh desert at sunset. Not only did the lighting have to capture these settings, but it also had to be consistent with the artists' shading on the background paintings. Under no circumstances could the lighting throw a shadow *against* the background. Museum lighting specialists experimented with each group before achieving the correct balance.

The Akeley Hall of African Mammals remains today one of the most remarkable halls in any museum in the world, displaying a level of realism not achieved before or since. In the center of the hall, Akeley's massive elephant group stands out on an elevated platform. The elephants are depicted in a state of alarm: the old bull faces the entrance, ears extended, trunk testing the air; a younger bull has wheeled around to guard the rear of the herd. All around the elephants, embedded in walls of black polished marble, are Akeley's habitat groups. They stand out in the darkened hall in a blaze of internal sunlight, as if one were looking through bright windows into another world at another time—the Africa that Carl Akeley wanted so desperately to save.

# EIGHT

# Fossils in
# Outer Mongolia

When Henry Fairfield Osborn succeeded Morris K. Jesup as Museum President in 1908, he became the first (and up to now last) scientist to hold that post. Osborn firmly moved the Museum in the direction of exploration and research, especially in the area of vertebrate paleontology—Osborn's specialty. Most of this exploration, as we have seen, took place in the American West, but this was more a result of the richness of those fossil beds than any kind of American chauvinism. On the contrary, Osborn took a global view of his science. In particular, he had developed an evolutionary theory involving a very different part of the world: Central Asia.

Around the turn of the century, Osborn published a prediction that Central Asia—Mongolia—would turn out to be the evolutionary "staging ground" in which both the dinosaurian and mammalian life of the planet had evolved and dispersed. He based his theory on the observation that related dinosaurs and mammals had been found in such divergent areas as New Jersey, the Western states, England, and Western Europe. If the animals had migrated across the Bering Strait,* then one could think of animals of New Jersey as occupying one extreme endpoint of dispersal and the animals of England as occupying the other. What land area occupied the midpoint—and therefore perhaps the dispersal point—of these extremes? Central Asia.

Osborn built his entire theory around, as he termed it, "this very interesting observation." Central Asia, he predicted, would turn out to be the birthplace of much of the fauna of the Northern Hemisphere. Most important, he believed that Central Asia would yield the earliest fossils of man—the so-called Missing Link.

Early in 1920, a young mammalogist at the Museum named Roy Chapman Andrews invited Osborn to lunch. After a pleasant repast (as Andrews reported later in his book, *Ends of the Earth*), President Osborn leaned back in his chair, lit his pipe, and said, "Well, Roy, what is on your mind?"

Andrews began to talk about his plan for a new expedition, a plan that he had been formulating for eight years. "We should try to reconstruct the whole past history of the Central Asian plateau," he said. "We ought to learn about its geological structure, fossil life, its past climate and vegetation. We should make collections of its living mammals, birds, fish and reptiles. We should map the unexplored and little-known Gobi Desert."

In short, Andrews not only wanted to confirm Osborn's own theory, he had even grander plans. With an unprecedented expedition, he wanted to make a complete scientific survey of this vast area. He proposed to lead a veritable army of scientific experts—from cartographers to paleontologists—to the heart of the unknown regions of Mongolia. As transportation, Andrews proposed a fleet of Dodge automobiles, which he felt could negotiate the level, grav-

---

*Before the days of plate tectonics and continental drift, this was thought to be the only dispersal route of fauna from the Old World to the New.

elly sands of Mongolia better than anything else. A caravan of 125 camels, loaded with tons of gasoline and provisions, would resupply the expedition every six or seven hundred miles. The expedition and its dozens of scientists and assistants would spend a minimum of five years in the field, using Peking as a base during the winter months.

After several minutes, Osborn's unheeded pipe had gone out and he was leaning forward in his chair, his eyes glowing. When Andrews was finished, Osborn began asking questions. Finally he looked hard at Andrews and said, "Roy, we've got to do it."

It was a bold idea. Nothing remotely like it had ever been attempted. Mongolia was a huge and nearly uninhabited area two thousand miles long by one thousand miles wide. It was split into two regions: the gentle hills and fertile plains of Inner Mongolia, controlled by China, and the parched wasteland of Outer Mongolia, which had been alternately controlled by China and Russia. The vast Gobi Desert lay across the entire central portion of Outer Mongolia, a formidable natural barrier to exploration. Politically, the area was notoriously unstable. Russia was just recovering from its revolution, and China was in the throes of an endless series of civil wars. Outer Mongolia, which was undergoing and consolidating its own revolution, existed in a state of anarchy, overrun by rifle-toting brigands.

As if political problems weren't enough, the Central Asiatic Expedition (also called by Andrews the Third Asiatic Expedition) would face some of the most extreme weather conditions on the planet. During the winter, the temperature in Outer Mongolia plummets to forty or fifty degrees below zero. Violent winds pile even a light snowfall into heavy, impassable drifts, and the snow usually doesn't clear up until June. Then, in July and August, daytime temperatures soar to 110 degrees in the shade, while nights remain cold. All year, sudden windstorms sweep down from the Arctic and Siberian steppes and scour the landscape.

Any expedition would have to cope with these dangers. But the greatest danger of all was that the expedition would be a failure. Only one fossil—a rhinoceros tooth—had ever been found in Central Asia. Although Mongolia had been crudely mapped and had been visited by Westerners, virtually nothing was known about it scientifically. Osborn knew his theory was speculative, based mostly on the distribution of fossil fauna in *other* parts of the world. Several conservative scientists dismissed the idea, and one said that the Museum might as well look for fossils in the Pacific Ocean as to expect to find them in the wastes of Outer Mongolia. Some geologists scoffed at the idea that anyone could determine the geology of an area known to be covered mostly with shifting sand.

Nevertheless, Osborn enthusiastically endorsed Andrews' plan. While it may seem in hindsight to have been a risky gamble, Osborn had a deep belief in himself and his scientific abilities. While the possibility of failure (especially after the recent Crocker Land Expedition) must have occurred to him, he dismissed it. Although Osborn realized he was putting his own reputation and, to a lesser extent, the Museum's on the line with such a highly visible expedition, he did it unhesitatingly, without looking back. This was a chance to associate the Museum with a grand project and possibly an unprecedented discovery, something that would be remembered in the annals of science.

Andrews began raising funds. He had no trouble obtaining the quarter of a million dollars required for the first leg of the expedition. Wealthy New Yorkers eagerly subscribed funds for the project, and Andrews found himself courted by society in an exhausting round of dinner parties, balls, and society teas. A short office visit to J. P. Morgan netted $50,000, and other large donations followed. Once the money had been raised, the Museum formally announced the expedition.

Newspapers across the country published the story on their front pages. What especially caught popular attention was the search for the Missing Link. During the next weeks, literally thousands of telegrams and letters poured into Andrews' office at the Museum, most seeking a job with the expedition. He got offers of assistance from every imaginable quarter, including letters from clairvoyants and seers who apparently specialized in locating bones. (One lady in St. Louis wrote that certain spirits had informed her of the whereabouts of a buried city in the Gobi Desert where a record of man's development from when he "crawled on all fours" to the beginning of recorded history could be found.) Over a thousand letters came from women, most of which were businesslike, but others contained proposals of marriage and other interesting "offers." Hundreds of hopeful young boys looking for adventure wrote to Andrews. One would-be explorer listed his qualifications as follows: "I want to help you find the Missing Link," he wrote. "I have always been interested in old clothes and things that people wore long ago. I can climb trees and I don't get dizzy. I know you will meet terrible dangers. Probably wild can-naballs will try to eat you."

The publicity, especially the emphasis on the Missing Link, raised considerable anxiety in the Museum. Human fossils were exceedingly rare, and both Andrews and Osborn knew that their chances of finding the Missing Link were uncertain. The Museum tried to play down the emphasis on human fossils, but the press would have none of it.

On the day that Andrews departed for Peking in March 1921, he had a final meeting with Osborn. The usually overconfident Andrews expressed his fear that the expedition would fail, that this might be his swan song in exploration. Osborn put his hand on Andrews' shoulder. "Nonsense, Roy," he said. "The fossils are there, I know they are. Go and find them."

## To the Ends of the Earth

The frontispiece to Andrews' autobiography, written some eight years after that meeting with Osborn in 1920, shows the author sitting on a desert hillock. He holds a 6.5 mm Mannlicher rifle in his right hand, and wears a cartridge belt loaded with bullets around his waist. On his feet are dusty leather jackboots. His rumpled wool shirt is rolled up at the sleeves. A worn ranger hat, sporting a pheasant feather, is perched on his head, cocked at an angle. The man is pictured in profile, his hard, clean jaw slightly elevated, his pale eyes gazing off into the distance. Behind him rise the Flaming Cliffs of Shabarakh Usu, in the heart of the Gobi Desert.

If this description sounds vaguely familiar, there is good reason. Andrews is allegedly the real person that the movie character Indiana Jones was patterned after. Andrews was an accomplished stage-master. He created an image and then lived it out impeccably—there was no chink in his armor. Roy Chapman Andrews: famous explorer, dinosaur hunter, exemplifier of Anglo-Saxon virtues, crack shot, fighter of Mongolian brigands, the man who created the metaphor of "Outer Mongolia" as denoting any exceedingly remote place. Where on earth did this man come from?

Andrews was born in the quiet Midwestern town of Beloit, Wisconsin. After graduating from Beloit College, he worked his way east with money earned from stuffing deer heads and birds. He often said that his only ambition in life was to work at the American Museum of Natural History. He talked his way into the Director's office, and the Director tried to shoo him away with the curt explanation that no jobs were open at the present time. Andrews persisted. "You have to have someone to scrub floors, don't you?" he asked. The Director allowed that he did. Andrews drew himself up. Of course, he explained, he didn't want to wash just *any* floors, "but Museum floors were different."

Accordingly, the Director assigned him to scrubbing floors in the taxidermy department. Soon, Andrews had graduated to collecting whales, in particular one record-size Atlantic right whale that had been brought ashore at Amagansett, Long Island. In a few years he went to Alaska, then Japan, Korea, and China, collecting marine mammals and, later, zoological specimens for the Museum. During this time he eked out an M.A. in mammalogy from Columbia and published two papers.

\* \* \*

In April 1922, fifteen years after polishing the Museum's floors, Andrews, with his motorcade, roared through the gateway of the Great Wall of China and headed out over the rolling grasslands of Inner Mongolia, bound for parts unknown. For several days the cars bumped and slid across the plains, stopping along the way to explore various outcrops.

On the fourth day, Andrews had arrived ahead of the rest at their rendezvous point. As he sat relaxing in front of his tent, the last two cars in the caravan careened wildly into camp. The men were obviously excited. The expedition's chief paleontologist, Walter Granger, leaped out of the lead car, puffing violently on his pipe. "Silently," Andrews wrote in his massive book, *The New Conquest of Central Asia*, "he dug into his pockets and produced a handful of bone fragments; out of his shirt came a rhinoceros tooth, and the various folds of his upper garments yielded other fossils." Granger laid them out before Andrews and held out his hand. "Well, Roy," he said, "we've done it. The stuff is here."

The stuff really *was* there—in surprising abundance. As they plunged deeper into Mongolia, they found more and more fossil evidence of dinosaurs and early mammals. In the flat desert, most outcrops could be seen miles away, and the caravan merely had to drive from one outcrop to another to discover new fossils. Their first truly significant find came several weeks into the expedition. A string of unprecedented discoveries had left the party in good humor, and they were sitting in camp, enjoying the sunset. Andrews wrote of this moment in his field journal:

> Nature, the greatest stage manager in the world, outdid herself in the display of changing color piling effect upon effect until we stood silent in awe—at first we had exclaimed breathtakingly at the theatricals but as it became more & more stupendous we all stood silent—I think most of us realized that we were standing on the threshold of one of the most extraordinary moments of our earthly lives—a moment which might never be

repeated. . . . To make our enjoyment complete, Walter and Shack had arrived with the two cars, just a moment before the curtain was lifted.

They had the dinosaur which Walter had found at Uskuk & which he says is one of the finest things he has ever collected. In the car they also had the end of a humurus, nearly all one side of a jaw & other fragments of a giant *Baluchitherium* the largest land mammal that ever lived [a kind of giant rhinoceros]. Wang, one of the chauffeurs, had discovered it lying exposed at the bottom of a V-shaped gully at the bad land pocket which they had stopped to investigate on their way to the camp.

Andrews was intensely excited about the find and talked far into the night about it. The next day they piled into the cars and drove back to the gully. While two men dug a trench near where the jaw had been found, Andrews went prospecting for more fossils along an adjacent ridge. Upon looking over the crest, he immediately spied bones on the other side. Andrews shouted and the others came running. After unearthing several small fragments, they came across the *pièce de résistance*, the giant skull itself, embedded in a huge block of sandstone. "I knew it was time to stop," Andrews wrote, "for I was too excited to do further prospecting."

At the end of the four days they managed to remove the block of sandstone that contained the skull, along with dozens of smaller bones of the animal. The paleontologists carefully divided the block into two sections and strengthened each with burlap soaked in plaster.*

Previously, the *Baluchitherium* had only been known from a few crumbly bone fragments and a piece of jaw. Now, with an almost complete skeleton, Osborn could tell the world what the animal looked like. It stood a full sev-

---

*These two blocks were carefully transported across Mongolia, defended from bandits, carried into China, loaded on a steamer, and shipped to New York. They arrived at the Museum December 19, 1922. When Osborn opened the two blocks, he found they contained an extraordinarily fine skull; the only *Baluchitherium* skull yet found. He wrote that the discovery and transportation of this skull halfway around the world was one of the greatest events in the history of paleontology.

enteen feet high at the shoulder—almost twice as high as the average elephant today, and a good deal larger than the extinct Imperial Mammoth. The animal grew to be twenty-four feet long. Its long, thick neck was graced by a giant skull sporting massive tusks, which probably allowed it to browse among trees and shrubs.

Throughout the summer of 1922, the expedition continued to unearth major fossils, and Osborn was well pleased. Although they had not yet discovered the Missing Link, they had found traces of ancient human camps—some 20,000 years old—from an unknown people they called the Dune Dwellers. Andrews hypothesized that the Dune Dwellers were the aboriginal descendants of the earliest man; he hinted to Osborn that they might find the Missing Link at any time now.

During the next field season, on July 13, 1923, the expedition made a discovery that caused everyone to forget about the missing "Missing Link." George Olson, the young assistant in paleontology, reported during the afternoon siesta that he had found some fossil eggs weathering out of the sandstone at the Flaming Cliffs of Shabarakh Usu. Since the strata dated from the Cretaceous (the last age of dinosaurs), Andrews dismissed the eggs as being natural sandstone concretions. Nevertheless, after tea Olson led them to his find. Sure enough, three unmistakable (if broken) eggs lay next to a sandstone ledge, with more bits of shell sticking out of the rock. The scientists began to argue. Could these be *dinosaur* eggs? No dinosaur eggs had ever been found, and scientists didn't even know how dinosaurs bore their young. (While many modern reptiles lay eggs, some bear live young.) They criticized the conjecture from every viewpoint. Could birds have laid these eggs? Probably not, as no fossil birds had been found there, and Cretaceous birds were exceedingly rare. Could the eggs be from a later deposit? No, as they were clearly encased in the original rock, in which the expedition had already found Cretaceous dinosaurs in numbers. Finally, the group was forced to accept the veracity of their find. If they hadn't been laid by a dinosaur, what other animal could have laid them? The question was settled.

With mounting excitement they began to brush the sand away from the ledge, exposing more of the fossils. Conclusive proof shortly emerged. Lying on top of the eggs was the fragmentary skeleton of a tiny, toothless dinosaur, which Andrews theorized had been feasting on the eggs when both beast and nest were covered by sand. The eggs were remarkably well preserved. The usual bumps, rugosities, and pores found on eggs were all clearly visible. More eggs appeared to be encased in the sandstone, and Granger carefully cut out a large block of stone, which was shipped intact to the Museum. Back in New York, paleontologists painstakingly chipped away the remaining rock, exposing a baker's dozen of large, oblong eggs in two layers, arranged in concentric circles just as the dinosaur had laid them millions of years before. The popular and scientific worlds were electrified by the discovery, and newspapers across the country reported the find.

The expedition dug up dinosaur eggs from a number of species by the gross, some of which contained delicate, fossilized dinosaur embryos.*

It is ironic that the expedition's greatest fossil discovery attracted little popular attention. In 1923 Granger discovered a tiny skull in a nodule of sandstone, which he labeled as "an unidentified reptile" and sent back for analysis to the Museum. A year later a paleontologist at the Museum chipped out the tiny skull and was astonished to discover that it was from a mammal, not a reptile—a mammal that lived during the Age of Dinosaurs. Very few mammal fossils from this era existed, and most belonged to a group that subsequently became extinct. This one, however, belonged to a placental (as opposed to marsupial) mammal, and thus appeared to be the antecedent of most mammal

---

*The eggs did bring grief from an unexpected quarter. When Andrews returned to the States the following winter to raise more money for the expedition, he was amazed at popular interest in the eggs. As a fund-raising stunt, he decided to "auction off" an extraneous egg. Spirited bidding followed, with Colonel Austin Colgate winning out with a $5,000 bid. (He gave the egg to Colgate University.) Unfortu-

life on the planet.* The Museum wrote back to Granger: "Do your utmost to get some other skulls." When Granger finally received the letter in 1925 from one of their camel supply trains, he casually strolled to the base of the Flaming Cliffs where so many other fossils had been discovered, including the dinosaur eggs. In less than an hour he discovered a second rare mammal skull in a sandstone concretion! The expedition dropped all work and spent the next seven days collecting and cracking open thousands of concretions, getting a total of six more skulls for their efforts. The seven skulls represented several different species of early mammal, from four genera and two families— quite a haul, scientifically speaking. "It was possibly the most valuable seven days of work in the whole history of paleontology up to date," Andrews stated in his usual hyperbolic fashion.

Back at the Museum, Osborn and his assistants eagerly studied the fragile skulls. Although the specimens were from different species, they looked very much alike—a small, furry creature with a pointed snout, about the size of a rat. As placental mammals, they were the primitive ancestors of all such life on the planet, including apes and man; ironically, these were the true "missing links" in mammalian evolution.

Since these animals lived during the Age of Dinosaurs and came from the same formation as the dinosaur eggs, paleontologists naturally wondered if they were responsible for the sudden extinction of the dinosaurs at the end of the Cretaceous. Perhaps, Osborn theorized, these tiny mammals ate the dinosaur eggs and finally drove the lumbering beasts to extinction, leaving a huge ecological niche to be

---

nately, the Chinese and Mongolians got wind of the auction and thought that each dinosaur egg was actually worth $5,000. Here was proof that the Americans, just as they had suspected, were plundering their country of priceless treasures. This was one of many factors that led to the cancellation of the expedition years later.

*Placental mammals are characterized by young that develop fully in the womb, nourished by the placenta. Marsupial mammals (such as the kangaroo) bear their young after a short gestation period, and the young develop in the mother's pouch. The true significance of Andrews' discovery wasn't that mammals lived during the Cretaceous, but that they had *already* evolved into two distinct groups at such an early date. It implied that mammals were a lot older than had been thought.

filled by the tiny mammals' descendants. (While today there are many theories about the extinction of the dinosaurs, this particular one is still considered viable, as a partial cause, by many paleontologists.)

The expedition was constantly beset by bad weather, bandits, and political troubles. Severe storms descended on the party without warning, tearing their tents to shreds and scattering their equipment. One such storm hit the expedition shortly after the discovery of the six mammal skulls, and nearly reburied them—along with the expedition. Andrews awoke suddenly one morning while they were still camped at the Flaming Cliffs, "with a strange feeling of unrest vibrating every nerve." In the dark, he buckled on his revolver over his pajamas and circled the camp, which lay in stillness. Nothing seemed amiss, so he slipped back into his sleeping bag but couldn't sleep. "At the end of fifteen minutes," he wrote, "I slowly became conscious that the air was vibrating to a continuous even roar, which was getting louder every second." He suddenly realized that a desert storm was on its way. The first blast of wind bellied in the tent, filling it with a choking sand, and Andrews pulled the bag over his head.

The wind passed suddenly, and at dawn the company arose to see a strange, tawny cloud hanging on the horizon and heading in their direction. Shortly the second storm struck, "like the burst of a high-explosive shell," Andrews wrote. "Even with my head covered I heard the crash and rip of falling tents. . . . As our tent swept away, [Granger] had leapt to save the box that contained the six tiny fossil Cretaceous mammal skulls."

The wind tore Andrews' pajama top right off his back, and lashed his skin with sand until it bled. When the gale at last ceased as suddenly as it had begun, the camp was a wreck. Basins, clothes, and ripped tents had been lifted by the wind and deposited in a half-mile swath across the desert. Smashed tables and chairs littered the campsite. If the cars hadn't been parked facing the wind, Andrews wrote, "they would certainly have been overturned."

Another particularly severe bout of weather occurred when the expedition was camped in a shallow basin at Ula Usu in Outer Mongolia. The group had struck several fossil deposits and were working them when the storm hit. It came upon them suddenly, like "a thousand shrieking demons," and caught Andrews several hundred yards from camp. The sand and gravel swirled so thick that breathing became difficult and seeing impossible. Andrews dropped to his hands and knees and began to crawl along the ridge at the edge of the basin, finally tumbling into a hollow depression where he lay huddled against the wind. The same storm caught Granger at one of the sites. He took refuge in a pit next to a *Titanotherium* skeleton. Propelled by hundred-mile-an-hour winds, gravel and sand buried him up to the neck and, according to Andrews, brought him to the brink of suffocation. The storm sandblasted the car windshields so severely that they had to be knocked out in order for the drivers to see where they were going.

The Chinese had repeatedly warned Andrews about Mongolian bandits, and indeed, almost weekly, in the more populated areas of Mongolia, travelers were being robbed and sometimes murdered by marauding brigands and soldiers. Andrews always packed a revolver and a cartridge belt, and often carried his 6.5 mm Mannlicher rifle when away from the camp. The guns were necessary for procuring food as well as for defense. One of the cars carried a mounted machine gun that could shoot two hundred rounds a minute. Andrews had no qualms about training his guns on an obstructive border guard or a petty Mongolian bureaucrat to get what he wanted. As for the bandits, he seemed to welcome an exciting confrontation.

Most encounters with bandits were short; once the Mongols realized that Andrews had guns and was going to use them, they usually fled. One incident—quite typical —occurred near Kalgan. Andrews had driven ahead of the other cars and was traversing a road where he knew some Russians had been robbed a few weeks earlier. Just as he was wondering if the brigands would attack him, he spotted a lone horseman on a nearby hilltop, apparently signaling to others on the far side of the ridge. He also saw the flash of sunlight on a gun barrel. Andrews drew his revolver and fired at the man twice, "whoever he might be." The man ducked behind the ridge and a moment later Andrews' car topped the divide. Sure enough, three mounted brigands were waiting at the bottom of the slope, blocking the dirt track and unshipping their rifles. Without a moment's hesitation, Andrews drew his revolver and gunned the engine, racing downhill directly at them at forty miles per hour. The Mongol horses took fright and began bucking madly, nearly throwing the men from their saddles. Andrews wrote with satisfaction, "The only thing the brigands wanted to do was to get away, and they fled in panic. When I last saw them they were breaking all speed records on the other side of the valley."

Another story is told in the Museum about a narrow escape from bandits. The expedition archeologist, Nels C. Nelson, had a glass eye. At one point the company was surrounded by hostile and well-armed Mongols. Nelson, the story goes, removed his glass eye and showed it to the natives, who fled in consternation and terror.

After months of hard living and comparative privation, the members of the expedition spent most of their winters in Peking, living a life of oriental luxury. In the legation reserved for foreigners, they rented a large compound from a Chinese prince, which consisted of eight courtyards with buildings on three sides of each. Andrews' building contained 161 small rooms, which he combined into about forty. Over twenty servants—more numerous than the members of the expedition—waited on them, as in China the custom was that each servant did only one kind of work. Managing the servants was a Byzantine task left to the head butler, who hired all the rest of the servants, took care of "squeeze" (small bribes essential to keep things running smoothly), and collected and distributed the wages. "It is a delightful Aladdin's Lamp sort of existence," Andrews wrote. "You say what you want and things happen. It is best not to inquire *how* they are to be done."

Their social life in Peking consisted of an endless round of lavish dinner parties with the British and Americans living in the legation. A typical dinner might include such wild game as snipe, woodcock, pheasant, roe deer, or boar, all washed down with the very finest French wines, Scotch whiskeys, and English beers.

For sport, Andrews and his group of friends rode to hounds, played polo, raced ponies, and played tennis. During the racing season, Andrews rented a temple near the racecourse. Called the Temple of Hopeful Fecundity, the five-centuries-old building was nestled in the hills outside Peking. Ancient cedars and a profusion of flowers tended by monks graced its courtyards. Apparently no one minded that the temple was rented to foreigners, and business was conducted as usual. Worshipers journeyed there from Peking to burn joss sticks and pray for male issue.

Aside from the usual prostitutes, which some expedition members patronized, there were more unusual amusements in Peking for the foreigners. In 1926 the gates of Peking were barred and sandbagged, while the city was assaulted by an army led by a rebellious Chinese general. The foreign population, Andrews wrote, "were having a glorious time." Every morning promptly at ten o'clock, an airplane droned into the city from the south, dropped a few gunpowder bombs on the city, turned around, and flew back from whence it came. "The roof of the Peking Hotel," Andrews wrote, "was the best place from which to see the show. 'Bombing breakfast' became the newest social diversion. A dozen guests would be invited to breakfast in the hotel at nine o'clock. At five minutes to ten they would adjourn to the roof, watch the planes do their stuff and then jump into motor cars to inspect the scene of devastation. As they were small bombs filled with black powder the damage was slight."

In the beginning the Chinese civil wars were more of a nuisance than a danger. But in 1926 things began to get serious, and "all tradition and good form were knocked into a cocked hat." For the first time the Chinese soldiers did not respect a foreign flag, and instead took it as an invitation to open fire, whereas previously the expedition could cross battlefronts unscathed merely by flying the American flag. That year, in fact, Andrews nearly lost his life attempting to cross enemy lines. He needed to get to Tientsin (later named Tinnjin) from Peking on expedition business. Andrews and three others piled into a car and headed for the outskirts of Peking. The gates of the city were heavily guarded, but the soldiers let them pass. On the road they met the retreating troops of one army, retiring in good order and "almost cheerful."

We drove on slowly and eventually passed beyond the rear of the retreating army. For three or four miles the countryside was deserted, houses closed, and all as quiet as the grave. We were five or six hundred yards from the ancient marble bridge at Tungchow when there came the sharp crack of a rifle and a bullet struck beside the front wheel. A second later a mass of soldiers appeared on the road and bullets began spattering around us like hailstones. They had opened fire with a machine gun but it was aimed too low and the bullets were kicking the dust just in front of us. The soldiers could see the American flag plainly enough but that made not the slightest difference.

Fortunately this spot on the road was wide enough for the car to be turned and I swung it about in record time. The bullets now were buzzing like a swarm of bees just above our heads. Forty yards down the road a sharp curve took us out of sight of the machine gun. . . . The ride became an exciting one. All the houses which had seemed so peaceful actually were occupied by the advance guards of Fengtien soldiers. They had let us pass because of the American flag but when they heard the firing in our rear and saw us returning at such a mad speed, they evidently thought that we were anybody's game. Each and every one decided to take a shot at us.

For three miles we ran the gauntlet of firing from both sides of the road. . . . The only reason why we were not riddled with bullets is because the Chinese is the world's worst rifle shot. . . .

New trouble began when they finally reached the rear of the retreating army. Thinking soldiers might be protection, Andrews let three or four ride on the running board of the car. One of them fell off and his arm was caught under the wheel just as Andrews slammed on the brakes, shredding his hand. Then more soldiers wanted to ride, and over Andrews' protests they piled on the car by the dozen. Inevitably, one soldier fell off and broke his leg. His enraged comrades cocked their rifles and were about to summarily execute Andrews and his companions when an officer arrived just in time to save them.*

The Russians and Buriats proved to be just as bureaucratic and dangerous as the Chinese.† On the 1925 expedition, the Russians decided that Andrews was engaged in a spying mission. In Urga (now called Ulan Bator), the capital of Outer Mongolia, one poor security agent ran himself ragged on foot trying to keep up with their motor cars. Andrews finally took pity on the man, inviting him to ride in his car. The Mongolian government insisted on assigning two Buriat security agents to accompany the expedition itself, Dalai Badmajapoff and John Dimschikoff. Dimschikoff, hoping to please his superiors, reported that Andrews was plotting with the American and British governments to annex Outer Mongolia. The other agent turned out to be a decent fellow and heartily contradicted Dimschikoff's reports, thereby saving the expedition from certain arrest. The Soviet government subsequently exiled Dimschikoff to Siberia for his fabricated reports; he was later "rehabilitated" and sent to Germany with Badmajapoff, where he reportedly robbed and murdered his companion.

The worsening political situation and rising antiforeign feeling in China finally forced Andrews to cancel the 1926 and 1927 expeditions. But Andrews had made up his mind

---

*It is ironic that the only time Andrews was actually shot, it was by his own hand. In 1928, he shot himself in the leg while drawing his revolver.

†The Buriats were the dominant Mongol tribes, to whom the Russians had given bureaucratic control of Outer Mongolia when they "helped" the Mongolians throw off the Chinese yoke during the Mongolian revolution.

that whatever happened, he was going to make one last try to get into Mongolia in 1928. By the spring of 1928, however, conditions in the Mongolian plateau had become very bad. Bandits swarmed over the area in such numbers that everyone who could be robbed had been, and the bandits themselves were starving from lack of booty. Finally the Chinese government made a truce with the bandits, allowing them to extract specified amounts of "protection money" from traders—five dollars per camel and $100 per car—provided it was done in a consistent and orderly fashion, with no loss of life. The expedition could only get into Inner Mongolia, where they explored a remote area in the northwest.

At the end of the 1928 expedition, the Chinese authorities at Kalgan seized their collections. A group called the Society for the Preservation of Cultural Objects accused the expedition of having "stolen China's priceless treasures" (among them, of course, the dinosaur eggs) and of being "spies against the government" and of "searching for oil and minerals and smuggling opium." Andrews spent six weeks negotiating with the Chinese authorities to get his crates of fossils back. In 1929 the same society required a list of onerous demands before it would authorize the expedition. Negotiations broke down, and Andrews reluctantly canceled plans for the 1929 expedition.

But Andrews persisted. In 1930, he finally came to an agreement with the society. Once again, the expedition set out to explore in Mongolia. They made outstanding fossil discoveries, especially of large mammals; among their finds was an entire graveyard of rare, shovel-tusked mastodons, previously known only from a few bones. On this trip they had their closest call with bandits, when three Chinese attacked a lone expedition member. The man drove the bandits away by shooting one in the face and killing another's horse.

The 1930 expedition was to be the last. It had now become too difficult and dangerous to continue scientific work in Mongolia. Although the expedition had been an outstanding success, it was a great blow to Andrews that they had not discovered the Missing Link. He was still convinced that it was out there, buried somewhere in the Gobi, the paleontological Garden of Eden.

# The Thirties
and Beyond

The Central Asiatic Expedition did, in a sense, turn out to be Andrews' swan song in exploration. He returned to great fanfare and popular acclaim, and four years later the Director of the Museum was asked to resign and Andrews took his place. Like other outstanding explorers, Andrews turned out to be a mediocre administrator.

Andrews' real accomplishments, though, live on in the Museum. Every fossil hall in the Museum is packed with his finds, and ten thousand more specimens remain in drawers and on shelves in the Vertebrate Paleontology section, still studied diligently by scientists from around the world.

The end of the Central Asiatic Expedition, 1930, also marked the end of the golden age of expeditions. It was the end of an era at the Museum in other ways as well. The immediate cause of the change was the Depression, but profound changes were taking place in the way the Museum—and similar institutions—conducted research and promoted exploration.

The Depression hit the Museum and its wealthy trustees badly. In 1933, Osborn retired from the Museum, frustrated by the chronic shortage of funds and the elimination of the grand projects he so desired. The Museum's endowments, one-half of which were in railroad bonds, took a plunge when many railroads defaulted. The trustees, who had traditionally made up the deficit at the end of the year by "passing the hat," found themselves dealing with their own financial problems.

F. Trubee Davison succeeded Osborn as President. A kindly man, Davison was not, however, a scientist and took only a casual interest in the Museum. At his request the trustees made the Director the chief operating officer of the Museum, leaving the President with overall responsibility but no administrative or scientific duties.

During the thirties the Museum cut salaries, curtailed publications, and eliminated staff positions. In 1932 the use of Museum funds for fieldwork and expeditions was banned entirely. Andrews became Director in 1934 at a low point in the Museum's history, and he proved incapable of handling what would have been a difficult job for anyone. According to Clark Wissler, a curator in the Museum's anthropology department during the Depression years, the Museum was infected with an "atmosphere of pessimism and defeat." Without a strong President or an effective Director, the Museum continued to slide downhill.

In 1941 the trustees finally took action and hired Alexander Ruthven, president of the University of Michigan and a systematic zoologist, to make a study of the Museum and its ills. After several visits and six months of poking around the Museum, Ruthven issued the recommendations he had hitherto kept secret, despite friendly requests from several nervous Museum officials. They were not complicated, and they boiled down to one major change—get rid of Roy Chapman Andrews. Andrews was asked to resign,

which he did with not a little bitterness. He lived the rest of his life in California, writing numerous books about his experiences at the Museum. He died in Carmel in 1960.

Andrews was replaced as Director by Albert E. Parr, who managed to pull the Museum out of its doldrums. The world had changed during the Museum's dark years, and it emerged a different kind of institution. The need for grant expeditions had passed. With that passage went the large-scale support from wealthy individuals, who liked to associate themselves with grand projects. Large, coordinated expeditions with supply caravans and native bearers were simply unnecessary—a curator could board an airplane and be anywhere in the world in a few days or a week. Little logistical support was needed. Efficient transportation and communications had taken all the glamour out of expeditions.

In addition, many of the curators who had lived under Andrews' directorship felt resentful of his style, his thirst for headline-grabbing discoveries. Some felt (probably unfairly) that he was a careerist who used the Museum for the advancement of his own fame. A consequence of this was that the Museum moved away from the showier kind of fieldwork and collecting for collecting's sake; a typical expedition would later consist of one curator who had a *specific* research question, and who as a result would make a very limited collection.

It is important to note that the collecting done before 1930, while not always directly related to current research, laid the groundwork for decades, if not centuries, of future scientific work. (In Part Two we will look at some of these modern-day explorers.)

Finally, the science of natural history itself, which had been ascendant in the nineteenth and early twentieth centuries, was being partially eclipsed by the newer sciences of cellular and molecular biology, and even medicine. In the minds of some, natural history, taxonomy, and evolutionary research seemed a little old-fashioned, a science in which most of the important questions had been solved.*

With the dramatic expeditions having ended, and the science of natural history sharing a more crowded stage, the Museum did lose national visibility. But today, its research and exhibition programs are stronger than ever before. The revolution in the theory of evolution—the so-called punctuated equilibrium theory—was born at the Museum, and today more than two hundred scientists and their assistants carry on research in all fields of evolution, zoology, animal behavior, and mineral science. As we will see later, the collections made before 1930 continue to support research programs in many disciplines, from planetology and systematic zoology to crystallography and evolution. The research that is being done today at the Museum is a synthesis of all that has gone before—all the collecting, storage, and expeditions, all the people who contributed in some way to the growth of the Museum—and has set the stage for the revolution in evolutionary studies and systematic zoology that has taken place over the past generation, much of which was and is centered at the Museum. We will take a brief look at some of this research in Part Two.

## Mountain of the Mists

Today, in a matter of forty-eight hours, a Museum scientist can get to almost any spot on the globe. No longer are huge supply caravans of camels needed, and no longer is it necessary to cut through miles of deep jungle or to traverse half a continent of ice and snow with dogsleds and Eskimo guides. Today, the real challenge isn't *getting* there, but obtaining the necessary funding, permits, and visas to go there (and, once there, sometimes dealing with military bu-

---

*Of course, anyone who has followed the recent developments in evolutionary theory realizes just how mistaken this belief was—as mistaken as Lord Kelvin when he claimed several years before Einstein appeared that virtually all of the problems in physics had been solved, and that future researchers would merely be adding digits to the right of the decimal point.

reaucrats or unstable revolutionary governments). There has been one exception to this rule: a place called Cerro de la Neblina, "Mountain of the Mists." An expedition there in 1984 and 1985 hearkened back in many ways to the age of Roy Chapman Andrews.

The northern section of the Amazon watershed—2,000 miles upriver from the sea—drains off a scattering of isolated tabletop mountains that rise sharply above the tropical rain forests. Called *tepuis*, these are the eroded remains of a vast plateau that covered the area hundreds of millions of years ago. One such *tepui*, straddling the border between Venezuela and Brazil, is the "Mountain of the Mists." Isolated by its sheer cliffs and deep canyons—and usually shrouded in a heavy cloud cover—Neblina floats like an island 6,000 to 9,000 feet above the jungle. Torrential rains soak the mountain and pour down its ravines, filling the blackwater swamps around its base.

Neblina is one of the most isolated places on earth, and one of the last areas still largely unexplored by biologists. Although the trackless swamps and nearly incessant rain together create an environment that fosters a diversity of animal life, Neblina and its surrounding rain forests have always remained uninhabited by humans.

In 1984, scientists from the Museum and a dozen other American institutions joined Venezuelan biologists and scientists from other countries in a major expedition. Its purpose: to conduct a complete biological survey of the Mountain of the Mists. Because of its extremely inaccessible location, the only way to reach Neblina and study it properly was through mounting a large expedition—not unlike the Central Asiatic Expedition of years before. This time, however, instead of camels and motorcars, the expedition used a combination of every sort of transportation, from military planes and helicopters to dugout canoes. The results of this research—thousands of animal and plant specimens—are now being intensively studied at universities, herbaria, and museums both here and in Venezuela.

The similarities of this expedition to the Museum's earlier extravaganzas are striking. The extreme remoteness of

Neblina demanded a large support team. Unlike most recent fieldwork, the Neblina expedition had no idea what they might find at the top of this isolated plateau. (They knew enough, however, not to expect live dinosaurs, as the more fanciful press has suggested might be found in such remote areas.) Like the Central Asiatic Expedition, the Neblina group included dozens of scientists from many disciplines and many institutions—including botanists, mammalogists, herpetologists, ichthyologists, entomologists, and ornithologists. And also like the Central Asiatic Expedition, it will take years—even decades—to study thoroughly the exotic plant and animal life brought back from the Mountain of the Mists. Funding for the costly expedition came from many sources, including the National Science Foundation and private donors (especially the William H. Phelps Foundation), as well as from the home institutions of the various scientists.

"The expedition had one basic purpose," explained Jerome G. Rozen, Jr., Deputy Director of the Museum and an expedition entomologist. "We wanted to get in there and find out what was living in this largely unstudied area—to take a detailed biological inventory. The expedition is part of a larger, worldwide effort to study and understand the world's rain forests before they are destroyed by man."

Sponsored by Venezuela's Foundation for the Development of the Physical, Mathematical and Natural Sciences, the expedition was led by Charles Brewer, a Venezuelan who has had years of experience exploring remote jungle areas. One of the few people familiar with the Neblina region, Brewer turned out to be an ideal leader—an old-fashioned, Roy Chapman Andrews type. Lean and muscular, comfortable with half a dozen Indian languages, Brewer was most at home, according to one expedition member, "hunkered down over a campfire with a group of Indians."

Although several decades of technological improvement have passed since the golden age of expeditions, transporting eighteen scientists and more than a ton of equipment and supplies to an area over sixty miles from any human

habitation proved to be a formidable logistical problem.*
U.S. scientists made the first leg of the journey by plane
from New York to Caracas, where they were joined by
their Venezuelan colleagues. From there, a small plane
took them to Puerto Ayacucho, the capital of Amazonas, a
territory in southern Venezuela. Brewer had lined up a
Venezuelan army Hercules transport and charter planes to
carry the scientists and their equipment to San Carlos, a
tiny settlement on the northern reaches of the Rio Negro,
one of the major tributaries of the Amazon.

At San Carlos the eighteen scientists of the first team
met for the final and most arduous part of their journey.
They loaded all of their supplies and equipment onto three
huge dugout canoes powered by outboard motors, and
headed upriver to Santa Lucia, an Army post consisting of
little more than a clearing sliced out of the jungle. From
there they flew helicopters across fifty or sixty miles of
unbroken, uninhabited swamp to their base camp at the
foot of Neblina. The first part of the expedition lasted six
weeks. Small parties sortied by helicopter up the sheer
walls of the mountain to establish mountain camps for
three- or five-day collecting forays. Armed with microscopes, specimen containers, nets, funnels, firearms, binoculars, tape recorders, preservatives, collecting jars, and
the like, they amassed tens of thousands of specimens and
gathered data on distribution, ecology, and behavior, as
well as documenting rainfall and temperature.

At one point a small collecting group dropped on the
mountain by helicopter for a three-day stint. When the time
had passed for their return and no helicopter arrived, they
were concerned and started rationing food. As the days
stretched on, they were forced to eat their bird specimens.
(Of course, they saved the skins and skeletons for study.)
"Every day, we would have a broth made out of one bouil-
lon cube and five little birds," said Richard Zweifel, a Museum herpetologist. "Unfortunately, all you can get out of a
bird is a little piece of meat the size of your pinky." They

---

*A total of seventy to eighty scientists studied Neblina in a series of team visits.

also discovered that a certain species of palm contained an edible heart—"a little like celery and about as filling." (The palm was a new species.) The helicopter finally arrived after nine days, the delay having been caused by mechanical problems and poor weather. Zweifel, who was built sparely to begin with, lost ten pounds.

Members at the base camp at the bottom of Neblina also had to go on short rations because of bad weather and helicopter breakdowns. They resorted to eating such rain-forest animals as the capybara (a large rodent: "tasty, like veal"); the caiman (a crocodile: "white and fishy, something like lobster"); the curassow (a chickenlike bird that tasted, not surprisingly, like chicken); and the peccary (a wild pig: "leaner than pork").

Although it will be years before comprehensive findings are published, major new animals and plants have already been identified and classified from the specimens brought back from Neblina. In terms of plant life alone, the results are stupendous. More than half of all the plant species found at the top of Neblina were unknown to science—and most may not exist anywhere else on earth.

Swept by chill winds, fog, and almost daily rainfall, the flat top of Neblina presents a landscape that looks like nothing else on earth. Its deep sphagnum bogs are filled with insect-trapping pitcher plants and sundews, and its marshy fields are sprinkled with previously unknown grasses and flowers. Spectacular orchids and bromeliads abound. Skinny palms rising only ten to fifteen feet punctuate the mountain's dense, chest-high vegetation of stubby trees and bushes. Foot-long earthworms grow in the springy soil, and tarantulas often crawled into the expedition's tents.

"Almost all the animals we brought back from the top of the mountain were unusual," said Rozen, "and many are certainly new species. These *tepuis* are like isolated islands, and it is quite possible that each mountaintop has its own set of unique species." (One of the few nonindigenous species of insect Rozen found at the top of Neblina was the

Africanized honeybee, the "killer bee" that has caused so much concern recently.)

Even at the base of Neblina, the expedition found new life. Gareth Nelson and Carl Ferraris, Museum ichthyologists, discovered dozens of new species of catfish and caracins (a small relative of the piranha) in the blackwater swamps that drain the *tepui*. They also identified a number of animals common to the jungle—fer-de-lances, giant anacondas, monkeys, toucans, macaws, caimans, capybaras, peccaries, deer, tapirs, and even a jaguar.

Many of the plants and animals found on the top of Neblina may derive from ancient lineages that stretch back hundreds of millions years to the time when Africa and South America were joined in the "supercontinent" Pangaea. Neblina and its surrounding *tepuis* may also provide the key to complex evolutionary questions, such as how new species arise and how fast they evolve. In the Galapagos Islands, for example, Darwin found dramatic evidence for his theory of evolution by studying different finch species, all descended from one common ancestor, that lived on separate islands. The *tepuis*, biologically isolated from one another by stretches of impenetrable swamp, form a similar "laboratory" for the study of speciation. Believed to have once been a large, unified plateau with the same species distributed throughout, the plateau eroded into a series of isolated mountain-islands, each possibly evolving a unique assemblage of plants and animals. By studying the similarities and differences among related species on these mountaintops, scientists may eventually be able to arrive at a more general theory of evolutionary change.

# Part Two

# THE
# GRAND
# TOUR

The Museum today is a very different place from the Museum of half a century ago. Now, high technology laboratories filled with computers and electronic equipment can be found next door to storerooms full of human mummies or snakes coiled in jars of alcohol. The collections are being cared for and studied in ways that Roy Chapman Andrews never dreamed of.

This next section of *Dinosaurs in the Attic* will take the reader on a grand armchair tour among the labs, vaults, and corridors of the Museum today. Along the way, we will often stop to chat with a curator, poke around in a storage room, or take a short excursion in space and time to the initial discovery of a particularly unusual specimen. Our first stop along this ramble will be the dinosaur bone storage room, certainly one of the more remarkable places in New York City—if not the world.

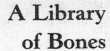

# TEN

# A Library
of Bones

To get to the dinosaur bone storage room at the American Museum of Natural History, we must first descend to the main basement. Here, the labyrinthine route follows dim passageways lined with rumbling steam pipes. Off one of these corridors is a padlocked door, with a grubby sign taped to it that reads DINOSAUR STORAGE ROOM. The door opens into a large, starkly illuminated chamber. Stacks of metal shelves reach up into the gloom. Everywhere, we see bones. Huge dark bones shrouded in plastic lie on the shelves, while large bones sit stacked on the floor or leaning against the wall. Slabs of rock containing twisted skeletons hang on the walls, and along the back of the room runs a workbench covered with dinosaur models, bones under study, and other odd-looking things. At the far end of the room and to the left, we see another door. Beyond this door is the basement to the Frick Building, a nine-story structure hidden in the center of the Museum's complex of buildings.

The Frick Building is the heart of vertebrate paleontology research in the Museum. The building was donated to the Museum by a corporation started by the millionaire Childs Frick. Frick, the Barnum Brown of fossil mammal collections, donated his outstanding collection to the Museum; later his corporation gave half of the ten-story building required to house it. Row upon row of green metal cabinets containing fossil vertebrates fill this basement room. But this is only a small fraction of the collection. Above it are seven floors of nothing but storage, comprising the largest collection of fossil mammals and dinosaurs in the world. The weight of this collection is so great that it would collapse a normal building; consequently the Frick Building was built with special steel reinforcing elements. On the top three floors are labs and offices.

In another area of the Museum—many winding passageways away from the dinosaurs—is the Whale Bone Storage Room. The whale collection is stored in an echoing, cavernous space that was once the Museum's powerhouse. Now, instead of massive generators, the room contains huge whale skulls and bones shrouded in plastic. The metal tracks and winches on the ceiling, once used for moving the giant machines, are now used for shifting the leviathans about. A peaceful light filters in through windows high on the walls, giving the room a hushed, mausoleumlike atmosphere.

But this is only the beginning. In a Museum attic, for example, rests the Elephant Room. Downstairs from that, one can find the tusk vault, the boar vault, and hundreds of metal cabinets containing the skeletons of everything from giraffes to shrews.

Moving even farther afield: In an office in the Anthropology Department stretch row upon row of cardboard boxes, all labeled and numbered, and each containing a human skull. Cabinets along the walls contain hanging human skeletons from all over the world.

Wherever one looks, there are bones—bird bones in the Ornithology Department, lizard and tortoise bones in Herpetology, fish bones in Ichthyology—bones from a large proportion of the vertebrate species on earth. Even the Museum's official logo shows two skeletons: those of a man and a horse.

If all the bones in the American Museum of Natural History were dumped into Central Park, they would form a pile well over three stories high and hundreds of feet in circumference. A *very* rough calculation indicates the pile would weigh at least 1,000 tons and contain about 50 million bones, representing the remains of more than 750,000 animals.

This mountain of bones has been gathered from every corner of the earth—from Outer Mongolia to East 59th Street. The people who brought this mountain together endured blizzards, sandstorms, bandits, and a host of other hardships. Some collectors even risked their lives or spent their personal fortunes in the effort. Almost all the bones —more than 99 percent—were collected for scientific purposes and are not on public display. More than two hundred scientists and their assistants conduct research in the Museum, much of which focuses on bones.

Why should such vast resources be devoted to collecting, cataloguing, storing, and caring for 50 million bones? Of what significance is this research? *Why study bones?* Perhaps the best way to answer this question is to visit one Museum scientist who does study bones: paleontologist Malcolm McKenna.

There can be no mistaking McKenna's office: boxes of fossil bones, all carefully labeled and numbered, cover most of the tables in the spacious room. McKenna himself has collected most of the specimens he studies, because such specimens are not present in the general collection. During his thirty-odd years in paleontology, McKenna has prospected for extremely rare fossils of early mammals just about everywhere—from Greenland to Patagonia.

McKenna brings out a plastic box filled with his recent

finds, which look like so many tiny chips of stone. Early mammals were small, and these pieces are actually hundreds of minuscule fossil teeth, tiny jaws a quarter-inch in length, and other irregular bits of fossil bone. In all, the box holds less than two ounces of fossils. They date, McKenna says, from about 66 million years ago, and were discovered in Cretaceous beds at Lance Creek, Wyoming. This type of collection is more typical of the Museum today than in the past. Although they lack the glamour of the huge dinosaurs, in many ways they may actually be more important.

These fossils are rare—exceedingly rare. "To get this little box of jaws and teeth," McKenna says, "a field crew of eight people had to process five tons of matrix every day for a week." McKenna spends most of his summers in the field collecting fossils such as these. Over the years, he has developed a collecting method that differs radically from the way Barnum Brown, for example, collected fossils. He doesn't collect *individual* fossils at all; instead, he collects entire fossil communities—fossil ecologies, so to speak. To accomplish this, McKenna has to extract almost every fossil larger than a small pebble from a particular deposit.

McKenna seeks a picture of the life of one entire community at a particular point in time. Since bones are usually the only things that survive into future eras, he must of necessity study them. Bones can provide us with an extraordinary amount of information, especially when combined with research in other areas such as astronomy and geology.

"My research," he explains, "requires the highest resolution data—the most detailed and complete picture possible." To accomplish this, McKenna needs thousands of bones, not just a few. To obtain such large quantities, he has his field crew dig up the fossil-bearing matrix, which at Lance Creek is made up of ancient channel sands cross-bedded with layers of clay, and dump it in water. (The highest concentrations of the fossils McKenna is after can be found in what he calls "fossil garbage dumps" in ancient streambeds, where flash floods and other processes have deposited a great assortment of bones, many of them originally contained in carnivore scat.) When the matrix has loosened in the water, it is sifted through a fine wire-mesh screen. The screen catches thousands of pebbles—and, if McKenna and his crew are lucky, a fossil tooth or two. In one day, working in assembly-line fashion, the crew can process 550 twenty-pound boxes of matrix. "It's very tedious work," McKenna says. "You have to go through a lot of beer and Cutty Sark just to find one fossil." Indeed, one of McKenna's colleagues named a toothy new species *Cuttysarkus mcnallyi* because the discoverer, a member named McNally, had been promised a bottle of the Scotch if he found a mammal jaw with six or more teeth in it.

McKenna's collecting method is tedious but wonderfully efficient. "The first day we spent at Lance Creek in 1956," McKenna says, "we collected more fossils than everyone else since the fossil locality was discovered." Yet the fossils are so rare that, even using McKenna's method, an entire summer's work could fit in a small piece of carry-on luggage for the return flight to New York.

McKenna pokes his finger around in the box of fossils. "This box represents," he says, "a picture of the animal life of one particular area at one particular moment in time—in this case, about 66 million years ago, around the time of the mass extinction at the end of the Cretaceous." Lance Creek has fossils of about eighty kinds of animals, including fishes, lizards, tiny and large dinosaurs, frogs, salamanders, birds, and early mammals. "I keep the mammal bones," McKenna says, "and spin off the rest of the fossils to other scientists."

He then explains what we can learn by looking at little bits of bone and tooth. "What can these bones tell us? An extraordinary amount, it turns out. There are many levels of 'boniness.' Bones have an exterior shape, which tells us about the anatomy of the animal and what it did for a living. Bones have an interior structure, which can provide clues about whether or not the animal was warm-blooded. Some bones have growth rings, which indicate whether the animal lived in a variable climate and had to slow down for a period every year. Bones also have a microscopic structure, which can show such things as the metabolism of the animal."

Since teeth, being extremely hard, survive better than bones, they make up most of the contents of McKenna's box. Fortunately, mammal teeth are almost a fingerprint of the animal—they are highly complicated structures with ridges, valleys, spikes, ribs, ripples, pits, and points. Few species have teeth that look exactly like another. Consequently, a paleontologist can sometimes identify an animal fairly closely by looking at a single tooth, and can usually identify it with certainty from a jaw with two or three teeth. Equally helpful is the fact that mammalian teeth remain constant for a given species.*

Once McKenna has identified the animals living in a specific community, he can start looking at some of the larger questions. Bones can reveal something about the behavior of the animal, for example. "Take foot bones," he says. "What was the animal doing with his feet? Was it hopping, swimming, galloping, climbing in trees?" Since bones have marks where ligaments and muscles were attached, the paleontologist can actually determine an extinct animal's musculature and reconstruct the form of the animal itself. (This landmark advance in paleontology was made at the Museum in the 1920s.)

Once paleontologists know what the animal looked like, they can start reconstructing its habitat. If the animal was a hopper, for example, it may have lived in an arid, sandy area. If the animal had tree-climbing limbs, its habitat must have been arboreal—even though, of course, no tree fossils may be found today. Bones, then, can shed light on past landscapes, climates, and vegetations.

"Much of this information can be found by studying this little box of fossils," McKenna continues. "You can actu-

*Those who study dinosaurs are not so fortunate. Reptilian teeth increase in size as the animal grows, and thus become a much poorer way to identify a species. Reptilian teeth are for the most part shaped like simple cones, making it impossible to identify a species from its teeth.

ally work out the 'census structure' of the community with these fossils." The census structure includes not only what animals were living when, but also the relative proportions of one species to another at that time. "How did the animals interact? For example"—he pauses to pick out a tooth from the box—"this mammal tooth passed through the alimentary tract of a big reptilian meat-eater, such as a crocodile. How do I know? The tooth has been etched by stomach acid—see, it looks frosted. I suspect it was a crocodile, because crocodiles have very acidic stomachs. So we even know what animals were eating what." Thus, bones can help reconstruct ecologies that may have been extinct for many millions of years.

And yet this is just the beginning, according to McKenna. "If you want to answer the largest questions in science—and this is the goal of most scientists—you have to study the highest-resolution data possible. You can spin theories with a bone here and a bone there; but what you really need are many, many bones of many kinds from one locality at one time period.

"By looking at fossil assemblages in a number of areas, you can correlate assemblages to within about one percent of their real age. Then, by studying successive layers, a paleontologist can learn how the community and the climate evolved over time. If a group of species suddenly went extinct, the paleontologist can look for the reason. Thus, even a small area can yield information about the earth as a whole." The study of bones can help date past events, and can show how evolution proceeded, including the evolution of entire ecosystems.

As with many scientific questions, there really is no end to how far one can go. By comparing two sets of layers in different sites, paleontologists can gain data that will help draw a hypothetical map of the earth as it appeared at some time in the distant past. "Let's say you're studying two localities, one in France and one in Wyoming," McKenna says. "In layers about 50 million years old in France and Wyoming, most of the animals are normally quite different. But about 60 million years ago, European and North American deposits had many animals in common. What do you conclude? Possibly that some sort of connection—a land bridge—was present between Europe and North America for a while."

The paleontologist, by looking at *other* scientific data, may recall that huge lava flows occurred when Greenland was closer to Scotland, possibly forming a land bridge. Europe and North America were much closer together 60 million years ago. Five million years later, the two faunas —in Wyoming and France—were different again. Thus he might hypothesize that a land bridge developed between 60 million and 55 million years ago across the North Atlantic, a bridge that lasted approximately 5 million years. When the sea encroached upon the bridge, it cut off that particular route of interchange, after which the faunas of the separated areas evolved independently. The above scenario is not imaginary; it is a theory that McKenna has developed through his research.

The amount of information that bones can provide is limited only by the questions we ask. Another question McKenna has been working on is whether the dinosaurs died out suddenly or gradually. Dating the exact time of the extinction, and how rapidly it occurred, is central to any extinction theory. A significant reason why McKenna collected at Lance Creek was that the fossil-bearing strata date from the very end of the Cretaceous, just when the dinosaurs were becoming extinct.

The results of McKenna's research are a bit startling. Up to now, one of the prime candidates for dubious distinction of the extinction of the dinosaurs is the theory of asteroid impact. In this theory, a large asteroid struck the earth about 65 million years ago, causing sudden atmospheric and climatic changes that in time caused the dinosaurs to vanish from the earth. The prime bit of evidence for this theory is a 65-million-year-old layer of iridium, and indications of ancient soot particles that appear in strata in various areas around the world. Iridium is scarce on earth, but rather more common in meteorites. Such a layer could thus most plausibly come from a meteorite impact, which—if large enough—could have spread a layer of iridium-enriched dust around the world. But McKenna's research contradicts this theory. His study of bones, combined with the research of many of his colleagues, indicates that the dinosaurs became extinct *before* the asteroid impact.*

"There is a small but significant thickness of rock without dinosaur fossils underneath the iridium layer," McKenna explains. "That dinosaurs could have been around but not found is possible, but the chance of that is about three percent or even less.

"Now, this is a fascinating observation. Could the various extinctions and the bolide† impact have been caused by the same thing? Here's where paleontology and other scientific disciplines can come together and provide important information. If we combine our data with astronomical data, we can tell something about the history of the earth in relation to the solar system.

"Paleontologists have noted a periodicity in mass extinctions. Astronomers have noted a periodicity in the path of the solar system as it passes back and forth through the galactic plane. Geologists have noted a periodicity in the formation of ancient meteorite craters on the earth. Geophysicists have suggested a periodicity in magnetic reversals. Could all these things be related?" McKenna noted that a number of theories do in fact relate some of these observations. One theory, now largely discarded, hypothesizes the existence of a dark companion star to the sun, named Nemesis, that periodically swings close to our solar system and sends comets plunging into earth-crossing orbits. Some of these comets, it is hypothesized, actually strike the earth.

"The point here is that all the various scientific disci-

---

*It is important to note that McKenna doesn't dispute the asteroid-impact theory per se; he merely contends that the dinosaurs were extinct *before* the asteroid struck.

†A bolide is a large meteoroid that either explodes in the atmosphere or strikes the earth, or both.

plines come together and test each other's theories. What we are doing—in the Museum and elsewhere—is putting together a general picture of the earth. We want to construct the entire history of our planet, not just the history of animal life. This is *real* natural history—not just biology. We're not the American Museum of Biology. What we are working on here in the Museum has consequences and implications throughout science, from astronomy to geophysics.

"The reason we collect bones is to build up a library of *facts*. It's not postage-stamp collecting by any means. Bones, and indeed all scientific collections, differ from books in that books are opinion and interpretation, while specimens are facts. In this way, museums are different from universities. Bones are one of our greatest links with the past—they are our record of extinct vertebrate life on this planet."

## Getting Bones

It is one thing to study bones, but quite another to get them. Paleontologists (as we have seen in several of the expeditions described earlier in this book) find their bones as ready-made fossils. In this respect, mammalogists are not so fortunate. They must collect from the living—and this means finding bones that are inconveniently encased in flesh and skin. At one time, before 1930, it was an easy matter for the Museum to send scientists out to Kenya or Tibet to shoot mammals for study. Today, with many animals becoming endangered, and amid a growing awareness of conservation, many of the Museum's specimens come from carefully monitored and licensed collecting forays— as well as from zoos.

Four flights down from McKenna's office, and at the end of a cul-de-sac in the Museum's African Hall, we come to a locked door with no knob. Through this door, down a twisting corridor, up one flight in a freight elevator, and down a quick right and a left, there is a locked steel door with a tiny window. This door is outside the mammalogy preparation area. Next to the door hangs a heavy coat, which one must put on before entering the room. The room's interior looks like nothing else on earth; it is like an exotic meat locker filled with rare animals. This room—the Museum's "freezer"—is often the first stop a dead animal makes upon entering the Museum. Lying on the floor at the time of our visit, arms outstretched, is the body of a female gorilla—frozen solid. Stretched alongside her, also frozen, rests a male leopard. On the far side of the room, a number of shelves hold stacks of elephant hides and other skins; some of these hides are from elephants shot by Teddy and Kermit Roosevelt. Assorted animal remains and skinned carcasses in plastic bags are stored about the room, and in a far corner, two mounted Siberian tigers stare at the scene with fierce but sightless eyes.

Most large natural history museums require a freezer to store perishable remains. Here animals are stored until preparators are ready to turn them into skeletons and skins for study or exhibition. Today the animals that end up in the American Museum's freezer almost always come from zoos with which the Museum has made special arrangements. (The gorilla, for example, lived at the Bronx Zoo until her death.) By the time you read these pages, the gorilla will probably be a numbered skeleton resting in a drawer in the collection.

It is here that we are very likely to run into Steve Medina, the man in charge of reducing animal carcasses to skin and bones. There are few people in the country in his line of work—perhaps no more than a dozen or two.

"There are," Medina explains, "two methods of preparing a carcass: bacterial maceration . . . and 'the bugs.'" Maceration is the preferred method for large animals whose bones will be disarticulated, while "the bugs" work best for smaller animals and for delicate parts of larger animals where curators want the skeletons to remain articulated.

Medina works mostly in the osteological preparation

lab, a sprawling, sunny room overlooking Columbus Avenue. Along one wall are the maceration vats—three tanks, two converted bathtubs, and one enormous stainless steel vat that looks as though it could hold a rhinoceros—and indeed it has.

Bacterial maceration of an animal to obtain its skeleton begins with a process called "roughing out," in which the body is gutted and excess muscle, fat, and tissue are trimmed off—but not too thoroughly, since the bacteria need something to work on. Then the carcass is lowered into one of these vats filled with warm tapwater. Small burners keep the water at just the right temperature for rotting to proceed at an optimum pace. During the next week or two, bacterial action "digests" the tissues, which float to the surface as a foul scum. When most of the meat has liquefied, the tank is drained, leaving behind a greasy pile of bones. The bones are boiled in a solution of cleaning soda, and any stubborn bits of flesh are picked off by hand. Although large vents above each vat carry off most of the hideous combination of gases that percolate up during maceration, Medina says that "it can get pretty bad in here." If the bones will be going on exhibition, they are then whitened in the big tank.*

"The bugs" are the second method of preparing skeletons for study. A humid closet adjacent to the preparation area houses a large colony of dermestid beetles. These small, voracious beetles have become famous in the press because of the way they are used to obtain skeletons. Most large natural history museums maintain a colony of these black, perfectly ordinary-looking beetles. The dermestids eat the flesh clean off a dead animal, leaving behind a spic-and-span skeleton. The great beauty of the process is that the skeleton remains articulated, held together by connecting cartilage, which the beetles won't eat—until, that is, they run out of meat. If left too long, the beetles will eat

*In the days before the Occupational Safety and Health Administration (OSHA) regulated the use of hazardous chemicals, Museum preparators often placed the skeleton in a shallow tray filled with benzene, which, when placed in strong sunlight, turned the bones a brilliant white.

not only the cartilage but also the bones, so they must be carefully monitored.

Contrary to popular belief, dermestid beetles are harmless to humans and are actually quite fastidious in their habits. As long as the Museum can supply a steady stream of specimens for cleaning, the colony maintains itself with little fuss. During occasional slow periods, Medina will supplement their diet with extra flesh cut from the animal carcasses.

The dead animal to be cleaned is placed in the dermestid room in a stainless steel box with slick sides and a bottom covered with cotton batting. The tubs rest some feet above the floor.

For maximum success, the animal corpse should be partially dried first with a fan, as the beetles don't like a sticky mess. The dermestids take about a week to polish off a large skeleton, but may finish a rodent or bat overnight. The Museum's colony can in fact handle many carcasses at one time. During my visit the beetles' assignment was about fifty small bats, a monkey, a fox, and an iguana. When a skeleton is more or less clean, Medina lures the beetles away with a fresh carcass, and the cleaned skeleton is immediately sealed in a cabinet with mothballs to kill any stray beetles, which otherwise might wreak havoc in the study collections. Finally, the skeleton is immersed in a water-ammonia solution, which removes grease and odor from the bones; then it is dried, numbered, and installed in the collection.*

The Museum's bones are in great demand for study. Not only do hundreds of scientists come from all over the world to examine them, but many thousands of bones are loaned to scientists at institutions as far away as India and China. For now, let us move on to some of the more unusual "remains" in the Museum—bones that have histories well worth telling.

---

*Although the foregoing methods may seem bizarre, they have been standard procedure in most natural history museums and large universities for many years.

## The Chubb Horses

Once obtained, bones are usually studied. But some are prepared especially for mounting and exhibition. The Museum houses a number of famous and unusual articulated skeletons. Some are on display; others remain hidden in storage behind various locked doors. Let's look behind some of those locked doors now.

Deep within the third floor of the Museum—in the preparation area—the corridors are lined with large glass cases of mounted skeletons. Most are of horses. In one case gallops the famous racehorse Sysonby, caught at the moment when all four hooves leave the ground. Other cases contain the skeletons of Lee Axworthy, a world-famous trotting stallion; a galloping Przewalski's horse being attacked by a wolf; four zebras mounted to show different gaits; and a grazing Shetland pony. There is, in fact, at least one mount of every species of *Equus*.

These mounted skeletons are the work of S. Harmsted Chubb, who created them at the rate of about one per year for the half-century he worked for the Museum. Many present-day osteologists acknowledge that Chubb was a master of the art of mounting bones, perhaps the greatest who ever lived. Many of these skeletons were first displayed in the Museum's old Hall of Osteology and later in the Biology of Mammals Hall, but several decades ago they were moved into storage. (In 1985, however, they were taken out for a special exhibition on Chubb, "Captured Motion," which was displayed in Gallery 1 for several months.) One of the Chubb mounts, showing the skeleton of a man trying to control the skeleton of a rearing stallion, has become the Museum's logo and is on all its letterheads and business cards. It is often mistaken by the ignorant for a dinosaur.

A slight, precise man with a neatly trimmed goatee, Chubb was a familiar figure at the Museum during the first half of this century. He was usually fussily dressed in a gold pince-nez, with waistcoat and tie covered by a white lab coat or apron. When he wasn't mounting bones in the Museum, he could usually be found at horse or dog races, not placing bets but taking photographs and chatting with the owners and jockeys.

Chubb's interest in bones, he reported in an autobiographical article, began as a child, when he found a dead cat under the porch of his Maryland home. He began looking for other dead animals, which he would spread out on the roof of his father's barn to decompose. When this arrangement quickly proved unsatisfactory to his parents, he hid the carcasses in the woods and returned later when they had been picked clean by scavengers and the elements. Since he lived in Maryland horse country, most of his bones came from dead horses.

Through sheer trial and error he taught himself how to mount skeletons, and this experimentation led him in turn to study the horse's movements, and how its bones articulated with one another. (In his first experiment with bone movement, Chubb reported, he attached a row of horse skulls to the edge of the woodshed roof. When he pulled strings attached to their jawbones, the row of skulls clacked their teeth in a wonderfully macabre fashion.)

At sixteen, just around the turn of the century, Chubb came to New York City and found work as a machinist. He spent much of his spare time, however, at the Museum. He quickly realized that the vast majority of skeletons in the Museum (and indeed in most museums) were carelessly mounted—often more poorly than his own early efforts. Chubb concluded that these professional osteologists simply hadn't studied how the animals *moved*—they had merely observed where the bones connected and then stuck them together.

He found his way into the office of Henry Fairfield Osborn, at that time the curator of the Vertebrate Paleontology Department, and with a few of his samples showed the paleontologist why some of the Museum's mounts were sloppy. Impressed, Osborn bought one of Chubb's mounted cats for forty dollars, and ordered a mounted opossum and

1. President Ulysses S. Grant lays the cornerstone to the Museum, June 2, 1874. (From *Leslie's Illustrated Newspaper*, June 20, 1874).

2. Benjamin Waterhouse Hawkins' studio in Central Park, showing models of extinct creatures to be included in the Paleozoic Museum planned for the park.

3. "The American Museum of Natural History as it will appear when completed." (From an architect's drawing, published in *Harper's Weekly*, 1897. The central tower, called the "Hall of the Heavens," was never built; neither were the north or west facades. As of today, the Museum is still only two-thirds complete based on this plan.)

4. The first Museum building, standing in a wasteland of undrained ponds and piles of rock (1878).

5. The Museum's first building on Manhattan Square (c. 1880). This photograph was taken from the rooftop of the newly built Dakota apartment building. Note the squatters' shanties in the middleground.

6. Albert S. Bickmore's official portrait, photographed on May 11, 1908. Bickmore was the founder of the Museum.

7. The completed first building in what was to become the 77th Street facade, 1893.

8. The Maritime Koryak tribe of Siberia, photographed on the Jesup North Pacific Expedition (c. 1900). The central post served as a ladder. The interior of the house is entirely coated with thick, greasy soot.

9. The Ahnighito meteorite on the shore of Melville Bay in Greenland, about to be slid across rails greased with tallow to Robert E. Peary's ship, 1897.

10. Unloading the Ahnighito meteorite at the 50th Street pier, Manhattan, around the turn of the century.

11. Automobile used to deliver collections to various schools for teaching purposes, 1908.

12. The Museum Taxidermy and Exhibition Department in 1905.

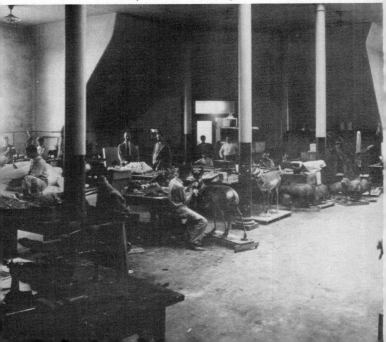

13. *Above:* The Crocker Land Expedition with their dog teams crossing a mountain on an island north of Greenland (1915).

14. *Below right:* A *Diplodocus* limb, the first discovery at Bone Cabin Quarry. The bones, fossilized remnants from an ancient Jurassic river bar, rested on and just beneath the surface.

15. The *Diplodocus* limb as shown on the Bone Cabin Quarry map.

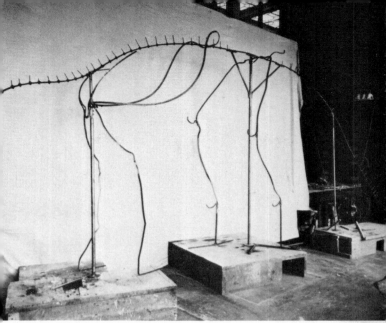

16. *Above:* The first step in mounting a dinosaur skeleton is the construction of the metal framework. Shown here in a 1908 photograph is a trachodont mount.

17. *Below left:* Henry Fairfield Osborn, the father of American paleontology. 18. *Below right:* Barnum Brown's dinosaur hunting houseboat, at a camp on the Red Deer River, Alberta, Canada, 1912.

19. Dinosaur hunter Barnum Brown among Lower Belly River rocks near Sweetwater, Montana, 1914. Even in the field, Brown was always immaculately dressed.

20. One dinosaur skeleton, as it appears before the fragments are assembled, cemented, and mounted. Barnum Brown (with bow tie) is in the background center.

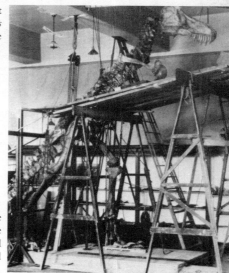

21. Assembling the great skeleton of *Tyrannosaurus rex* in the Hall of Late Dinosaurs, 1915.

22. Carl Akeley puts the finishing touches on the clay model for the big bull elephant in the Akeley Hall of African Mammals, 1914.

23. Carl Akeley at the edge of a volcano in the Belgian Congo, filming with the camera he invented, c. 1920s.

·

24. Carl Akeley after being attacked by an elephant, in the bush in Kenya.

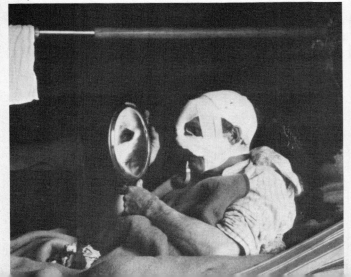

25. An example of an early Museum hall: the Morgan Hall of Minerals and Gems, 1922.

26. Roy Chapman Andrews, leader of the Central Asiatic Expedition, in Mongolia (1928).

27. The expedition just outside the Great Wall of China at Wan Chuan Hsien, 1928. Lined up behind the expedition is the Chinese cavalry escort that protected the expedition from marauding soldiers and bandits in Inner Mongolia.

28. The supply caravan of camels for the Central Asiatic Expedition crossing the dunes of Tsagan Nor. Tserin, the Mongolian guide, heads the caravan (1925).

29. The Central Asiatic Expedition attempted to cross an apparently dry lake, but broke through the crust. Mongolia, 1928.

30. Roy Chapman Andrews scans the desert in Mongolia for trails leading east into the Gobi Desert, 1928.

31. The Central Asiatic Expedition just inside Nankan Pass with the Great Wall of China in the background, 1928.

32. Roy Chapman Andrews and Walter Granger excavating dinosaur eggs at Erhlieu, Mongolia.

33. *Above:* "The mongol men of Hat-in-Sumu prefer to listen to the radio signals being received by Hill. We are greatly indebted to the radio station at Cavidi, Philippines, who kindly sent us time signals twice a day and which we received remarkably well at a distance of two thousand miles." (Original expedition caption. The time signals were necessary for the Central Asiatic Expedition to calculate their exact position by the sun and stars. Mongolia, 1928.)

34. S. Harmsted Chubb in an elaborate rigging set up to photograph the back of a trotting horse for one of his osteological preparations.

35. A rare photograph showing Ellis Hughes, the Welshman who stole the Willamette meteorite, and his son. The meteorite—the largest ever found in the U.S.—rests on the handmade cart Hughes used to transport the meteorite to his own land.

36. The Willamette meteorite arriving at the Museum by horsedrawn cart. Note the right wheels sinking into the roadway from the meteorite's immense weight.

a raccoon. In 1901, Osborn decided to hire Chubb full-time to help prepare the Museum's planned Hall of Osteology.

Naturally, Chubb decided that mounts of the horse would be the best way to teach visitors about animal locomotion; mounts of famous racehorses would be even better. Chubb made the rounds of some of the famous racehorse owners of the time, delicately suggesting that they donate the bodies of their prize horses if they should happen to die. While some owners immediately ejected Chubb from their offices for such a morbid suggestion, others liked the idea that their best horses might end up in a museum. Chubb didn't have to wait long; the owner of the famous stallion Sysonby, James R. Keene, wrote to him in 1906 that his champion stallion had unexpectedly died, and shortly thereafter the dead horse arrived at the Museum.

Chubb wanted to capture Sysonby at the peak of his speed. At that time it had only recently been established (in a famous bet) that for a split second during full gallop, all four of a horse's hooves leave the ground. But before mounting the animal in such a position, Chubb wanted to establish the position of its legs and body during various phases of its stride. Using a borrowed racehorse on the grounds of the Museum, he painted white stripes and spots on the horse's body. While the horse trotted or galloped along, Chubb photographed it from every conceivable angle. One photograph of Chubb shows him dangling about thirty feet directly above a trotting horse, photographing straight down onto its back, which had been strangely painted with dots and lines.

Chubb spent eleven months mounting Sysonby. Following the usual procedure (described in the previous chapter) he roughed out the carcass and dumped it in one of the maceration vats. During the first few nights, Chubb lived in an adjacent room so that he could tend the small Bunsen burners that kept the water at an even 98 degrees Fahrenheit. In two weeks most of Sysonby could be drained out of the vat, and Chubb put the bones in benzene for another six to eight weeks.

Chubb assembled the skeleton under a complex scaffold

he called his "osteological Christmas tree." He dangled each bone from the scaffolding by a string and made adjustments to its length until it was hanging in its correct position for the mount. A flexible rod, threaded through the spinal cord, anchored the mount, and the other bones were attached, one by one, with slender pins, pipes, and wires. During the months-long process, Chubb adjusted and readjusted each bone numerous times, using his marked photographs as a guide. When he was finally satisfied that everything was correctly in place, the ribs were hung and pinned to thin metal bands along the inside of the ribcage. Every bone of the horse became part of the mount, including several vestigial ribs no larger than a toothpick.

Innovative mount followed innovative mount as Chubb's career progressed. At last, in 1949, forty years after mounting Sysonby, Chubb began his most challenging—and his last—mount. This time he chose a less glamorous subject: a donkey nibbling at botfly eggs on his left hind leg. The donkey is twisted in one of the most contorted and asymmetrical positions the animal could assume, making it an extraordinarily difficult mount. As Chubb was making the final minute adjustments to the mount, he collapsed. The most accomplished osteological preparator in the Museum's history died two weeks later, at the age of eighty-five.

Chubb's horses now trot along a twisting corridor, each one enclosed in its own glass case. Bringing up the rear of this lively procession is the giant skeleton of an elephant, its head nearly bumping the ceiling. This skeleton comes from one of the most famous animals of all time, whose name has become synonymous with immensity—Jumbo.

The story of Jumbo the elephant, although perhaps somewhat peripheral to that of the Museum, illustrates the fortuitous way in which many odd specimens can end up in its collections.

# Jumbo the Elephant

*The pillar of a people's hope,*
*The center of a world's desire.*
— from a newspaper obituary of
Jumbo, the King of Elephants

A little over a century ago, Jumbo the elephant arrived in New York aboard the ship *Assyrian Monarch*. The great beast was paraded up Broadway, accompanied by brass bands, dancing girls, wildly cheering crowds, and all the fanfare that P. T. Barnum's formidable publicity machine could unleash. Three years later, Jumbo was dead—struck down by a speeding freight train.

Barnum scattered Jumbo's remains far and wide. His tusks, badly shattered in the accident, were mostly sliced up for souvenirs, or eaten (more about that later). His heart was reportedly sold to Cornell University for forty dollars. His stuffed skin (mounted by the great Carl Akeley) was given to Tufts University, where it became the school's beloved mascot until it burned in a fire in 1975. And his bones—after a brief tour—were deposited in the American Museum of Natural History. His skeleton was exhibited now and then for seventy years, but as the memory of Jumbo faded from children's minds, it was eventually taken off exhibition permanently in 1977.

Jumbo's journey from Africa to the mammalogy section of the Museum began in nineteenth-century Abyssinia (now Ethopia), along the banks of the Settite River. It was here in 1861 that a group of Arabs trapped him, possibly for sale to a European zoo. (Another account has him captured on the shores of Lake Chad.) At the time, Jumbo was a calf, standing only forty inches high at the shoulder. The elephant first traveled to the menagerie at the Jardin des Plantes in Paris, which later traded him to the Royal Zoological Gardens in London, reportedly for a rhinoceros. At the zoo, Jumbo was a perfectly ordinary elephant until he reached the age of seven, when his keeper began noticing a vast increase in his appetite. His intake of food soon reached a point at which he consumed, on a daily basis, two hundred pounds of hay, two bushels of oats, a barrel of potatoes, several quarts of onions, and ten to fifteen loaves of bread. His keeper, Matthew Scott, allegedly said that for medicinal purposes Jumbo was sometimes allowed two gallons of whiskey. (Scott himself was a teetotaler.) Jumbo's fame grew with his size, and soon he had become the most famous animal in England.

In 1882, Phineas T. Barnum quietly approached the director of the London Zoo and offered him $10,000 for the elephant, a staggering sum for the time. When the deal was legally concluded and "securely buttoned up" in Barnum's vest pocket, news of the sale leaked out. The British public reacted instantaneously and furiously; the sale was denounced across the country. Barnum fanned the fires of controversy by making various provocative statements, which resulted in his public damnation by the Prince of Wales. The publicity was invaluable, and by the time Jumbo arrived in the States he was already a household name. Wherever the Barnum, Bailey & Hutchinson Circus went, Jumbo drew huge crowds. Barnum was to claim that more than one million American children rode on his back.*

Jumbo was cut down at the height of his fame. On September 15, 1885, the circus animals were being loaded on a train at the railroad yards of St. Thomas, Ontario. To allow the large animals to cross the tracks and board the train, a section of railside fence had been taken down. Jumbo and a baby elephant named Tom Thumb had just been brought alongside the cars when an express freight train came thundering toward them along the other set of tracks. Scott, the keeper, scrambled out of the way and screamed to Jumbo to run. With his trunk high in the air, the alarmed elephant charged down the track away from

*Jumbo lived only three more years after his arrival in America, so that would work out to an unlikely one thousand a day. Since Barnum tainted any facts he came in contact with, most of the stories about Jumbo are suspect.

the train, but in his panic he ran past the gap in the fence. When Jumbo realized his mistake he wheeled about, galloping back along the tracks toward the opening. The train first struck Tom Thumb and knocked him, hurt but alive, down an embankment. Then it struck Jumbo head-on. The collision killed Jumbo instantly and derailed the train.

Barnum suddenly had to face the loss of his most profitable attraction. Drawing on his remarkable resources, he immediately began shamelessly concocting stories about Jumbo that would ensure the elephant's (and Barnum's) place on the front pages everywhere. In one account of Jumbo's death, he wrote, "Jumbo sacrificed his life to save that of Tom Thumb, a pigmy elephant. [He] had snatched the little elephant from in front of the thundering train and hurled the little fellow twenty yards to safety." Sure enough, Barnum struck gold again, and the front pages of newspapers all over the world poured out column-inches of heartrending copy that repeated many of Barnum's apocryphal stories.

Scientifically speaking, Jumbo was an important animal. When he attained record size, zoologists believed that he represented a new species of elephant, and accordingly, though still alive, he was designated the type specimen for his species. After his death, it was imperative that zoologists be able to dissect the animal and obtain its skeleton for future study.*

Jumbo's carcass was therefore immediately removed to Henry Ward's Natural Science Establishment in Rochester, New York, for dissection, mounting, and stuffing. A man named Peters performed the "inside work," climbing into the elephant's body cavity and dissecting various organs. One witness described poor Peters as emerging from the mess every few minutes "looking a little white around the gills." (Transportation was slower in those days, and Jumbo had started to decompose.) When Peters sliced open the stomach, out spilled a "hatful" of English pennies, a

---

*For an explanation of type specimens, see page 7. It was later concluded that Jumbo did *not* represent a new species, but only a variant of an already known species. He was, alas, reduced to a subspecies, a much less important designation.

crown, several rivets, a bunch of keys, and a bobby's whistle. The hide weighed 1,538 pounds and the bones 2,400 pounds. Although the entire elephant was never weighed, he was estimated at about six tons.

Barnum gave Ward strict instructions concerning the stuffing of Jumbo. "By all means," he wrote, "make him show like a mountain." Carl Akeley did a fine job of increasing the animal's height in death by about a foot. He also repaired the shattered skull and mounted the bones.

Barnum, determined to squeeze every ounce of publicity out of the elephant, planned a gala for the unveiling of the stuffed elephant and its mounted bones. He invited a crowd of reporters and high-society ladies to a fancy hotel. During a series of flowery speeches, Barnum served his guests a gelatin dish made from a pound and a half of Jumbo's finely ground tusks.

Jumbo's remains traveled with Barnum's circus for several years; he eventually gave the stuffed skin to Tufts, where he was a trustee, and the scientifically important bones to the Museum. When Jumbo was taken off exhibition, his aged and crumbling skeleton was wrapped in a plastic shroud and stored in the bowels of the Museum. Just a few years ago the Mammalogy Department refurbished the skeleton, repaired its mounts, and moved it into the same corridor as the Chubb horses. Now Jumbo brings up the rear of a parade of skeletons along the hall, a silent memorial to one of the most famous animals of all time.

## The Warren Mastodon

Another sort of elephant parade can be seen in the Museum's Hall of Late Mammals. (By "late," the Museum means recently extinct, not deceased.) Four mastodons and mammoths parade single-file down the center of the hall, frozen in taxonomic sequence. The most famous of the quartet is the Warren Mastodon, second in line, named after the scientist who acquired it for his personal collec-

tion. One of the most complete mastodons known, it is the remains of a beast that wandered along the shores of the Hudson River perhaps ten or twenty thousand years ago. The hapless animal came to an untimely end in what is now Orange County, New York, by venturing too far into a boggy patch of peat moss.

The discovery of this venerable skeleton dates from before the Civil War. The summer of 1845 was dry and hot in upstate New York, and a number of shallow ponds and bogs had dried up. The local farmers began digging up some of these bogs, since the peat and marl they contained made excellent fertilizer for their fields. One of these farmers was Nathaniel Brewster of East Coldenham, New York, who hired a gang of workmen to cut the peat out of one bog and spread it on his fields. The men had dug about three feet into the soft peat when one of them struck something hard. Further digging exposed a four-foot-long skull with a pair of gracefully curving, almost flawless ivory tusks.

Not knowing what to do, Brewster called the local doctor, a man named Prime, who lived in the nearby town of Newburgh. Dr. Prime sped down to the Brewster farm in his carriage to supervise the excavation. As the workmen dug, they gradually brought to light a beautifully preserved skeleton of a mastodon, standing upright just as it had sunk in the mire hundreds of centuries before. The skeleton's position gave an indication of the animal's last terrifying moments as it sank into the bog. Its legs were thrust forward and slightly apart, and its skull was tilted upward as if straining for the last breath of air.

While most mastodon bones turn black with age, these bones were remarkably well preserved and only lightly stained. One paleontologist described them as "beautiful" and the color of "old human bones." Although the animal's flesh had decayed and vanished, the contents of its stomach remained.

Dr. Prime later described the discovery of the mastodon's last meal:

In the midst of the ribs, embedded in the marl and un-mixed with shells or carbonate of lime, was a mass of matter, composed principally of the twigs of trees broken into pieces about two inches in length, and varying in size from very small twigs to half an inch in diameter. There was mixed in with these a large quantity of finer vegetable substance, like finely divided leaves; the whole amounting to from four to six bushels. From the appearance of this, and its situation, it was supposed to be the contents of the stomach; and this opinion was confirmed on removing the pelvis, underneath which, in the direction of the last of the intestines, was a train of the same material, about three feet in length [and] four inches in diameter.

When the beast was finally exhumed, Prime had the bones carried to Brewster's barn. During the weeks that followed, neighbors came to watch the enthusiastic doctor carefully fitting and wiring the bones together in the gloom of the barn. In classic nineteenth-century style the mounted bones went on tour, stopping at various small towns in new England and upstate New York, where it drew crowds of amazed viewers. (Unfortunately, the original tusks had crumbled to pieces upon drying out, and the mastodon had had to be fitted with a pair of fakes.)

By this time, New York State had already yielded a number of mastodon fossils. As early as 1705, according to an article by Henry Fairfield Osborn, Governor Dudley of New York mentioned in a letter to Cotton Mather that several mastodon bones and teeth had been found near Albany. In 1782 the first mastodon bones found in Orange County were unearthed on a farm outside Newburgh. (George Washington even made a special trip to see these bones during his sojourn at Newburgh in the winter of 1782–83.) In 1802 a complete mastodon skeleton came to light on John Masten's farm near Newburgh. It was excavated by Charles Willson Peale and his sons, Rembrandt and Titian.*

*The excavation was immortalized by Peale in a painting showing the beast

The Warren Mastodon was the fifth complete probiscidian found in Orange County, and the locals were proud of their mastodon heritage. *An Outline History of Orange County*, by Samuel W. Eager (published the year after the Warren Mastodon was found), contained a section on mastodons. The subject strained the author's somewhat limited literary gifts, but it provides a fascinating pre-Darwinian view of paleontology:

> We cannot, without disrespect to the memory of a lost but giant race, and slighting the widespread reputation of old Orange as the mother of the most perfect and magnificent specimens of terrestrial animals, omit to tell of the mastodon. Contemplating his remains as exhumed from their resting place for unknown ages, we instinctively think of his great and lordly mastery over the beasts—of his majestic tread as he strode these valleys and hilltops—of his anger when excited to fury— stamping the earth till trembling beneath his feet— snuffing the wind with disdain, and uttering his wrath in tones of thunder,—and the mind quails beneath the oppressive grandeur of the thought, and we feel as if driven along by the violence of a tornado. When the pressure of contemplation has subsided and we recover from the blast, we move along and ponder on the time when the mastodon lived,—when and how he died, and the nature of the catastrophe that extinguished the race; and the mind again becomes bewildered. Were they preAdamites, and did they graze upon the fields of Orange and bask in the sunlight of that early period of the globe?—or were they antediluvian, and carried to a common grave by the deluge of the Scriptures?—or were they postdiluvian only, and till very recent periods wandered over our hills and fed in these valleys.

In 1846, John Warren, a wealthy professor of anatomy at Harvard College, bought the mastodon for $5,000. He had it crated and shipped to Boston, and hired a Mr. Shurt-

---

being taken out of its pit, bone by bone. For years, Peale exhibited the mounted skeleton in his museum in Philadelphia. The skeleton was later lost—God knows how—and remains missing to this day.

leff to remount it for display in his small paleontological collection. Several famous nineteenth-century scientists viewed the Warren Mastodon, including Louis Agassiz and the Scottish geologist Sir Charles Lyell.

Apparently, Warren became dissatisfied with Shurtleff's mounting, because three years later he hired a Mr. Ogden to dismantle and remount the fossil. Ogden had his own ideas about what a fossil should look like, and he painted the bones with a layer of black varnish. Next he decided the beast wasn't large enough for his taste, and so he arbitrarily raised the ribcage and backbone two feet above the shoulder blades, thereby increasing the mastodon's height from nine feet to twelve. Finally, he sculpted a brand-new set of papier-mâché tusks, which curved in precisely the wrong direction.*

In the small but famous museum he established at 92 Chestnut Street in Boston, Warren exhibited the mastodon along with his rapidly growing collection of probiscidian remains from all over the United States and Europe. Warren died shortly after the turn of the century, leaving his museum in the hands of a trustee, Thomas Dwight. In 1906, Dwight wrote a discreet letter to Henry Fairfield Osborn, President of the American Museum, suggesting that the collection "might be offered for sale under certain conditions." Osborn, who had had a greedy eye on the Warren Mastodon for some time, set out for Boston on the same night he received the letter, arriving at the Warren Museum the next morning. (Extinct elephants were Osborn's true passion, more than dinosaurs or anything else. He spent fifty years of his life, off and on, writing his massive work *Proboscidia*, the two volumes of which weigh forty pounds. Its publication reportedly cost the Museum over a *quarter-million*—in pre–World War II dollars.) Osborn poked around the museum with Dwight, and after a friendly chat they settled on $30,000 for the whole lot. On

---

*A number of mastodons and mammoths were mounted with their tusks reversed in the nineteenth century, all based on an erroneous mounting done by the Russians in St. Petersburg. The Warren mounting, of which an illustration still exists, was probably based on the St. Petersburg mount.

Monday, Osborn telephoned his good friend J. P. Morgan, and asked if Morgan wouldn't send the Museum a check to cover the cost of the entire collection. Morgan readily agreed.

So, after an absence of half a century, the mastodon was at last dismantled and sent back to its home state. Osborn immediately issued directions to have the skeleton remounted, and especially to have the varnish cleaned off the bones, which he considered a desecration. After experimenting with various chemicals, Museum technicians built a series of large vats and filled them with benzene, in which the bones soaked for many weeks. This was followed by a scrubbing with alcohol. The process worked; it bought out, as Osborn reported with satisfaction, "all the purity and beauty of color that characterized the skeleton."

Repairing the original tusks presented a more serious problem. They arrived in many fragments, filling up two boxes. Piecing them together took an assistant several months of tedious labor.

Adam Hermann, then chief preparator at the Museum, remounted the skeleton. One of the trickier questions he was faced with was to figure out exactly how the shoulder and backbones articulated, which would indicate how tall the beast had been. Hermann solved the problem by riding an elephant all day at the zoo while feeling its bones and taking notes. His notes led him to calculate that the mastodon was nine feet two inches high at the shoulder and fourteen feet eleven inches from skull to tail. He posed the skeleton in a walking posture, head held high, a reminder of the days not so long past when mastodons roamed the Hudson highlands.

The procession of proboscidians in the hall illustrates the evolution of these curious mammals, and especially the changing shape of their large tusks, which began as enlarged, flat teeth in their lower jaw. Elephant remains have been discovered all over the world, having spread outward over the centuries from their hypothesized origin in Africa. In America they did quite well, ranging over much of the continent. There were dozens of now-extinct forms, from tiny, pig-sized elephants to the huge Imperial Mammoth. Mastodons died out in North America a scant ten thousand years ago—yesterday, by evolutionary standards. It is thought that humans may have contributed to their demise, just as we are now doing to elephants in India and Africa.

# ELEVEN

# Mammals

While the Museum has a dozen or so extinct elephants, it possesses over one hundred living elephants (the word *living* is evolutionary jargon, meaning existing as opposed to extinct; the specimens themselves are hardly alive), housed in the Mammalogy Section of the Museum. It is not easy to store even one elephant, let alone one hundred. Nor is it a simple matter to find space for the half-dozen preserved gorillas, the fifteen-foot whale skull, or the hundreds of rats in jars of alcohol\*; or the giraffes, lions, platypus skins, narwhal horns, and 250,000 other specimens that constitute the Museum's mammalogy collection.

For over eighty years mammals had been accumulating in the Museum, filling up an alcove here, an attic there,

---

\*This collection of rats represents most of the species of *Rattus* in the world and is a highly important series from a scientific standpoint.

until parts of the collection became virtually unmanageable. A scientist looking for a particular bear, for example, often had to open a dozen or so fluid-filled tanks just to find it. Skeletons were separated and scattered throughout several storerooms, taking hours of detective work to link one bone to another. During the last twenty years, and especially in the last five, the department, under Guy Musser, took the matter in hand and launched an overhaul of the collection. For a year the senior technicians in the department moved tens of thousands of specimens, from elephant skulls to shrews, into newly renovated storage areas. Now, for example, if a researcher needs to locate that jar containing the mummified contents of a mastodon's stomach, or the tusks from an elephant that Teddy Roosevelt shot, it takes only a few minutes. The collection is arranged as meticulously as books in a library.

It is indeed an overwhelming collection. Our grand tour continued with a talk with Helmut Sommer and Bill Coull, the two technicians primarily responsible for the curation. The mammals are stored in a number of rooms. They include bones, "alcoholics" (i.e., specimens preserved in alcohol), skins, trophy heads, and other odds and ends.

We first visited the alcoholics, arranged on shelves in an immaculate storage room on the third floor of the Museum. The smaller mammals (and pieces of mammals) are in glass jars, while the larger animals inhabit a series of stainless-steel tanks. The alcoholics are arranged in taxonomic order—that is, according to their evolutionary relationships. A researcher need only know the place of a species on the phylogenetic "tree" of Mammalia in order to locate it in the collection. Not surprisingly, then, we found the most primitive mammal—the duck-billed platypus—at the farthest corner of the room, on shelf number I. A stroll down one aisle and up the next is, in a sense, a stroll through mammalian evolution. Primates, including *Homo sapiens*, are located in the middle (not at the other end, as one might think—Ptolemaic thinking has disappeared in evolution as well as astronomy), since that is where we fall in terms of familial relationships with our fellow mammals. At the far end are the bovines—the antelopes, cows, oxen, and so forth.*

The small *Homo* collection in Mammalogy (there is much more in Anthropology) occupies only one shelf, and includes fetuses, some of which are nearly a century old, several brain sections, and a skinned-out human foot in a rectangular glass container. None of these old specimens are thrown out, however, as one never knows when they might be useful. (As an example from another area of Museum research, several years ago high levels of mercury were detected in tuna fish. It was believed that the oceans may have been badly contaminated by mercury, and that the fish were unsafe to eat. Examination, however, of the mercury content of century-old tuna flesh in the Museum's ichthyology collection showed an equally high mercury content—indicating that it wasn't pollution but a biological characteristic of tuna.)

The *Homo* collection is rarely consulted. On the shelves directly above us, on the other hand, rests an important collection of chimpanzees often consulted by researchers from around the world. Many of these specimens came from zoos as well as from early expeditions, and some of the Museum's best chimps were donated by the Barnum & Bailey Circus.

The bigger mammals rest in an adjacent room, soaking peacefully in huge tanks bolted shut. Sommer pointed out the highlights of the collection. "We've got a couple of tigers in there," he said, pointing at one crate, "four lions —or at least heads of lions—and some panthers. In there is a giraffe and a camel head—a big one. In this crate are the gorillas." We asked to have a look at the gorillas, and he unbolted the lid. Immediately, the fumes from about one hundred gallons of 150-proof grain alcohol filled the room. "You don't smoke around here," Sommer advised.

The gorillas, soaking in the brown liquid, were covered

---

*Many people erroneously think of evolution as a path from extinct animals to living animals, with humans at the top. Actually, evolution is thought in terms of relatedness more than progression.

by a piece of burlap. Sommer lifted it to expose the skinned and seemingly grinning face of a gorilla and an apparent confusion of dissected body parts. "Many of the big animals here have been dissected by researchers," he said. In fact, he explained, scientists prefer to examine dissected rather than whole animals in the vats because it can save them a lot of trouble if they wish to study the internal organs. Staring up at us with sightless eyes was one of Carl Akeley's gorillas, from the slopes of Mt. Mikeno, as well as a lowland gorilla collected by Harry Raven, a Museum curator about whom we will hear in the next chapter. The others in the crate—and in fact most of the rare mammals —came (and still come) from zoos.

Sommer next showed us other animals in the collection. From one shelf he brought out a jar containing the eight-inch-long fetus of a baleen whale. The next jar held the eyeball of a full-grown baleen whale, larger than a grapefruit. Nearby were elephant parts, and a jar containing the mummified remains of the contents of a mastodon stomach discovered in Ecuador. Another contained a seemingly chaotic mass of flesh, labeled GIRAFFE TONGUE AND EYE. Against a wall was the carefully dissected reproductive tract of a female walrus.

Next door to the alcoholics is a vast room filled with thousands of hanging skins. (The really valuable skins, such as the vicunas, are locked in a separate vault.) "We've got just about everything," said Sommer, "even a rug made out of platypus skins. Can you believe that some idiot killed about forty platypuses just to make it?"

Even though the Museum accepts only scientifically useful material, the walls of some of the storage rooms are covered with trophy heads. "Scientists come in and measure them," Sommer said.

Next, Sommer led us up through a labyrinth of stairs to an attic room under a Museum roof, illuminated by skylights—the incomparable Elephant Room. Arranged meticulously on a tier of metal shelves are dozens of giant elephant skulls. Nearby, a second group of shelves houses the bones. The room is spotless, and all the bones are cov-

ered with plastic sheets. Along one wall are drawers of
various smaller elephant bones: several dozen ten-pound
teeth, an Adam's apple, and Jumbo's sesamoid bones,
which were too small to include in its mount. A bound
folder lists all the specimens and where they came from.
Up here are elephants shot by Theodore and Kermit Roosevelt, Carl Akeley, and Martin and Osa Johnson; gifts from
P. T. Barnum and the Barnum & Bailey circus; one from
former New York Mayor John Lindsay (given to him by
the president of Chad); and a dozen or more from zoos.
Each elephant is represented by a half-ton or so of bones,
many with two-hundred-pound skulls. "Moving these elephants," Sommer said, "was no joke."

None of the skulls have tusks; those are stored in the
Tusk Vault, where they are safe from robbery. This secret
vault—a tiny room with a green steel door—is so carefully hidden within the Museum that few Museum employees even know of its existence. In this dim room, tusks
are laid out in neat rows on shelves from floor to ceiling.
Some of the tusks have been grotesquely mounted on
stuffed elephant feet (the donations of early elephant
hunters), but most are simple tusks, polished with use and
slightly yellowed with age. One set, from a circus elephant, sports a ball at each tip, while several others have
freakish congenital deformations. On a top shelf lies an
even more valuable kind of ivory: a dozen or so narwhal
horns. Each tusk has been numbered to correspond to the
rest of the skeleton, stored elsewhere in the Museum.

Along the same corridor with the Tusk Vault are other
bone rooms—the hippo room, a room full of pig skeletons, and many more. Taken together, these collections
constitute a gold mine of information for comparative anat-
omists, evolutionary biologists, and systematic zoologists,
who make this one of the most heavily used and researched
collections in the world.

This is not to say that everything in the Mammalogy Department is dead. For a number of years the department
was home to a family of ferrets. Two of these small, wea-

sellike creatures, a male and an albino female, were given to the Museum for the collection. But the tannery technician certainly didn't want to kill them, so he adopted them as pets instead. The two animals had several litters before they died, and one of their offspring, named Jeb, became a Museum favorite. He had the run of the place and even learned to ride the elevator from floor to floor. One day he met with misfortune. Impatient to board the elevator, he missed his footing and fell down the elevator shaft.*

During the Museum's history, many curators have kept various exotic animals in the Museum, especially, it seems, insects (which we will deal with later).† The best-remembered pet in the history of the Museum, however, was a chimpanzee owned by a curator in the 1930s.

## Meshie Mungkut

In the far corner of the Museum's Hall of Primates, a mounted chimpanzee is shown sitting on a plaster log, its chin cupped pensively in its hand. The label identifies the anonymous animal merely as *Chimpansee troglodytes*,†† with a catalog number of 148201. The label makes no further mention of this animal or of its short life on earth, and most visitors to the Museum hurry past without a second glance. But let us remain for a moment.

Over half a century ago, the Museum sent a small field party to Africa to make zoological collections, particularly of lowland gorillas. The expedition included one man, Harry Raven, who was a curator in the Anatomy Department at the Museum. In February 1930, Raven was estab-

*The excruciatingly slow elevators in the Museum are infamous.

†One of our librarians told me that on one occasion, several guards were discreetly poking around an office in the library looking for "a big black snake." The snake was reportedly found in the basement, quite a bit fatter from a plentiful diet of mice.

††Since the placement of this exhibition label, this animal has been renamed *Pan troglodytes*.

lished in a temporary field camp in the great forest of the French Cameroons. He had just finished lunch when two Africans emerged from the bush, carrying a baby female chimpanzee. They explained that they had shot the mother for food, with a poisoned dart, and that when they had retrieved the body they found the terrified infant clinging to the dead mother's fur. They had kept the chimp for about a month as a pet, and they wanted to know if Raven would like to buy it.

"I approached the man," Raven later recalled, "and put out my arms. The little animal looked at me a moment, then stretched her arms toward me and I took her. She grasped me tightly as if she feared she might fall. She looked at me curiously and stroked the hair on my bare arm."

Raven was greatly taken with the animal, and bought her after a long negotiation over the price. Raven carried the chimp with him for more than two thousand miles through the jungle, putting one of his African assistants, a little boy, in charge of the animal. When Raven finally returned to his main camp at Djaposten, the chimp had the run of the town, and she became very popular among the African children. Raven had initially been worried that the many hungry dogs roaming the town would find the tiny chimp a delicious meal, but he soon discovered that the dogs seemed to regard the chimp as just another annoying human child: "If she pulled their ears or their tails or their legs," Raven wrote, "they would simply whine and walk away." The chimp exploited her advantage: the African dogs were very fond of bananas, and if the chimp saw a dog eating a banana she would rush the poor animal, making a loud noise. Usually the dog would flee with its tail between its legs. The local children began calling the chimp "Meshie Mungkut," which translates loosely as "little chimpanzee who fluffs her hair up to look big."

When Raven finished his work in Africa, he decided to bring Meshie back to the States with him on board a steamship. This was the unwitting beginning of a new experiment—raising a chimpanzee as a human child in a family. It wasn't a scientific, or even a deliberate, experiment, and Raven could not foresee the inevitable—and ultimately tragic—result of his decision.

One cold February day in 1931, they arrived in Boston. "Meshie was very much excited," Raven wrote. "The outstanding incident of Meshie's arrival in the United States was her alarm on seeing . . . a team of great, dappled gray draft horses blowing steam through their nostrils. . . . She uttered a little scream and grabbed me around the neck . . . Meshie actually got down on the floor once in an effort to get as far away as possible, but a moment later she was back looking out the window." Raven arrived at his house, and after the first greetings with his wife and children, he reached into a large pouch and—much to everyone's astonishment and delight—pulled out the baby chimp.

One anthropologist in the Museum, a colleague of Raven's named Harry Shapiro, remembers Meshie very well. "All of us in the Museum were just fascinated with how human this chimp was," Shapiro recalls. "She did all the things human children do. Harry treated Meshie just like another child in his family and raised her accordingly." The Raven children simply treated her as a sibling. In the backyard of his Long Island home, Raven built Meshie a house that consisted of a box attached to the crossbar of a swing set. The box had a sliding door and stood eight feet off the ground; chimpanzees, being arboreal, are nervous about sleeping near or on the ground. Every evening, before going to sleep, Meshie climbed to the top of the crossbar and sat in the doorway to her box. Raven stood under the box, holding a pile of blankets, and Meshie leaned out the door and caught them one by one as he tossed them up. Inside the box she twisted the blankets into a nest. Every morning, upon rising, she carefully picked up the blankets and dropped them one by one to the ground.

Raven brought Meshie into the Museum on a regular basis, and the chimp had the run of the long fifth-floor corridors where the staff offices were. "She would ride down the corridor on a little kiddie-car with pedals," Shapiro says.* "At lunchtime she would go down the elevators and eat with us in the old staff dining room. She had perfect manners. She always ate with a knife and fork, although she sometimes was a little impatient with the waitresses." She also learned to buzz for the elevator operator, much to that gentleman's disgust, as Meshie would impatiently press the button repeatedly until the operator came. On such occasions the operator's annoyed protestations could be heard up and down the elevator shaft.

Shapiro remembers one incident at lunch that particularly impressed him with the near-humanness of the animal. "After lunch," Shapiro says, "Harry got out a cigarette and put it in his mouth. He tossed a book of matches at Meshie and said, 'Meshie, light my cigarette.' Meshie sat there and looked at the matches with fear. Harry repeated his order in a strict, firm tone of voice. This time, Meshie picked up the matches, then dropped them in fright. Harry again repeated the order and Meshie picked up the matches again and took out a match before dropping them. Finally, after Harry insisted several more times, Meshie lit his cigarette. She obviously knew what the matches were and was afraid of fire."

Raven took home movies of Meshie, which are now part of the Museum's film archives. In the films, the resemblance of the chimp's behavior to that of a human child is striking. One scene in the movie shows Meshie, dressed for winter with a coat and gloves, pulling a sled and a child through the snow. In other scenes she is bouncing on a bed with the Raven children, eating with a spoon and drinking with a straw, riding a tricycle around the neighborhood, taking a bubble bath, playing tug-of-war, and spraying a hose into the upper-story windows of the Raven home. In one extraordinary sequence, Meshie picks up the family baby, carries her to a high chair, brings over her food in a bowl, and then feeds her with a spoon. After the baby is finished eating, Meshie fetches a damp cloth and neatly

*This corridor, stretching a long West Side block, is alleged to be the longest straight corridor in New York City.

wipes clean the baby's tray. A favorite trick of Meshie's was to remove a person's shoes, put them on her own feet, and stomp around with a grin on her face, much to the amusement of everyone.

Meshie hated cages and chains, and often devised ways of escape when necessary. She learned ingenious ways to untie complicated knots. In her favorite method, caught on film, she loosened the knot with her teeth and pulled out the loop until it was several feet in diameter. Then she actually *climbed through* the open loop, which thereby untied the knot. If the rope was double- or triple-knotted, she learned how to climb through the different loops two or three times—a rather sophisticated piece of topological reasoning. Meshie also learned how to spring open a padlock by packing it with sand, how to break an iron chain by knotting it and yanking, and how to remove leather collars by wetting them over and over again with her tongue until they became brittle and could be snapped.

To Shapiro, one of the most striking things about the movie is that Meshie attempts to walk upright, rather than hunched over with her knuckles touching the ground, like other chimps. She was curiously human in another way: Raven reported that her exposed skin, usually white, became deeply tanned during the summer. She reportedly used tools without prompting; to retrieve a roasted potato from the fireplace, she grabbed a poker and fished it out. She often used sticks to pull things to within her reach.

If primatologists were to study the movie today, they would probably decry the lack of blinds, double blinds, and controls, and disagree about how much Meshie was being "cued" and to what extent her actions were imitative. How much English she actually understood is also debatable. But no one seeing the movie could disagree that Meshie acted in an uncannily human way.

Meshie's short life in New York was extraordinary by any standards. She became a minor celebrity, and was invited to lunch with such prominent people as the publisher Ralph Pulitzer, the novelist Edna Ferber, and two Museum Presidents, Henry Fairfield Osborn and F. Trubee Davison.

The high point of the chimp's social career was described by Raven in a 1933 article in *Natural History*:

> Not long ago, Meshie had the honor of being the guest of President F. Trubee Davison of the American Museum of Natural History at a formal banquet at the Waldorf-Astoria. What could be stranger, more unlike her former home in the African forest, than the ride across Manhattan in a taxicab, the brightly lighted hotel with the gaily dressed people everywhere, the brass band and the Negro minstrels! But she rode her kiddie car through the foyer, into the banquet hall crowded with strangers, and took her place at the table with the rest of the guests. She politely ate some of each course as the dinner was served, sat quietly while the speeches were made, blinked while the press photographers took more than a dozen flash-light photographs of her, and did not get home until long after midnight.

Meshie spent about five years with the Ravens. Then things began to fall apart. "When Meshie became sexually mature," Shapiro recalls, "she became a real problem." Today, such behavioral changes at puberty are well known in chimpanzees, but at that time it was unexpected. She became increasingly restless and uncontrollable, and would often throw violent tantrums, break things, and even threaten to bite. She had grown quite large and was very strong, probably stronger than a human being. Mrs. Raven tried to lock her in the basement when she had tantrums, but the chimp became particularly violent when locked up.

"She thought of Harry as her father," Shapiro says, "and he was the only one who could control her. I remember Mrs. Raven began calling Harry regularly at the Museum, and he would have to rush home to handle some crisis or other with Meshie. They didn't know what to do. Finally, Mrs. Raven absolutely insisted that Meshie go." With great reluctance, Raven sold Meshie to a zoo in Chicago. Raven loved the chimp and, according to Shapiro, experienced a loss that remained with him for the rest of his life.

"About a year after that," Shapiro says, "I ran into

Harry in the Museum, and he looked very upset." Raven told Shapiro that he had just returned from a trip out west, and that he had decided to stop by the zoo in Chicago before returning to New York. When he had asked the keeper if he could see Meshie, the keeper explained that the animal was extremely dangerous and had been taken off public view and moved to a large cage in the basement. When Raven went down to the basement he could hear high-pitched screaming and a loud banging coming from Meshie's cage. He told the keeper to unlock the cage and let him inside. The man refused, saying that it was far too dangerous, since Meshie had attacked several people and tried to bite others. Raven absolutely insisted, and the keeper finally gave in, washing his hands of all responsibility.

"When Raven did go into the cage," Shapiro says, "Meshie threw herself into his arms and clung to him tightly. She began crying. The tears were streaming down her face."

Meshie died in childbirth a year later, and the zoo shipped her body back to the Museum at Raven's request, where he had it mounted and put on display in the Hall of Primates. It is said that Raven stopped by the hall once in a while and gazed thoughtfully at the sad little chimp with the glass eyes. "I suppose," says Shapiro, "that it was kind of a memorial for him."

# TWELVE

# Insects

It's time to leave the vertebrates for a while and rummage around in a far different corner of the natural world —that of the insects. After all, there are only some 40,000 known species of vertebrates, including everything from fishes to chimps. On the other hand, there are at least a *million* known species of insects, and probably several million more that remain undiscovered as yet. It has been said that insects will inherit the earth, but most entomologists would tell you that they have already done so. Insects and spiders were the first animals to emerge on land, and they have held sway ever since. In both sheer numbers and diversity, almost all animal species on the planet are insects—at least 60 percent and perhaps as many as 90 percent, in fact.*

---

*And most insects are beetles. Thus, an alien visitor to our planet could accurately report back that animal life on earth consists of beetles, with a few strange variants.

In keeping with their importance to life on the planet, insects and spiders (a spider, by the way, is not an insect but an arachnid) make up fully 45 percent of the Museum's entire collection of 35 million specimens. Today the insects are housed in row upon row of gleaming white cabinets on the fifth floor of the Museum. At last count there were 16,167,000 insects and spiders in the collection. Despite the small size of insects, over 90,000 square feet of Museum space are required to house them in safety.

A brief sampling of the collection would turn up over 1 million spiders (the largest collection in the world), 1.6 million beetles, 8 million social insects (such as ants and termites), and 2 million butterflies. As we stop briefly at the Department of Entomology, three Museum entomologists, Pedro Wygodzinsky, Lee Herman, and Jerome Rozen, have agreed to give us an inside view of their profession.

Entomologists are fond of statistics; in any contest of numbers, insects always win hands down. While most other animal species have been discovered, at least half of all insect species remain unknown to science. Some entomologists believe there are probably 2 to 5 million *more*. Even worse, one entomologist recently reported that an exhaustive, random sampling of insects in the upper canopy of a rain forest indicated that there may very well be 30 million undiscovered species of beetle alone. The figures start to climb when you begin to look at numbers of individuals in a particular species. Lee Herman recalls a collecting trip he made to a salt flat in Oklahoma. "The flat," he says, "was about forty-three square miles, and it was inhabited by two species of burrowing insects. I counted about 250 burrows per square foot. Now that may not sound like much until you do the arithmetic—and realize that there are 300 billion burrows of *just* those two species living on that salt flat." These are the sort of figures one encounters in nuclear physics, not biology.

Rozen explained life according to the entomologist. "Vertebrates," he says facetiously, "are merely a blip in evolutionary diversity. They are a tiny, specialized sub-group of the invertebrates."

Such astronomical figures, when applied to specimens in a collection, don't mean very much, according to Pedro Wygodzinsky. "If you go out," he says, "and collect one termite nest, you may increase the collection by a million individuals. The fact that you *collect* specimens means nothing until you observe and *study* them."

How do entomologists study insects? At the Museum they do what most systematic zoologists do: they study the life histories, distribution, comparative morphology, ecology, and evolutionary relationships of insects and insect groups. This research is highly important in the control of crop parasites and other destructive (in our anthropocentric view) pests. In many ways, insects figure much more prominently in our lives as humans than do mammals, birds, and so forth. The study of insects differs, however, in several important ways from the study of—for example —mammals.

"Insects aren't like mammals," Herman explains. "You can't open them up and look at their teeth, take them apart, and measure every bone and organ. Some insects are so small you can't even observe their behavior in the wild. If you see a particular structure on a mammal, you can find out what it is for by watching how the animal uses it in the wild. You can't do that with many insects. We often discover strange-looking structures on insects and we can't even *imagine* what they're for.

"We sometimes dissect insects under a microscope with scalpels we make from tiny pins. Sometimes the pulse in your thumb will cause the scalpel to jump at every beat. You learn to dissect between heartbeats."

While mammalogists and most other Museum scientists study animals that are often well known and widely studied, there are simply so many insects that entomologists end up studying species about which nothing is known except their species names and a few spots where they have been found. "We often find ourselves looking at things no one has ever seen before," says Herman.

Yet there are advantages to studying insects. "You can," says Herman, "collect thousands of the same species or genus to study variation. I remember a collecting trip to Nebraska, when in a half-hour I attracted enough insects with a black light to fill to overflowing a thirteen-quart bucket. It's a great advantage in systematic studies to have the luxury of examining many specimens."

Because the majority of insect species remain unknown, some entomologists have discovered and named hundreds of new species by the middle of their careers. We asked Wygodzinsky how many new species he had discovered. He shrugged. "I couldn't even guess," he said. A very rough estimate might put the number at about five hundred, judging from a random sampling of the papers he has published over a long and productive career.

Herman, who is much younger, has discovered more than one hundred new species. "It's a big deal," he says, "when you discover your first new species. You always remember that one. But after a while the numbers get so high you completely lose count." He even says that finding unknown species in a collection under study can be an annoyance, since it means each one has to be described and named before it can be "officially" recognized. In this respect, entomologists contrast with some birders who keep "life lists" of all the bird species they have sighted. Most entomologists consider such lists unimportant, even a little ridiculous. Indeed, it is highly unfashionable in entomology to admit that you care or even know how many species you have discovered.

The naming of new species can be a problem, especially if you have twenty or thirty in a single paper. Strict rules governing nomenclature are set forth in a volume called the *International Code of Zoological Nomenclature*. Within the tortuous rules set forth therein, however, there is some room for personal expression. Often the entomologist will name the species after a friend, colleague, or spouse. (Entomologists like to joke about the man who named a parasitic worm after his mother-in-law.) Museum entomologist

Jerome Rozen named a new species of bee *filiorum* (Latin for "children") because his children waited patiently in the sun while he dug up the nest. Other waggish entomologists choose humorous names—within bounds, of course. One fellow who discovered a wasp of the genus *Lalapa* named the species *lusa*, just for the hell of it. Really outrageous names, even if they conform to the Latin rules, have been thrown out by the committee on nomenclature that decides such matters.

Most entomologists end up with many species named after them by colleagues. Rozen had to consult a fat catalog of bee genera names when we asked how many species had been named after him. There were five *rozeni*. He said that he wasn't sure offhand whether any other genera had species named after him. (When we asked whether an entomologist would name a species after himself, we were told in a shocked voice that such a thing "just isn't done.")

Insects are highly specialized, even to the point of co-evolving with plants, and thus are unusually sensitive to habitat destruction. Thousands of unknown species may be becoming extinct every year as forests are cut down and habitats are destroyed. People don't normally think of endangered *insects* (except butterflies), especially since the extinction of some insect species would be heartily welcomed by most. Nevertheless, the rapid and uncontrolled extinction of insect species could be a tragic loss. "Nature," says Wygodzinsky, "is finely balanced. Any unprovoked attack can throw everything off in ways we cannot predict. When forests are burned, you destroy species." Thus the food chains on which higher animals depend may be disrupted.

We asked Wygodzinsky why he devoted his life to studying insects, a question entomologists are often asked. "I suppose," he said, "it would be nice for me to say that we study insects for altruistic reasons—to save crops and prevent disease. But I think most entomologists would tell you that they study insects because of a love for pure knowledge. We *like* insects."

## Peripatetic Roaches (and Other Insects)

Paradoxically, the study of insects, while seemingly obscure, is the systematic science that most often has direct consequences for the average person. While a new discovery about, say, gorillas may be fascinating, a new discovery relating to cockroaches could affect millions of people. Indeed, the Museum's Entomology Department receives thousands of queries and requests a year for information on insects—mostly on how to get rid of them. One such problem is worth recounting. Several years ago a Museum research associate was called upon to solve a tricky problem for the New York City Transit Authority. The problem was brought to the attention of the TA by dozens of letters, of which the one below is an example:

Dear Sir,

I'm hoping this is not another exercise in futility. Letters of complaint are so easy to ignore, so I rarely, if ever, write them. It seems only the danger of public exposure produces any effect.

Most of the time, despite momentary flashes of anger, one can shrug off the indifference, hostility, and even outrageous rudeness unleashed by bus operators on the unfortunate riders of the New York City bus system.

But roaches!!! And from the many sizes, second generations of them!! How dare you inflict this on those who support your system, pay your salaries, and put their trust in you. Roaches—I will not sit still for them. This horde of roaches was on bus number 8553, October 4, 1979, at 2:50 P.M.

This obviously bespeaks gross negligence as well as total indifference. Littered buses, soiled windows—bad enough. But vermin? I can't imagine the heyday the media would have with such a news item, and unless something is done, and fast, I shall do everything in my power to see that it is publicized.

A Disgusted Rider

Cockroaches, as it turns out, have been riding the city's buses for over fifty years. Generally they have kept a low profile and stayed out of trouble. But around 1979, a minor population explosion took place on the city's buses. The Transit Authority tried one ineffectual remedy after another without any success, until finally, in desperation, someone from the TA called the Museum.

Joseph DeVito, director of safety at the TA at the time, explained the problem: "A few years ago, the TA embarked on a program of bus washing. But believe it or not, the more we washed the buses, the more complaints we got about the roaches." In response, the TA stepped up its insect bomb and fumigation program; but the itinerant roaches, like roaches everywhere, held fast to their domain, and bus drivers complained of the fumes. Other remedies were attempted. One ingenious engineer even rigged up a grid of live wires at a roach hangout on a bus, but after several roach electrocutions the bugs learned to avoid the trap.

It was at this point that a TA executive suggested that an entomologist might be able to help. "We hoped," explained DeVito, "that by studying roach behavior, perhaps there would be a way—something like the Pied Piper of Hamelin—to get the insects to march right off."

Dr. Betty Faber, a research associate in the Entomology Department, offered her expertise free of charge. The TA gave her a transit pass and she began riding the buses and visiting the terminals, jotting down the behavior of the stowaway roaches in her field notebook.

Faber is experienced in roach-watching. For her research she keeps a colony of wild roaches in the greenhouse on the roof of the Museum, where they share quarters with electric eels, black-jawed fish, and various plants. Faber provides her roaches with protection from insecticides (with large warning signs posted around the greenhouse), but the roaches have to shift for themselves when it comes to food and water. Faber herself traps most of the wild roaches, and affixes number strips of tape to their backs so she can tell one from another. At night,

Faber observes her wards using a sophisticated infrared scope similar to the kind the army uses for seeing in the dark. She has also set up closed-circuit TV cameras so that she can watch the roaches from her office.

The cockroach, Faber explained, is one of the earth's most venerable animals. A cockroachlike insect was one of the first animals to colonize the land hundreds of millions of years ago, and its decendents have thrived ever since. Its survivability is due, in part, to the fact that it has been able to adjust to changing environments. For example, fossil roaches have been found within the same strata with dinosaur bones, indicating that they probably ate dinosaur flesh. They seem equipped to survive as well in spotless Park Avenue kitchens as in steaming Cretaceous swamps. Hungry roaches have even been known to eat the inner organs of television sets and refrigerators.

The roach's adaptation to city life is nothing short of remarkable. Despite vigorous efforts to eliminate them, they can still be found at some of the best addresses and some of the finest restaurants in New York. (Faber told us about one exclusive New York restaurant that discreetly contacted her about a desperate roach problem.)

Faber explained that the bus-riding bug is usually the German cockroach. Long a victim of wanderlust, this peripatetic creature immigrated to New York City from Asia (not Germany) at least a century ago, and has since established itself as the dominant species. (The larger American roach, sometimes erroneously called a waterbug, is still very much around, however.) Like most cockroaches, the German roach is strongly attracted to water. After looking into the TA's problem, Faber suggested that the bus-washing program, which started before the infestation, might actually have exacerbated it by making the buses a wetter and more appealing environment for roaches. People eating on buses provide roaches with food, and Faber noted that eating on buses has gradually increased over the years. The third ingredient for cockroach comfort—warmth—is provided by the engine and heating system.

But the real question Faber faced was how roaches got on the buses in the first place. "A roach," said Faber, "could conceivably climb on a bus while it is sitting in the terminal. But the terminals are actually kept very clean, and most are unheated. Anyway, it would be like climbing Mount Everest for a roach to get on a bus."

After some thought, she came to a definite conclusion: "Roaches get on the bus riding the passengers, and then get of the passengers once on the bus. These German roaches will hang on for dear life when disturbed or upset, and a perfectly clean person could be carrying a roach around in his clothing this way."

Unfortunately, Faber had to tell the TA that there was nothing it could do to eliminate roaches. She recommended simply that the buses be kept as dry as possible, and free of rubbish, especially in the rear seat areas, where the roaches were most noticeable. This approach may prevent roaches from staying too long on the bus, but it won't prevent them from getting on with riders. That problem, Faber felt, was insoluble. "After a point," said Faber, "there isn't much you can do about roaches except to learn to live with them. Roaches are a lesson in humility for all of us humans."

Roaches are not the only live insects in the Museum, however. One of the most celebrated "pet" collections belongs to Alice Gray, Senior Scientific Assistant Emeritus at the Museum. Gray and her menagerie live in a sunny tower office on the Museum's third floor, commanding spectacular views east across the park and south down Central Park West.

Miss Gray is a kindly lady in her seventies, a little hard of hearing, and a veritable storehouse of information about insects. Anyone who calls the Museum with questions about insects is referred to Miss Gray. Visitors with scurrying things in shoeboxes and jars are told to go to Miss Gray. She and her menagerie have appeared on such TV programs as "To Tell the Truth," "What's My Line?" and "The Mike Douglas Show."

Scattered about Gray's office, which she shares with the

Origami Society of America, are mayonnaise jars, glass cages, and plastic boxes crawling and rustling with exotic creatures. One of her favorites is a colony of three-inch-long Madagascar hissing cockroaches, surely one of the most horrific insects in existence. When disturbed, the Madagascar cockroach emits a loud, evil hiss by drawing air through spiracles in its chitinous shell. (Gray explains that the spiracles are also used in molting; the insect simply sucks air into them until the pressure bursts the skin along its back.) Cockroach enthusiasts, of which there are many on the Museum's staff, are delighted to find numerous rare species in Gray's collection, including bright green Cuban roaches, lobster roaches, and species from Central America, as well as the old standbys—the American and German cockroach.

The grande dame of Gray's collection, though, isn't an insect at all, but a large tarantula named Blondie. Gray raised Blondie from infancy in the Museum, and the giant spider—the size of a small salad plate—is tame enough to be picked up and handled. Gray has other tarantulas, but most are too "frisky" to tolerate handling, she explained.

With such a large collection of insects, some are bound to escape. Many years ago, one of her tarantulas escaped from its cage and was gone for several weeks. Then one day she received a call from someone who had found a tarantula wandering about in Central Park about four blocks north of the Museum. Gray recognized it, she said, "by the balding pattern of hairs on its abdomen."

Another famous escape scene occurred in 1979 during the Museum's special exhibition, "Pompeii A.D. 79." One of Gray's favorite scorpions managed to squeeze out of its box and disappear. "I knew it was in the Museum," Gray explained later, "since it was born and raised here." One day about three weeks later, someone burst into her office and said that a scorpion was loose in the crowded exhibition, causing panic. Gray rushed to the scene and found a large crowd gathered around the insect, which sat in the middle of the exhibit, stinger raised in fear. Several burly men had taken off their shoes to crush the insect, but they just couldn't work up the courage. Gray forced her way through the crowd, clucking disapprovingly, and picked up the scorpion in her bare hands. She is reported to have said, "There you are, I've been looking for you for weeks!" Then she turned to the crowd, dangling the insect by its stinger. "It can't hurt you," she explained, "if you pick it up by the stinger."

Gray's collection is periodically augmented by gifts from visitors. Several summers ago, she added two praying mantises to her collection: one picked up on the forty-fifth floor of the Empire State Building, the other discovered on a window ledge on the thirty-eighth floor of a Wall Street office building. Apparently, Gray surmises, the hapless insects were caught in updrafts of air from the hot city streets.

Gray recalled one of her strangest cases, that of a large grasshopper found on the observation deck of the Empire State Building. Gray recognized it as a species that could be found only in the South. The story was published in a newspaper, and eventually a woman came forward to solve the mystery. She worked as a secretary in the building, she said, and had received a box in the mail from a friend in Florida. Upon opening the box the grasshopper had popped out, and before the horrified woman could recover her wits the insect had escaped out the window. Normally this grasshopper inhabits the tops of rushes, and it instinctively climbs upward when confused. Thus, mistaking the Empire State Building for a lovely tall rush, the poor insect climbed several dozen stories to end up on the observation deck.

The Museum's only Insect Hall closed in the early 1970s. The remains of it can be seen in a storage area outside Gray's office—a series of dusty dioramas and various aging wax models. There are plans to create a new Insect Hall, but it may be years before it opens. According to entomologist and Deputy Director Jerome Rozen, it could include live material—like the Smithsonian's Insect

Zoo—or just models. But live insects are expensive to maintain, and models expensive to build. Someday, though, insects are sure to take their proper place in the Museum. "The Museum," said Rozen, "simply can't neglect nine-tenths of the animal kingdom in its exhibits forever."

# THIRTEEN

# Amphibians and Reptiles

T he Herpetology Department is tucked away, apart from most of the other offices, in a warren of rooms off the Museum's second floor. A sign on the department's main door discreetly points out that the offices are not open to the public.

One of the most interesting areas of the department is the office of its chairman, Dr. Charles Myers, which usually echoes with the sounds of chirping frogs. Along the walls are several terraria full of brilliantly colored and actively hopping frogs. Myers' research focuses on a group of animals popularly named poison-dart frogs—so called because Indians in northwestern South American use the frogs' skin secretions to poison blowgun darts. So far, Myers and his collaborators at the National Institutes of Health have discovered a dozen new species of these frogs

199

—one of which is in fact so poisonous that it produces one of the most toxic nonprotein substances known to man. Appropriately, the vivarium containing this most poisonous and most beautiful of species—a brilliant golden yellow creature—includes a moss-covered human skull.*

Myers and colleagues discovered this new species in western Colombia in the early 1970s. Two other poisonous species were previously known to be in this area, and a few writers had commented on the use of the frogs by the Indian population for poisoning darts. The poisoning method involved catching the frogs in the forest and bringing them back to camp. To obtain the maximum amount of poison, one witness reported, the Indians impaled the unfortunate animal on a sharp stick passed through the throat and out one leg. The dying frog might even be held close to a fire. This torture caused the frog to "sweat" the poison in large quantities off its back, and the Indians collected this secretion for their darts.

The new species of yellow frog that Myers discovered turned out to be twenty times more poisonous than its relatives—so toxic that Indians poison their darts simply by wiping the points across the animal's back. No torturing of the frog was necessary. "We didn't realize just how poisonous this frog was," Myers explains, "until our contaminated garbage killed a chicken and a dog." Back in the United States, the scientists named the new species *Phyllobates terribilis*—for obvious reasons—and the toxin, when analyzed at the National Institutes of Health, was found to contain large quantities of a recently discovered class of compounds labeled *batrachotoxins*, or "frog poisons." Poisoning by these alkaloids swiftly results in blurred vision, convulsions, gagging, muscle rigidity, heart failure, and death. The skin secretions of a single frog may in fact contain two dozen different poisonous compounds, and there are no known antidotes. So far, over two hundred previously unknown compounds have been identified from the group of poison-dart frogs.

"In the rain forest," says Myers, "there could be over a

*One of the favorite resting spots for the frogs is inside the skull's eye sockets.

hundred possible predators of frogs—snakes, birds, opossums, you name it. But most animals learn to avoid this frog very quickly. A snake, for example, will take one bite, drop the frog immediately, and go into convulsions. The snake usually doesn't die, so it learns to avoid the frog in the future." There is, however, one species of snake, Myers has discovered, that seems to be almost completely immune to the poison. Myers fed a young frog to the snake, which ate it without apparent ill effects. When he gave the snake a larger frog, it chewed on it a while but couldn't swallow it. "The snake went limp and I could hang it over my finger like a piece of spaghetti, but twelve hours later it seemed fine. It just proves that nothing is immune from predation. But this frog comes close."

Myers is working on a related group which shows other intriguing problems. For example, a given species may come in hundreds of different colors, patterns, and sizes. Why a single species would show such tremendous variation is a mystery that Myers is still working on. "This could shed light on some fundamental problems in speciation—how species occur—as well as problems in genetic variation," Myers explains.

The Herpetology Department employs two other curators and two scientific assistants. One curator, Charles J. Cole, keeps a colony of live parthenogenetic lizards in the department. These unisexual lizards (of which there are about thirty species) live in all-female populations that reproduce without the benefit of males. The egg of this lizard develops unfertilized, and the resulting offspring is an exact genetic copy of its parent. Among other things, Cole is trying to discover how these lizards evolved.

In addition to their research, these curators of the Herpetology Department (like all of the Museum's curators) are in charge of caring for the collections and the planning of exhibits. The collection itself dates back to well before the Museum was founded.

On May 17, 1832, Prince Alexander Philipp Maximilian of Wied-Neuwied set sail for America with a Swiss artist, Karl Bodmer, on a grand expedition to explore the West.

For thirteen months the prince and his companion traveled up the Missouri River, from St. Louis to the Rockies, through five thousand miles of largely unknown territory. Along the way, the prince kept his celebrated journal (which swelled to 500,000 words), while Bodmer created his splendid watercolors of the Indians and landscapes. A lesser-known accomplishment of their travels was the collection of jars and jars of pickled animals, including strange new species of snakes, lizards, and frogs.

In 1870, when the Museum was barely a year old, it bought Prince Maximilian's collection of amphibians and reptiles. The venerable collection spent its first few years in the Arsenal Building while the Museum was being built, and was later moved uptown to a small storage area in the Museum's first building, where it formed the distinguished nucleus of what is now one of the best herpetology collections in the world.* As of November 1, 1982 (when the most recent count was made), the collection comprised 263,529 cataloged specimens, not including some 10,000 recent arrivals still awaiting admittance to the catalog. Of the 9,200 or so species of "herps" known to exist, over 60 percent can be found in the Museum, and an average of fifty-one species per year are being added to the collection. Most of the storage areas for the collection were recently overhauled, and new cabinets in Day-Glo orange were installed for the benefit of the frog collection. (Charles Myers explains that the whimsical color choice was based on the brilliant skin color of his favorite poison-dart frog.)

The new storage space and offices include a sound studio crammed with fancy electronic equipment for analyzing frog calls ("Some frogs," says Myers, "can best be identified by their calls"); a half-dozen computer terminals; a separate room for type specimens; a tape library for storing animal sounds; a live-animal room (filled with king snakes, from curator Richard G. Zweifel's research); a breeding colony of mice for the king snakes; a breeding

*The Greek word *herpeton*, from *herpo*, to creep, denoted something that crawled; herpetology is the science that embraces reptiles and amphibians.

colony of beetles; and various other storage areas. (Since this was originally written, the department has switched to using more convenient frozen mice.)

The Herpetology Department has responsibility for one hall in the Museum, the Hall of Amphibians and Reptiles. While the actual layout of this hall is unexciting, the exhibits are among the most remarkable in the Museum. The new hall opened in 1977, but many of the specimens were painstakingly recycled from the old 1929 hall. Where earlier models didn't exist, pickled specimens were cast and painted. One live snake even made an involuntary contribution.

The case showing this particular snake—a python—was prepared by a Museum technician. The nine-foot snake itself was arranged through a Singapore agent, who acquired the snake and sent it via jet to New York's Kennedy Airport. A museum staff member met the snake at the plane, and it was later taken to the New York Zoological Park animal hospital. There it was anesthetized with halothane administered with a mouth cone. The unconscious animal was then wrapped around a clutch of plaster eggs, a veterinarian inserted a breathing tube down the animal's throat, and plaster was smeared over the snake, layer by layer. Work had to proceed quickly, because the natural heat of the setting plaster could not be allowed to exceed 100 degrees without danger of harming the snake. As soon as the snake was removed from the mold, a few whiffs of oxygen revived it. The Museum donated the live snake to the Bronx Zoo. (Unlike most reptiles, this snake incubates its eggs. Being cold-blooded, it generates metabolic heat when necessary by flexing its muscles while coiled around its eggs.)

Not far from the python—either in the hall or in world geography—is the Komodo Dragon. A group of these ancient-looking beasts was salvaged intact from the old hall, and placed in a new habitat setting showing the creatures eating a dead boar. These specimens were the first such animals brought back to the West from the Dutch East Indies (now Indonesia), where the animal lives on several small, nearly uninhabited islands. We shall pause here for a moment, because the story of the discovery and capture of these animals is a particularly fascinating tale.

## The Dragon Lizards of Komodo

West of Timor and east of Java lie the Lesser Sunda Islands. One of the smallest of these islands is Komodo, sandwiched between Flores and Sumbawa in the Lintah Straits. Komodo, a twenty-two-mile-long series of eroded volcanic plugs, rises several thousand feet above the sea. It is covered with grass, tall gubbong palms, and pockets of jungle. Because of the island's position in the Lintah Straits, tidal currents, driven by monsoon winds, rip past its shores and churn about its treacherous coral reefs at speeds of up to thirteen knots. It is likely that these currents are what prevented human settlement on the island, and are certainly what discouraged Europeans from exploring the island until the twentieth century.

In 1912 some Malay pearl divers risked the currents and anchored in a harbor on Komodo, hoping for a rich haul from its virgin oyster beds. After landing, they saw giant lizards roaming about the island's uplands and volcanic slopes, and returned to tell their neighbors about it. The story reached a man named P. A. Ouwens, then director of the Zoological Museum in Buitenzorg (now Bogor), Java. Ouwens had heard rumors of "dragons" in the Lesser Sundas for years, and he finally decided to investigate. He sent several collectors to Komodo, who killed and brought back specimens of a nine-foot-long black lizard. Ouwens described the new species and named it *Varanus komodensis*; the public started calling it the Komodo Dragon.

In 1926, one of the American Museum's wealthy trustees, a young adventurer named W. Douglas Burden, brought an idea to the Museum's president, Henry Fairfield Osborn. Burden wanted to finance and lead a Komodo expedition to bring back the first dragons to the West. And he wanted to bring at least one back alive. Burden, an enthusiastic hunter, had frequently volunteered his money and services to the Museum to shoot exotic and dangerous animals for habitat groups. By the time he was twenty-eight, he had stalked elephant, tiger, rhinoceros, and water buffalo in the jungles of Indochina; Asian roe deer and Mongolian argali along the Sino-Mongolian frontier; and ibex, red bear, and Marco Polo sheep in the high Himalayas.

Osborn thought the idea a splendid one, and approved it as an official expedition for the Museum, provided Burden paid for it with his own funds. Osborn was especially keen to have the first live film footage, in addition to study specimens of the strange beast.

Burden found the expert hunter he needed in the person of F. J. Defosse, a scruffy, taciturn man who had spent years hunting dangerous animals in the jungles of French Indochina. He hired E. R. Dunn to be the expedition's herpetologist, and as they steamed around the world toward Komodo in the *Dog*, a ship provided for the expedition by the Dutch Colonial government, Burden picked up a Chinese cameraman in Singapore and fifteen Malay assistants.

On June 9, 1926, after a journey of 15,000 miles, Burden and his crew sighted the peaks of Komodo rising above the horizon. The *Dog*'s captain, a Dutchman, expertly brought the ship through the tidal currents and into Python Bay, a calm harbor on the lee side of the island. "The shore was a curving ribbon of sand," Burden later wrote. "With its sharp serrated skyline, its gnarled mountains, its mellow sun-washed valleys and the giant pinnacles that bared themselves like fangs to the sky, [the island] looked as fantastic as the mountains of the moon. . . . We seemed to be entering a lost world."

Burden soon discovered that the island was overrun with game, including deer, wild boar, and dangerous water buffalo. For the first few days, all he saw were tracks and spoor of the giant lizard—not the beast itself.

After several preliminary explorations, Burden established his camp on a 2,000-foot plateau near a pool whose muddy shores were crisscrossed by tracks of the Komodo dragon. Shortly afterward, Burden spied his first lizard. "A large dark object moving in the distant grass caught my eye," he wrote. "Sure enough, it was a varanid—a giant lizard. There was something almost unbelievable about it . . . it looked enormous. . . . He swung his grim head this way and that, obviously hunting, his sharp eyes searching for anything that moved. A primeval monster in a primeval setting."

Burden began setting out bait for the lizards. Although they occasionally ambush boar, deer, and even buffalo on the jungle trails, dragons prefer to feed on dead and rotting carcasses. In setting up the bait, Burden would lash a dead boar to a heavy stake driven into the ground. Then he would set up the film equipment to catch the lizards when they came to feed. Once at the bait, the lizard would clamp its jaws on the carcass, sinking its recurved, serrated teeth deep into the flesh. By rocking back and forth and tugging at the carcass, the lizard could tear off thick slabs of meat, which it then swallowed whole. Burden watched one lizard actually rip a boar in half and gulp down the hindquarters —legs, hooves, and all.

Despite their frightful appearance, the lizards were slow, and stalking and shooting them was hardly a challenge. Burden described the typical process of bagging a specimen.

> About fifty yards up the sandy draw a very large lizard strode ponderously into view. This was a real dragon. He would do perfectly, I thought, for the Museum group. I started the movie camera and obtained some wonderful footage. . . . [He was] a ragged customer, black as dead lava, every aspect spoke of infinite existence. . . . He took the whole boar in his jaws and started rocking back and forth with all his power, trying to wrench it free. It was a seesaw motion so violently performed I felt the rope might break at any moment and I would lose the animal. . . . So I picked up my rifle and shot him.

The real challenge, Burden discovered, was *capturing* the dragon. Burden wanted to keep the biggest, best specimens alive, and one day the Malay hunters reported seeing just such a creature—a huge, battle-scarred lizard—on the edge of a thicket. Burden and Defosse began rigging up a trap at the spot, hoping to catch the beast during its daily hunt. They killed a fat boar for bait, and the Malays pounded a stockade of thick stakes around it, leaving only a narrow entrance. Defosse selected a nearby tree as a spring pole, and with fifteen Malays pulling, the tree was bent to the ground and lashed in place. A noose was set at the opening of the stockade and tied to the end of the bent tree, and the whole contraption was then camouflaged with leaves and grass. A release string attached to the bent tree ran along the ground to a boma that hid Burden, Defosse, and the Malays.

The first visitor was a small lizard, which was soon chased away by a bigger one. The second lizard went into the trap and tried to drag the boar out, but Burden, feeling that this was an inferior specimen, held off cutting the release string. After a few minutes the lizard in the trap fled "as if the devil were after him," and the old giant crept into the clearing. "He looked black as ink," Burden wrote, "his bony armor was scarred and blistered. His eyes, deep set in their sockets, looked out on the world from beneath hanging brows. . . . Here at last was a real monster." The beast eyed the trap for about thirty minutes before deciding to enter. Suddenly, without warning, the lizard charged into the stockade and sank its teeth into the bait. Burden tugged the release.

Immediately the dragon found himself sailing through the air. A moment later there was a terrible cracking, for, as the beast fell again, the rope tightened and under his weight the spring pole broke and bent so far down that our prize, instead of being suspended in mid-air, was on the ground, tugging at the tether which held him about the middle. Then as the natives ran out to surround him, the ugly brute began vomiting.

The Malays backed off and refused to go near the animal, but Defosse was ready with a lasso. "A strange pair they made, the old hunter and his grim antagonist—who by this time was lashing himself into a frightful rage, the foam dripping from his jaws."

After a few tries, Defosse neatly dropped the lasso over the dragon's head and another around its tail. After much effort, they finally were able to tie the lizard to a pole and carry it into camp hanging upside down, where they had a specially built cage waiting for it. Once the lizard was free in the cage, it worked itself up into another fury of snapping, clawing, and vomiting. The smell became so offensive that Burden had the cage moved a quarter-mile downwind of the camp.

They went to bed that night congratulating themselves on their catch, but when they visited the cage the next morning, they saw that the beast had escaped. The animal had actually bitten and clawed its way through the steel mesh at the top of the cage.

Burden was now even more determined to get a live dragon. He eventually managed to get two smaller ones using the same methods, but nothing quite like the dragon that got away. He also shot twelve others, for a total of fourteen specimens. The fourteen specimens would allow scientists to study interspecific variations in such things as size, shape, and color—all of which allow taxonomists to determine the characteristics of the "typical" Komodo dragon. His collections were now complete, and not long afterward, Burden and his prizes arrived in New York City.

The two live dragons were deposited at the Bronx Zoo, where, until they sickened and died, they drew thousands of visitors. But on the third floor of the Museum, at the rear of the Hall of Amphibians and Reptiles, today's visitors can still see several of the specimens Burden brought back. One dragon has just sunk its jaws into a dead boar, while two others lurk nearby, their beady glass eyes surveying the landscape in a tireless search for prey.

# FOURTEEN

# Birds

A curious nineteenth-century photographic portrait hangs in the Ornithology Department at the American Museum. Made up of many little photographs cut up and pasted together, this photomontage shows a group of solemn Victorian gentlemen—some with drooping mustaches, others with long beards—dressed in dark frock coats and high, starched collars, who were the founders of the American Ornithologists' Union.

In the center of the picture is a peculiar-looking man, Joel Asaph Allen, who started the Museum's bird department. By all accounts, Allen was a remarkable man and a brilliant scientist. During the latter part of the nineteenth-century he became not only one of America's leading ornithologists, but the dean of American mammalogy as well. He also helped initiate the Museum's collection of birds, later to become one of the finest in the world.

Born on a farm in Massachusetts to rigidly strict parents

of Puritan stock, Allen began collecting birds and other animals at an early age. He later financed his education at Harvard, under Louis Agassiz, by selling this collection. He soon became Agassiz' assistant and, in 1865, traveled with him on an expedition to Brazil. (The philosopher William James was also a member of this expedition.) Another Harvard expedition that Allen accompanied was the 1873 Yellowstone Expedition, during which several scientists of the party were killed by Sioux.

During this time Allen suffered a nervous breakdown, and poor health plagued him all his life. His eyesight was poor, and he was so painfully shy in the presence of strangers that he could barely bring himself to speak at public meetings. According to most accounts he was a kind and gentle man who never spoke ill of anyone, but could —and did—destroy a colleague's scientific reputation with the flick of a pen if he disagreed with his theories. One of his assistants wrote, "I have seen him treat with fatherly kindness a man whose theories he had subjected to fatally destructive criticism."

Allen joined the Museum in the early 1880s as curator of both birds and mammals. In 1888 he hired Frank M. Chapman, a young man of twenty-six, to help him sort and catalog birds. It was a wise choice. Chapman would become the greatest ornithologist of his day, and his *Handbook of Birds of Eastern North America* was later to introduce the techniques of "birding" to the general public. He also founded the magazine *Bird Lore*, which eventually grew into *Audubon*. Yet one of Chapman's greatest contributions was in exhibition, not ornithology. He is credited with introducing the idea of the "habitat group" into museums.

Old photographs and engravings of the interior of the American Museum of Natural History show rows upon rows of cases. One can barely make out, in the dim recesses of each case, an undifferentiated mass of specimens lined up like ducks at an arcade. To many visitors, birds were particularly boring; while a stuffed lion skin or a large fossil did have its appeal, rows upon rows of stuffed bird skins could only capture the interest of the most dedicated ornithologist.

Around 1900, Chapman changed this. Several donors to the Museum gave Chapman $1,200 to help finance the new Hall of North American Birds, and Chapman used the money to start work on habitat groups. The first, finished in 1902, showed the birdlife on Cobb's Island, Virginia, with a beach made of actual sand, graced by both natural and artificial plants. The most novel and startling aspect of the habitat group was the background. Painted on a double-curved surface, it imperceptibly merged the three-dimensional foreground with a two-dimensional background of sea, birds, and sky, with the entire display illuminated by unseen internal lighting. While others had created museum displays with one or more realistic elements, Chapman was the first to pull it all together.

In this day of movies, television, and fine color reproduction, it is hard to imagine the kind of popular excitement the habitat group could provoke. Here, in the middle of a huge urban area, visitors could suddenly step into a museum and find themselves looking through a sort of magic window at the wildlife and scenery of a remote New Hampshire lake, or a high cliff above a surging Labrador sea.

Predictably, some conservative scientists criticized the habitat group as being unscientific, and even labeled the painted background "sensational" in the pejorative sense. Chapman defended it, saying that the backgrounds were "realistic productions of definite localities, [which] thus in themselves possess a scientific value." President Jesup thought they were splendid. In the following years the Museum would greatly expand its habitat groups, culminating with the great Akeley Hall of African Mammals. Museums all over the world would follow suit.

During Chapman's tenure the Museum's bird collection was built up from about 10,000 specimens to over 750,000, to make it the greatest such collection in the world. Chapman once said that the Museum's bird collection was better than all the rest of the world's put together.

212 DINOSAURS IN THE ATTIC

It was greatly enhanced by a single acquisition, one of the largest in the Museum's history—the birds of an eccentric English baron.

## Lord Rothschild's Birds

In 1931 the Museum's already fine and still-growing collection was augmented by the extraordinary bird collection of Lord Walter Rothschild. Ever since he was a little boy, Rothschild had had a grand passion for natural history, and in 1889 he started a museum at the family estate in Tring, England. In the years that followed, it was to become the largest and most famous natural history collection ever assembled by one man. Eschewing his family's banking business, Rothschild devoted himself full-time to collecting, and over the years sent more than four hundred men into the field for his museum. Rothschild was particularly interested in birds and butterflies. By the late twenties, the Tring collection of birds—which numbered well over a quarter-million—had become the most studied bird collection in the world.

Then, on March 10, 1932, in a move that stunned the British public and scientific circles, he announced that he had sold his bird collection to the American Museum of Natural History for an undisclosed sum of money. Indeed, at the time of the announcement, the sale and transfer of the collection was already close to completion, and had been accomplished with such secrecy that even Rothschild's family had no idea that it was under way.

The secret sale was initiated in October 1931, when a trustee of the American Museum and patron of the Ornithology Department, Dr. Leonard Sanford, received a letter from Rothschild offering him the collection for $225,000, or about a dollar a bird. "It requires thought and courage," Rothschild wrote to Sanford, "to tear one's being out by the roots. . . . This debacle would not have happened had my brother been alive for as you know I was disinherited & he inherited my father's fortune & always helped me when he was alive. . . ."* Rothschild hinted that he was forced to sell the collection because he owed three years' back taxes to the Crown, and was being pressed by the government.

Sanford immediately wrote to Henry Fairfield Osborn that the collection was "now worth between $1,500,000 and $2,000,000 and is offered to us for $225,000. This offer is largely due to the fact that I have promised Lord Rothschild we will keep the collection intact and develop it according to his ideas."

Following that correspondence, negotiations and arrangements were made, all with the secrecy that Rothschild requested. The family of Harry Payne Whitney agreed to donate to the Museum the funds necessary to acquire the collection, and Robert Cushman Murphy, a curator in the bird department, was put in charge of the monumental task of cataloging the collection at Tring, packing it, and shipping it to the States.

Sanford, who knew Rothschild, undertook the delicate negotiations, made all the more so by Rothschild's strong emotional attachment to the collection. Rothschild wanted to keep some of the birds for sentimental reasons, including a peerless collection of birds of paradise. The Museum especially wanted the birds of paradise, however, and Sanford was charged with the task of getting them. When Sanford finally persuaded the baron to give them up for the sake of science, Rothschild broke down and wept. (According to Robert Cushman Murphy, "Old Doc Sanford was close to weeping as well.") Later, Murphy wrote to the Museum's assistant director:

Getting everything we wished, and more than we dared hope for, was a great feat, but still more remarkable is the good will, not to say enthusiasm, that [Sanford] has aroused in Lord Rothschild. A week ago the old gentleman looked as though hanging would be a relief to him. Now he acts and talks rather as though the transfer of

*Rothschild's father had disinherited him, according to Walter, because he had not gone into the family banking business, but his father could not deprive him of his title and estates.

his life-long love to the American Museum was its most desirable apotheosis . . . and he is fully "sold" regarding the care, protection, and scientific use that his treasures will inherit in the Whitney Building.

Murphy and his wife spent four months at Tring cataloging and packing the collection. Rothschild had managed to fill four rooms and a capacious basement with birds. They were arranged in systematic order, but Rothschild's prodigious memory had obviated the need for a written catalog. Many specimens weren't labeled, and the information was stored only in the baron's head. Thus, before the collections could be moved, Murphy had to count every bird (all 280,000 of them) and prepare a catalog containing information on each specimen. He wrote that

> any hitch, any unrecorded gap, would lead to hopeless confusion, especially since only one or two specimens in many series of one kind had had the scientific name written upon the field label. A thousand packs of cards, turning in a lottery barrel, would be a simple task of reassortment compared with a possible jumble of partly unnamed Old World warblers and thrushes, represented by subspecies extending across Eurasia from Ireland to Japan.

The larger specimens were wrapped in newspapers, "mostly of wartime vintage," and later, when those ran out, Dutch newspapers. (When they switched from English to Dutch papers, Murphy noted that the work of the packers speeded up considerably.) The catalog, when finished, took up 740 foolscap pages.

When most of the collection had been shipped to America, Rothschild finally announced that it had been sold. He merely indicated, in a terse statement, that he had found it necessary to dispose of part of his collections, and that the birds were the only easily sold asset.

The American Museum worried about how the British Museum would react to the sale, as there had always been (and continues to be) an excellent relationship between the two institutions. Although there was some grumbling, the British Museum took the sale with grace. One scientist even declared that the collection belonged to the world, not to any country, and that it would be more accessible and better cared for in America. Rothschild, who was actually a trustee of the British Museum, had quietly approached several of his co-trustees, including the Archbishop of Canterbury, to explore the possibility of a British Museum purchase. He apparently was told that there was no hope that it would be purchased by the British Museum. Rothschild wisely decided that if he sold it abroad, he had better keep the deal secret until it was consummated. The collection was so large that, back at the American Museum, it took many years to unpack and install in the new Whitney Wing.

It wasn't until after Rothschild's death, in 1937, that the real reason for the sale of the Tring bird collection came to light. Rothschild's niece, Miriam Rothschild, reported the discovery in her memoir about her uncle, entitled *Dear Lord Rothschild*:

> Walter, who was then thirty-six years of age, had decided he could no longer bear to read his personal correspondence . . . He obtained two large wicker baskets (five feet by three feet) from the Tring Park estate laundry, and when the mail was brought to him with his early morning tea he sorted the letters into two piles, one large and one very small, the latter with a well-known dreaded handwriting on the envelope, and dropped them unopened in their respective baskets. When the baskets were full, he shot the iron bar through the two pendulous metal loops, secured the padlock and turned the key. Over the months which followed a large number of similar baskets accumulated in his room, one piled on top of the other. . . .
>
> It was not until thirty years later, after Walter's own death, that the last of the linen baskets divulged its ugly secrets. His greatest act of folly was the decision to set aside, securely locked, this one basket into which he had dropped the smaller packets of letters. It fell to the lot of his horrified sister-in-law to discover the existence

of a charming, witty, aristocratic, ruthless blackmailer who at one time had been Walter's mistress, and, aided and abetted by her husband, had ruined him financially, destroyed his mind for forty years and eventually forced him to sell his bird collection.

Miriam Rothschild never identified the blackmailer. She wrote that the baron

seemed to shrink visibly in the period following the sale. . . . He felt tired and distrait, and spent only about two hours before lunch in the [Tring] Museum. It was winter—his birds had flown.

Before Murphy left, Rothschild gave him a large photograph of himself. Murphy wrote in a letter:

After getting him to sign it and add the date of the contract [with the Museum], I promised him that it would be framed and hung forever in the department. He is as jubilant over it as a school boy on the "honor roll"! In many ways he is as naïve and shy as a child, anyway, and, although he always carries the front of a lord, he is also an extraordinarily simple man. . . .

True to the promise, that photograph still hangs in the department, showing a plump, bearded, and avuncular old man with a kindly face: this nobleman who built up—and then lost—the greatest private bird collection ever assembled.

## The World's Biggest Nest

In addition to birds themselves, the ornithology collection also includes birds' eggs and nests, which are cataloged together for convenience. But we will find what is by far the strangest bird nest in the Museum on display at the back of the Sanford Hall of Biology of Birds. Taking up an entire case, this social weaver bird's compound nest was collected in South Africa in 1925. At 300 to 400 cubic feet, it may be the largest bird nest in any museum.

The history of this nest begins in the 1920s, with James Chapin, a curator in Chapman's bird department, who was particularly interested in African bird nests. When a colleague of his at the Smithsonian Institution, Herbert Friedmann, was arranging a trip to South Africa, Chapin pressed him to collect a nest of the social weaver, which he felt would make an excellent addition to the collection. Friedmann accepted the challenge and set out for Africa in 1924.

The social weaver is a bird architect *nonpareil*. Flocks of these birds build huge "apartment house" nests in the flat-topped acacia trees of the South African veldt. Crafted out of coarse grass and twigs, the nests are not woven but rather thatched, much like a haycock. The result is a large, hanging mass of straw whose underside is perforated by the entrances to individual nests. Every year the flock adds to the nest, contributing to massive domiciles that occasionally grow so heavy they collapse parts of trees. The very largest can reach 2,000 cubic feet. Often they can rival human dwellings in longevity; some nests have been observed to be in use for over one hundred years.

Friedmann's search for the perfect nest began in January 1925, near what was then Maquassi, in the Transvaal. A railroad had recently opened the area, and Friedmann journeyed by train, searching a swath of land about five miles deep on each side of the tracks for a distance of some one hundred miles. The veldt was so flat and open and the nests so large that they could be spotted miles away. Friedmann claimed to have examined every nest in the 1,000-square-mile area—all twenty-six of them—before selecting a large, shapely, compact nest that looked as if it might travel well. The nest, which was nine feet high, seven feet wide, and eight feet deep, hung in a twenty-five-foot acacia, and covered about 25 percent of the tree.

Friedmann and his assistants realized that collecting the nest meant collecting the tree as well, so they trimmed off the excess branches, tied several guy lines to the crown, chopped through the trunk, and gently lowered the tree onto a horse-drawn cart. (Friedmann makes no mention of how the resident birds might have viewed this procedure.)

Borrowing a technique used in collecting dinosaur bones, Friedmann first covered the nest with burlap, then wrapped it with plaster-soaked burlap. This was followed by a layer of chicken wire and more layers of plaster. Following Chapman's example, Friedmann collected all the fixings of a habitat group, including some of the birds, made plaster casts of the acacia leaves, and even dug up a tubful of red earth near the base of the tree—all so that preparators back at the Museum could re-create the setting.*

Chapman had authorized $100 in expenses for Friedmann to get his prize to the port at Capetown. But when he found out that shipping the nest from Capetown to New York was going to cost hundreds of dollars more, he was so horrified he wanted to instruct his shipping agents to dump the nest then and there. But he changed his mind—probably under Chapin's influence—and the nest duly arrived at the Museum.

The nest was first displayed in the 1940s, when the Hall of Biology of Birds opened. Chapin was in charge of erecting the exhibit, and after it opened he used to pose as a visitor and mingle with the crowds admiring the nest. A story is told that one day Chapin, finding a large and excited crowd in front of his exhibit, sidled up to drink in their praise. To his dismay, he found that the people were watching the activities of a mouse that had made the nest its home.

In 1982 the hall was renovated, and along with it the nest was given a thorough cleaning and refurbishment. The nest was washed with detergent, which was flushed out with water and then blow-dried with fans. Finally the

---

*The tree was to go in the middle of the hall, surrounded by a bit of its nativ habitat, but the exhibition department truncated the exhibit and today only the crow is on display in a case.

whole thing was cemented together with a spray consisting of a solution of Elmer's Glue-All and glycerine. Altogether, it took several hundred man-hours to refurbish the nest, which is now safely back on view in its familiar setting on the Museum's first floor.

# Anthropology

**N**o one really knows exactly how many anthropological artifacts are in the American Museum of Natural History. The official number given to the press is about 8 million, but many curators will privately admit that this is mostly a guess. Whatever the number, they fill well over fifty storage rooms, and the Museum has been spending millions of dollars to renovate, conserve, and computerize this extraordinary collection. Yet these are merely the physical collections. There is another collection that is, in a sense, invisible. It has no catalog numbers and is not cross-referenced or indexed in a computer system. It cannot be displayed, photographed, or insured.

This collection is the vast body of myths, songs, dreams, sacred texts, and visions gathered by Museum curators from hundreds of living and extinct cultures, from New Guinea to Manhattan Island. Both in published works

and in reams of unpublished notes stored in a fifth-floor vault, one can find hundreds of creation stories, descriptions of afterworlds both heavenly and hellish, epic tales of gods and demons, magical formulae, chants and songs, dreams of the past and future, visions of prophets and shamans, recipes for potions to heal the body and mind, and much more.

The collection contains such things as the creation myth of the Hackensack Indians (who once lived on Staten Island), accounts of the dream cults of the Oglala Sioux, and shaman chants of the Tsimshian Indians of the Northwest Coast. Here too one can read the epic tale of the San Carlos Apaches, the love poetry and death songs of the Ojibwa Indians, songs recorded on old wax cylinders of the Yukaghir people of Siberia, and dozens of myths of a Great Flood and an arcadian age when animals spoke like people.

No one really has any idea of just how much—or exactly what—mythological material might be stored in the Museum. Most of the myths were gathered before 1930. Today, with several notable exceptions, the Museum's anthropologists are less interested in mythology, partially because many of them are working in literate societies where myths have already been written down. One of the exceptions is Robert Carneiro, a curator specializing in the cultures of Amazonia. In a visit to South America in 1975, he collected a dozen myths from the Kuikuru, a Carib-speaking people who lived in a single village in the upper Xingu basin of central Brazil.

By far the most complete body of myths in the Museum comes from the Indian cultures of North America. Between 1880 and 1930, myth collectors from New York traveled west with pen and paper to capture the Indian myth cycles before they became hopelessly garbled by Christian influences or were lost entirely. While Franz Boas was busy recording the entire myth cycle of the Kwakiutl Indians of the Northwest Coast (a staggering body of myths, as voluminous as the Bible), his contemporary, Robert H. Lowie, was tramping across the West from Alberta to Arizona, collecting hundreds of myths (as well as artifacts) from the Hopi, Assiniboine, Blackfoot, Cree, Shoshone, and Ojibwa cultures. Pliny Earl Goddard, another Museum curator, spent twenty years studying the dancing societies of the Sarsi and the many dialects of the Athabascan family of tribes, of which the Apache are most prominent. Clark Wissler, also a myth collector and chairman of the Department of Anthropology, built the Museum's collection of Plains Indian material into one of the greatest in the world, and in addition edited several numbers of the *Anthropological Papers of the American Museum of Natural History*, in which many of the myths were published.

The myths that are now bound into silent volumes in the Museum still retain their freshness and vitality. Some are mysterious and obscure, some sacred, some obscene, some humorous, and some historically straightforward. Many explain how the earth was created and why things are the way they are. In rummaging around among dozens of old volumes in the library, I came across the following passage, collected by Robert Lowie in 1907. It is the story of Genesis according to the Assiniboine, a culture of the northern plains:

Long ago there was water everywhere. Sitconski was traveling in a moose-skin boat. He saw the muskrat coming towards him, holding something in its paws. "What are you holding there?"

"Nothing."

"Let me see, and I'll take you into my boat."

The muskrat showed him the mud it was holding in its paws. Sitconski took it, saying, "I am going to make the earth out of this." He rubbed the mud between his palms, breathed on it, and thus made the earth. . . .

Inktonmi was wearing a wolf-skin robe. He said, "There shall be as many months as there are hairs on this robe before it shall be summer."

Frog said, "If the winter lasts as long as that, no creature will be able to live. Seven months of winter will be enough." He kept on repeating this, until Ink-tonmi got angry, and killed him. Still Frog stuck out seven of his toes. Finally, Inktonmi consented, and said there should be seven winter months.

Inktonmi then created men and horses out of dirt. Some of the Assiniboine and other northern tribes had no horses. Inktonmi told the Assiniboine that they were always to steal horses from other tribes.

Many of the tales that Lowie and other anthropologists recorded involved things that would be considered highly obscene in European culture. Bowdlerizing the tales would be contrary to scientific principles, but they certainly couldn't be printed as they were, with passages describing in precise detail such things as coprophagy, incest, and bestiality. The anthropologists solved the problem by translating the sensitive passages into (often execrable) Latin; presumably, only the most dedicated scholar would take the time to translate them, and thus the morals of society would be protected. The following passage illustrating this practice has been taken verbatim out of another Assiniboine myth, just as it was published in the Museum's *Anthropological Papers*. It again involves Inktonmi, who discovers an unknown village inhabited only by women who have never seen men. Inktonmi enters the chieftainesses' lodge and sits down:

"Are there any men here?" [Inktonmi asks.]

"No, we don't know what men are."

Inktonmi thought, "I am going to show them something." Sublata veste mentulam erectam eis demonstravit. The rabbit's mother [one of the chieftainesses] first noticed it, and stooped down to look at it more closely. The other chieftainess also looked down. "Istud quid est, cui bono?"

"Ad copulandum."

"Qua in parte corporis coire oportet?"

"Prope accedite, et vobis demonstrabo." Sublatis vestibus, earum cunnos indicavit. "In hunc locum si penam inseram, vobis dulce erit."

As the story continues, Inktonmi gives the women a demonstration, using two chieftainesses and several other women as subjects, and goes on to explain sexual matters to them. When he has more than gratified his desires and wishes to leave, the "uninitiated" women capture him and hold him back. Finally he makes good his escape, with the women frantically pursuing him. When he reaches his friend, who has been waiting for him in a canoe, he says, "Well, brother, let us go on, I found nothing there but rocks."

As European culture began to disrupt the Indian way of life, many myths became altered, and new tales sprang up involving the white men and their ways. One Menomini tale recounts the Indians' discovery of a particularly insidious white man's vice, transforming it to the Indian point of view:

Very long ago, in the early days, the Menomini Indians saw the white people drinking and making intoxicating liquors. The Indians seeing the white men in delirium because of the liquor thought it great and surmised it caused a good feeling during the time of its effects. The young men, anxious to experiment, said, "Let us first try it on our old grandfathers; let them drink first, and if it poisons them there will not be much loss for the old fellows have reached the limit of their lives. If the fire water works well on them and they do not die from it, then we will use some of it ourselves."

... The old fellows drank and were overcome by a strange feeling. They talked on and on and could not stop and tears flowed from the eyes of some of them. Soon all of them were paralyzed drunk, motionless, and only breathing. The young men's eyes opened to see their old people die from the poison and they said, "Alas, they are dead," and were frightened. However, to the young men's surprise, after some hours the old fellows revived. They said, "How is it? How did you feel when you were dead?"

"Oh no," said the old men in laughter, "it is very

nice and good. There are funny feelings and a merry go of the brain and you can know more than you ever knew."

The young men thought it to be so and commenced to use liquor and have continued up to now, knowing the consequence, but they do not believe it, until the end comes. Liquor acts as a go-between between mankind and all powers of good and bad, above and below. The closer a shaman is to the powers, the more he needs liquor to get them to guide and tell him what he cannot know in his soberness. This is the way of all Indian medicine doctors of different sorts and descriptions, as the powers accept this method of coming to them.

Of course, the myths came not just from American Indians, but from all over the world. Waldemar Jochelson collected hundreds of myths in Siberia during the Jesup North Pacific Expedition of 1901 through 1903, mentioned in Chapter Three.

Jochelson, like Boas and other museum anthropologists, was shocked at the rate with which primitive cultures were being destroyed, even in the remotest areas of Siberia. In one of his ethnographies, Jochelson frequently consulted census documents to find statistics on baptisms, deaths from white diseases, and other benchmarks of the creeping influence of European ways. When he was among the Koryak in northeastern Siberia he noted with alarm that an 1897 census of northeastern Siberia showed that 45 percent of the Koryak had been baptized as Christians. "The new ideas represented in the mode of life of the Russians," Jochelson wrote, "are destroying the Koryak beliefs at an ever accelerating rate.... Their religious myths are changing into meaningless tales and fables, or are being forgotten entirely."

Jochelson transcribed hundreds of Koryak myths, along with Yukaghir and other tribal mythologies. Some of these he captured on wax-cylinder recordings, while others he transcribed and/or translated. He also asked questions about every aspect of their lives, and even had one Koryak informant name the stars for him and draw a star map showing the major Koryak constellations.*

Many Koryak myths—like myths of other cultures around the world—involve what are known as "trickster cycles" or "trickster tales." These tales usually include a physically weak but wily and clever character who outwits much more powerful opponents. A familiar example would be the B'rer Rabbit tales, essentially a black American trickster cycle that many feel has African roots; others include the trickster Monkey of Chinese mythology and, indeed, many European and Scandinavian folk myths. The Koryak trickster tales usually include two characters, the Creator and Miti, his wife, who is usually the trickster. In one tale, "How Miti Played Tricks on Her Husband," Miti is cast out of their house in a quarrel, and she takes revenge by rearranging her body and putting her breasts on her back, her buttocks in front, and her vagina behind. When she returns and her husband sleeps with her, he is astounded: "Is it possible that you have your breasts on your back?" he asks. Miti puts him in his place with a scornful reply: "Don't you know that they are [supposed to be] on my back?"

These were not just tales and amusing stories. Many of the myths collected were prayers and chants that held great power for the worshiper. They were as important as, for instance, the Bible was to medieval Europeans. Though a great number of these prayers and chants are obscure unless placed within their proper ceremonial context, some are quite beautiful as poetry. Here, for example, are several excerpts from a long and hauntingly beautiful prayer gathered by Washington Matthews among the Navajo in the 1880s. It forms part of the Navajo Night Chant:

In the house made of the dawn,
In the house made of the evening twilight,

*The Koryak called the constellation *Ursa Major* "The Wild Reindeer Buck"; their name for the Morning Star was "Suspended Breath," and they called the Milky Way, "Clay River."

In the house made of the dark cloud,
In the house made of the he-rain,
In the house made of the dark mist,
In the house made of the she-rain,
In the house made of pollen,
In the house made of grasshoppers,
Where the dark mist curtains the doorway,
The path to which is on the rainbow,
Where the zigzag lightning stands on high,
Oh, male divinity!
With your moccasins of dark cloud, come to us . . .
With the far darkness made of the dark mist on the ends
      of your wings, come to us soaring,
With the far darkness made of the she-rain over your
      head, come to us soaring,
With the zigzag lightning flung out on high over your
      head, come to us soaring,
With the rainbow hanging high over your head, come to
      us soaring . . .
With the darkness on the earth, come to us.
With these I wish the foam floating on the flowing
      water over the roots of the great corn. . . .
Happily abundant dark clouds I desire.
Happily abundant dark mists I desire.
Happily abundant passing showers I desire. . . .
Happily may fair blue corn, to the ends of the earth,
      come with you.

The Museum's collection of myths may turn out to be at least as valuable and irreplaceable as the physical collections. Artifacts can survive the extinction of a culture; pots, house foundations, knives, carvings, and burials can last thousands of years. But when a nonliterate people comes in contact with Western culture, the shock often destroys its religion and mythology first. Myths are a culture's most delicate artifacts, and among its most important and revealing.

## Little Finger Nail

The word *artifact* comes from the Latin *arte factum*, meaning something made with skill. The word hardly conveys the rich associations that are invested in each artifact. Museum collectors did not make aesthetic decisions when collecting artifacts; they were much more interested in what the artifact signified to the people who created it. An ordinary wad of feathers tied in a bundle would not be collected because of its beauty, but because it was considered an object of magic and power. As recently as several years ago, a group of Indian chiefs visited the Museum and conducted ceremonies with some of the magical objects from their tribes that are stored in the sixth-floor vaults, as these were objects of greater power than anything which survived in the tribes today.

In our own somewhat spiritually barren culture, we do not think of objects as being charged with spiritual power or meaning. Most primitive cultures, however, believe in some form of animism, a class of religions in which a spirit or power dwells in everything, including such "inanimate" things as stones and earth. Thus the so-called artifacts of a culture are not just an inert group of objects to be taken apart and studied by anthropologists. Anthropologists do not normally study *artifacts*; instead, they try to understand the great invisible body of meaning that lies behind and within an object. The concept of an object being art—that is, a skillfully made object that excites aesthetic pleasure in and of itself—is foreign to most cultures. "Art" is a peculiarly Western idea. Philosophically, this is where the American Museum of Natural History differs from an art museum: Artifacts in the Museum are displayed in their cultural context, so the visitor can understand how they were used and *what they meant*. An art museum will often display pieces more or less divorced from their historical and cultural context, because the viewer is meant to appreciate them for their aesthetic qualities alone.

An example of an "artifact" that is highly charged with

history and meaning can be found in the Plains Indians Hall at the Museum. It also shows how the histories of many artifacts have become entwined with the history of our own culture—the native culture of the anthropologist. If we look into one of the cases toward the back of the hall, we will find a ledger book of the kind made during the nineteenth century—tall and narrow, with a cloth binding and ruled pages. The book has been pierced by a bullet, and faint marks—bloodstains—are on the cover. Inside the book are drawings by a young Northern Cheyenne Indian named Little Finger Nail, depicting, in scenes of courtship and battle, the last months of his life.

This ledger was one of two given to the Museum by the estate of Joseph Cuyler Hardie. Hardie's brother Francis was a cavalry officer during the Indian wars, and he had found the bullet-pierced ledger on Little Finger Nail's body following the massacre of the Indian's tribe. He sent the two ledgers to his brother with the following letter, which has been preserved in Museum archives:

Post of San Antonio, Texas
September 21, 1889

Only the canvas covered book has any special history, the book with the bullet hole in it. It was, or rather the pictures were, drawn by a Northern Cheyenne Indian while in confinement at Fort Robinson, Nebraska during the winter of '78, '79. I was then Post Adjutant. I endeavored to get the book but its owner and maker refused to part with it for any price. So I gave the matter up. It purports to depict the deeds of several of the Northern Cheyennes during their famous march from Indian Territory to Wyoming Territory. The outbreak of the Cheyennes is well known, and [as] a consequence of the outbreak, I got the book in this manner. Four troops ... commanded by Captain Wessels, who by the way was severely wounded, surrounded the hostiles and charged upon them killing all the bucks and unfortunately in the melee, some women and children, but previous to the charge I saw an Indian with the book pressed down between his naked skin and a strap around his waist, another strap went between the middle of the book and around his shoulder. I turned to private Laselle of H troop who was near me and said, "I want that book if we come out all right." Several other of the enlisted men heard me also. When the fight was over, and as the dead Indians were being pulled out of the rifle pit, they drew out finally my Indian with the book, apparently dead; the book was injured to the extent of a carbine ball through it and was more or less covered with fresh blood. This fight took place near Bluff Station, Wyoming Territory, January 22, 1879. This fight was the closing one of a series of fights with the Indians, and they perished to a man.

> In haste,
> Frank

Little Finger Nail was probably born in the late 1850s, and came of age while the Cheyenne and other Native American tribes were engaged in the final struggle to retain what remained of their lands and way of life. The history of the ledger really begins in 1876, during the Indian Wars, when General Ranald Mackenzie surprised the settlement of Northern Cheyennes at their camp on Crazy Woman's Fork of the Powder River. Mackenzie's attack was sudden and swift, and the Cheyenne fled into the fastnesses of the Bighorn Mountains, leaving behind their winter stores, teepees, and other belongings, which Mackenzie burned. The Cheyenne were led by two chiefs, Dull Knife (also called Morning Star), and Little Wolf. That winter the Cheyennes suffered so badly from frostbite and starvation that in April 1877 the tribe voluntarily surrendered at Fort Robinson, Nebraska.

At that time the government had plans to resettle many of the Plains Indian tribes in Indian Territory (now Oklahoma), where they were to learn farming, build houses, and generally behave like the white settlers. Thus the government ordered the tribe moved south, claiming that the Cheyenne had agreed to the resettlement in a treaty signed with General Sheridan in 1868. Dull Knife protested, saying that if there was such a clause in the treaty, Sheridan had lied to them about the contents of the document. But the government insisted, and at last pressured Dull Knife into acquiescence by promising him that he and his people could return if they didn't like life in Indian Territory.

In August 1877 the Cheyenne arrived at their new home, the Darlington Agency, in present-day Oklahoma. Here they were told to settle down, live in cabins, grow crops, and in general act like the white man. But it was miserable, barren land, and the Indians were unused to this foreign way of life. Almost immediately, two-thirds of the tribe came down with malaria and other diseases. The water was bad and the rations scarce, even inedible. The government, which had promised to support the Indians until they could adjust to their new, forced way of life, couldn't even provide them with enough food to survive. Mackenzie himself—that veteran Indian fighter—protested to Washington about the terrible conditions imposed upon the Indians, and called it "a great wrong." He asserted that the Indians were "starving."

Nothing was done. The Cheyenne finally told the head of the agency, "We are sickly and dying here, and no one will speak our names when we are gone. We will go north at all hazards, and if we die in battle our names will be remembered and cherished by all our people."

At dawn on September 9, 1878, the Cheyenne carried out their plan. Led by Dull Knife and Little Wolf, most of the band decamped from the reservation and started the eight-hundred-mile journey north. Thus began the famous Cheyenne march from Indian Territory to Wyoming Territory—and the events that Little Finger Nail recorded in his ledger.

Little Wolf had been fighting white men since 1856, and he warned the younger warriors that they were not to start any battles with soldiers, or attack settlers or cowboys. Any provocative actions, he realized, would likely bring swift retribution. As the march north continued, they were attacked by soldiers again and again, the tribe fighting defensively and retreating whenever it could.

When they neared Dodge City, however, the Cheyenne were again attacked, this time by soldiers and cowboys. Although the Cheyenne repulsed the attack, many of the young warriors, including Little Finger Nail, felt angry and wanted revenge. They needed horses and food, and were tired of restraint and retreat. The next day some of them raided a cow camp, killed four whites, and captured some horses and mules. As the band moved northward, the young men continued to raid settlements north of Dodge City, especially along Sappa and Beaver creeks. There, three years earlier, buffalo hunters and soldiers had massacred Cheyenne women and children. In retaliation, Little Finger Nail and his companions shot the same number of whites as the whites had killed of Indians. In a single raid they captured over two hundred horses.

Little Finger Nail later recorded many of these incidents in his book. In one drawing we see a warrior galloping through a hail of bullets, a young man on a horse counting coup on a fallen settler, a camp of buffalo hunters, and a smiling warrior galloping off with stolen U.S. Cavalry horses. One scene depicts a major battle with government troops, probably one of several skirmishes outside Dodge City. Scattered among the battles and raids are scenes of courtship, since Little Finger Nail was apparently courting one or more of the young girls of the tribe.*

In the closing years of the Indian Wars, ledger-book Indian art became increasingly common. Earlier warrior art had usually been painted on buffalo hides and tipi covers, and represented important scenes in the life of a warrior. Some warriors painted their own scenes, but more often a warrior would ask an artist in the tribe to outline the figures in paint. He would recount to the artist the incidents he wanted depicted, giving specific details such as descriptions of horses, number of troops, and brands on captured horses and cattle. The figures would then be colored in by the warrior himself. To prepare black paint, the artist

---

*We know that most of the warriors depicted are young because their clothing is unadorned and their shirts are of white manufacture.

would mix ashes and buffalo blood; for various earth colors, he would blend different iron-bearing clays with the gluey residue of hide scrapings. When pencils, crayons, and watercolors became available, the Indians quickly adopted them, as they offered both convenience and a wider range of colors. The Indians also acquired ledger books in which to draw. From the Indians' point of view, these were superior to hides for several reasons: first, when U.S. soldiers raided Indian villages during the Indian wars, they often burned the tipis, thus destroying the buffalo hides and the artwork upon them. The ledger books, on the other hand, could be carried away to safety. More important, the Indians believed the drawings offered magical protection and—unlike hides—could be carried into battle.

The Cheyenne continued north and finally crossed the South Platte River on October 4, 1878. Here, Little Wolf and Dull Knife disagreed as to where the tribe should go. Little Wolf wanted to head farther north toward Canada, while Dull Knife wanted to go to the Red Cloud Agency, where he thought the Sioux were encamped. So the group split, and Little Finger Nail joined Dull Knife in heading toward Red Cloud.

Winter came early, and before the Cheyenne reached their destination, U.S. soldiers surprised them during a blinding snowstorm and captured the entire group. While being escorted to Fort Robinson, Nebraska, the Indians secretly took apart their best firearms and hid the parts, with ammunition, among the clothing of the women and children.

At Fort Robinson the Cheyenne were given a great deal of freedom as long as they stayed within the fort, while the fort's captain, Henry Wessels, waited for word from Washington about what to do with the Indians. It was here that Frank Hardie noticed Little Finger Nail making drawings in his ledger book.

All went well until one of the Cheyenne disappeared. Wessels immediately imprisoned all the Cheyenne in their barracks, and kept them there even after the Indian returned several days later. Meanwhile, Wessels had also received orders from General Sheridan that the Cheyenne were to go south. When Wessels relayed this message to Dull Knife, the Chief gave his famous and eloquent reply:

> All we ask is to be allowed to live, and to live in peace. I seek no war with anyone. An old man, my fighting days are done. We bowed to the will of the Great Father and went far into the south where he told us to go. There we found a Cheyenne cannot live. . . . To stay there would mean all of us would die. . . . We thought it better to die fighting to regain our old homes than to perish of sickness. Then our march was begun. You know the rest.
>
> Tell the Great Father that Dull Knife and his people ask only to end their days here in the north where they were born. Tell him we want no more war. . . . Tell him if he tries to send us back we will butcher each other with our own knives. I have spoken.

Wessels relayed Dull Knife's message to Washington and received the following reply from General Sheridan: "Unless they are sent back to where they came from, the whole reservation system will receive a shock which will endanger its stability."

When Dull Knife was told of Sheridan's response, he said: "Great Grandfather sends us death in the letter. You will have to kill us and take our bodies back down that trail. We will not go."

Wessels decided to force compliance by securely locking the Indians in one barracks and cutting off all their food, fuel, and water. What he didn't know about was the Indians' secret cache of weapons parts and ammunition. On January 8, 1879, the Indians covered the windows of the barracks with blankets, in preparation for reassembling the rifles and pistols. Thinking the Indians might be planning an escape, Wessels increased the guard on the barracks and hired a blacksmith to wrap chains across the locked doors. The Cheyenne ripped up the floorboards to make clubs, and were able to assemble twelve rifles and three pistols from the cache of parts. Then, on the evening of January 9, the Indians painted their faces and made ready for their escape.

At 9:45 P.M., two Indians, one of whom was probably Little Finger Nail, knocked out two windows and killed the sentries at the southwestern and western ends of the barracks. Within seconds, the other Indians opened fire on the guards as the rest of the tribe began climbing through the broken windows.

The soldiers were taken by surprise, but recovered quickly. As the Indians fled, the soldiers piled out of their quarters and began firing at the fleeing figures. The Indians made easy targets as they stumbled across a level snowfield in full moonlight. About half were shot down and killed almost immediately, including a large number of women and children. Wessels sent his soldiers in pursuit of the rest, who had scattered into small groups and become separated. Little Finger Nail and his group made it across White River, and fled southwest into a series of low bluffs behind the camp. They had no horses, little food, and poor clothing, and the weather was bitter cold. Despite these handicaps, they managed to evade the cavalry soldiers (who were on horseback) for almost two weeks.

On the thirteenth day, however, they realized that escape was hopeless. They had only managed to put thirty-five miles between Fort Robinson and themselves, and were just across the border in Wyoming Territory. The soldiers were fast closing in. The Indians determined to make a last stand at a dry streambed along the edge of a bluff. Uncharacteristically, they chose a poor defensive position; the soldiers had a clear line of fire, and the Cheyenne did little to conceal their presence other than piling up sod and digging a few shallow rifle pits in the frozen earth.

The pursuing soldiers—Frank Hardie among them— quickly discovered the hideout. As Hardie mentions in his letter, he was close enough to identify Little Finger Nail before the battle.

Wessels gave the order to fire, and the soldiers charged to the edge of the streambed, firing directly into the scattered shrubbery, rifle pits, and crude breastworks that hid the Cheyenne. They charged again and again, all the while saturating the streambed with fire. For an hour the greatly outnumbered Indians—a total of thirty-one men, women, and children—fought back with what little ammunition they had. The soldiers continued firing until return fire from the Indians had ceased. Wessels then ordered a cease-fire and approached the edge of the streambed. The Indians were scattered about and all appeared to be dead. Suddenly a warrior looked up and fired directly at Wessels with what must have been his last bullet, striking him in the head. The captain fell back, gravely wounded, and was carried off while the soldiers resumed peppering the hollow with fire for another quarter of an hour. Finally the soldiers paused and approached the streambed. Within moments, three bloody warriors leaped up and, armed only with knives, charged at the troops. They were promptly shot down.

Once more the nervous soldiers crept up to the side of the streambed. Only a few badly wounded women and children were alive; all the rest had perished. Many had been literally riddled with bullets.

When the soldiers had hauled the last of the corpses out of the dry streambed, Hardie untied the ledger book from Little Finger Nail's body. During the saturation fire, a carbine ball had passed clean through it. The Museum received the ledger in 1912, and put it on display in 1934. We can still see it there today: a young Cheyenne man's remarkable account of the last days of his great people.

## Faces from the Past

While looking at artifacts from the other side of a thick sheet of glass, it is hard for us to keep in mind the human beings that created them. There is, however, one collection in the Museum that, at least to me, suddenly brought home this fact. It is a collection where one comes literally face to face with the people who created these artifacts. We reach this particular collection, which is stored in an attic vault underneath a Museum rooftop, by climbing up a narrow flight of stairs from the Anthropology Department's fifth-floor offices. As we ascend the staircase, the incongruous sound of a mountain waterfall comes echoing down, created by water circulating in a sprinkler tank. At the top of the stairs is the tank itself, guarded by a grotesque wooden statue of a woman—carved by the Northwest Coast Indians a century ago—and a pile of silent, slit-log drums.

The tower attic room to the right, illuminated by ancient skylights, contains the Museum's large collection of life casts.* Shelf after shelf is lined with the plaster busts of actual people who once lived—Indians, Siberians, Eskimos, Patagonians, even Museum presidents and trustees. They look out over the garret room with blank eyes. Each cast is identified when relevant by tribe, and sometimes by name as well. Here is the face of Mene Wallace as a small child, wrapped in protective plastic, staring out sightlessly. Next to Mene is his father, Kissug, who died of tuberculosis while in New York, and a cast of the Eskimo who returned to Greenland and told of what he saw, only to be nicknamed—as we've seen—"The Big Liar." Here we can also make out casts identified as Mrs. Lost Horse, Thomas Pretty Back, Ghost Face, and Maggie Old Eagle—all Oglala Sioux. On another shelf rests Lumbango, a Congo Bahumba; Annie McKay, a Tlingit Indian; Shenandoah, an Oneida Indian; Bonifacio, a Patagonian; and hundreds of others. In the far corner is a stack of cast arms and legs, looking like a broken heap of dolls. These were cast from life in various positions—flexed, extended, relaxed, gripping imaginary objects, and so forth.

Most of these life casts were collected in the field around the turn of the century by various scientists and explorers, including Franz Boas, Waldemar Borgoras (on the Jesup North Pacific Expedition), and Casper Mayer.

The life casts arrived at the Museum along with the

*Anthropologists made life casts of the faces, and then sculpted the eyes, hair, ornaments, and shoulders to make a conventional bust portrait.

other collections. During this period, the Museum cast copies of the busts for other institutions for twelve dollars each. The faces became useful not only for research, but for model-making and Museum exhibitions. In the Plains Indians Hall, for example, the creased and melancholy faces of once-living men and women gaze imperturbably out of glass cases. Other real faces can be seen in the Hall of Eastern Woodland Indians, the Hall of Eskimos, and the Hall of Asian Peoples.

And, in what is perhaps the most comprehensive use of life casts in a Museum exhibition, the great Haida canoe at the 77th Street entrance to the Museum is propelled by figures whose faces are life casts of Northwest Coast Indians. The Norwegian-American sculptor Sigurd Neandross was commissioned by the Museum in 1908 to create the figures for this canoe. He not only took casts from some of the faces Franz Boas had collected along the Northwest Coast, but he also made body casts of willing volunteers.* Since the weight of plaster distorts soft parts of the body, Neandross began by covering a subject's entire body with paraffin to create a stiff base for the plaster, working from the feet to the head. But before applying the paraffin, he placed threads strategically along the body so that when the plaster had just begun to set on top of the paraffin, he could draw the strings and cut the mold into parts. To complete the illusion of reality, he even made casts of blankets, clothes, and other ceremonial objects for the canoe.

These melancholy, peaceful faces will continue to remind us that real people created the artifacts on display, and that these people and many of the cultures they came from no longer exist. The Museum tried to preserve everything it could—even the faces of the people themselves. But what it could not save were the actual cultures—those

*This practice of making life casts—often by attaching real but ethnically incorrect bodies to correct faces—continues to this day. In the Asian Hall, the faces of several nineteenth-century Yakut are attached to casts made from the body of a young curatorial assistant in the Anthropology Department. Another figure was made out of the head and hands of a Buddhist monk who is still very much alive.

intricate systems of belief, tradition, technology, morals, religion, and habit that make all of us human.

## Mummies

We can't take leave of the Museum's vast anthropology collections without touching on that most fascinating section—the mummies. Recently, mummies have become a problem for the Museum, and at the present time none are on public exhibition. Most natural history museums around the country have faced strong protests from Native Americans and other groups of people who—with good reason —object to the displaying of the remains of their people. Thus, when the Margaret Mead Hall of Pacific Peoples opened in 1984, the Museum decided not to include the Maori shrunken heads.

The Museum's Hall of South American Peoples, slated to open in the late 1980s, may be the only hall that will display human remains. The Museum's most famous mummy—the Copper Man—may be featured in the hall, along with Jívaro Indian shrunken heads and possibly an example of the Peruvian "mummy bundle," a burial in which the body was interred in a flexed position and wrapped in cloth.

At present, we can find most of the mummies stored together in a single room, in large black metal boxes. These human remains include mummy bundles from the Americas, trophy heads wrapped in exquisite textiles, and several dozen Egyptian mummy heads loaned by the Metropolitan Museum of Art over half a century ago. Not everything is hidden away, however; resting in one glass case is the Copper Man, a striking sight indeed.

It is not hard to see how he got his name. The mummy is dark green, and oozing fluids have created the illusion of a shiny metallic surface over parts of the body. Unlike other mummified corpses, which look shriveled, the Copper Man shows few signs of shrinkage and looks quite fresh indeed. You can actually see the details of his musculature and facial features. His hair is neatly braided, and he wears two strips of coarse cloth as a loin covering.

The history of the Copper Man was pieced together some years ago by the late Junius Bird, a Museum curator. The story is long and quite involved, beginning almost a century ago at a small mineral claim at Chuquicamata, Chile, known as the Restaradora Mine. The body was discovered wedged in a collapsed shaft along with his tools—four coiled baskets, a stone hammer, and a stone shovel. He was certainly a pre-Conquest Indian who had been removing copper ore from the shallow hole by hammering and prying out pieces of rock. Apparently the ceiling of the narrow crawlspace he was in suddenly shifted, pinning the poor miner down. His arms were still extended in a working position, and his hand clutched one of the coiled baskets, which he was apparently filling with ore.

The Museum's accession file for the mummy contains a most interesting letter giving much of the history of the Copper Man. Dated June 18, 1912, the letter is from a man named Edward Jackson—who for a time owned the mummy, much to his later regret—to a Mr. F. D. Aller. According to the letter, the discovery of the mummy started an argument between the American owner of the mine, William Matthews, and the Frenchman who was renting it, a Mr. Pidot. Both claimed ownership of the mummy. To bolster his claim, Pidot had a piece of the body assayed—and it turned out to be almost one percent copper. Pidot declared the mummy was his because it was copper ore; Matthews replied that he had rented the *mine*, but not the *miners*. Edward Jackson (the writer of the letter) happened to be in Chuquicamata when the mummy was unearthed and immediately offered $500 for it, but was turned down. About a year later, after Matthews and Pidot had worked out a deal for splitting the profits, Jackson was finally able to buy the mummy for $1,000. He arranged for it to be shipped back to his house in Antofagasta, Chile. "When I received it in Antofagasta," Jackson reported in his letter, "it was already minus a toe which I think someone cut off in Chuquicamata for a keepsake." With characteristic Yankee enterprise, Jackson set up the mummy in his house and charged admission to sightseers. Later, one of Jackson's friends, Perez de Arce, offered to take the mummy on tour of several Chilean cities and split the profits with Jackson.

"It was exhibited in Valparaiso and Santiago," Jackson wrote, "and then I began to get offers. As I never saw any of the profits I decided to sell it through my brother, John Stewart Jackson, who eventually did so to two gentlemen who formed a society, 'Torres y Tornero,' for the sum of $15,000 Chilean, this sum to be paid $5,000 in cash and $10,000 in two months."

The two men, Torres and Tornero, brought the Copper Man to the United States for the Pan-American Exposition in Buffalo. After a prolonged hassle with U.S. customs officials (who took a dim view of letting a mummy enter the country), the two men put the Copper Man on exhibition from May 1 to November 2, 1901. To stir up interest, they printed a pamphlet entitled "Human Petrification: The Only Specimen in Existence of a Perfectly Preserved Body from a Race which is Now Entirely Extinct."

During the exhibition, excited spectators swarmed into the Chilean Pavilion, sometimes climbing over the railings and standing on the furniture to get a better look at the green mummy. At one point the police had to rope off the exhibit after the mummy's glass case was shattered by the frantic press of the crowds. After the Pan-American Exposition closed, Torres and Tornero put the mummy up for sale at a fantastic price, expecting to become rich men, but there were no takers. As their stay in the United States lengthened, they sank deeper into debt until one of their creditors seized the mummy as security against an unpaid debt. The two had to return home with their passages paid by the Chilean consulate in New York.

Jackson was still owed the $10,000 for the mummy, and it was legally his if he could satisfy the U.S. creditor. He wrote in his letter to Aller:

When Mr. Raimundo Docekal of Antofagasta went to the States, I gave him my power of Attorney to recover it and gave him $500 U.S. gold. He was shipwrecked in the Straits of Magellan but arrived in New York. From New York I had several encouraging letters from him but when he began to ask for more money, I refused to send him any. He then made some sort of an arrangement with the creditor, cancelled the $10,000 still owing me and sold it in New York and never sent me a cent.

I looked for him when I was in New York but found it rather too big a place to find him.

Jackson then concluded his letter on a philosophical note:

My books show that I received $2,500 and paid out about $2,300 so that I made only $200 on it, and I came to the conclusion that it is a sin to deal in dead men's bodies, and shall not do so again.

Mummies went up terribly in the market after our find.

Kind regards to Mrs. Aller.

Yours very sincerely,
Edward Jackson

The Copper Man apparently bounced around New York for a time, and was finally bought by J. P. Morgan in 1905, who gave it to the Museum. How much Morgan paid for the mummy is a mystery, but records show that the owner was asking $100,000 for it. (He probably got only a small fraction of that amount.) The proud Director of the Museum put the Copper Man on display almost immediately. A good deal of publicity surrounded the opening, and the mistaken notion arose that the mummy was female, probably because of the braided hair. One 1905 newspaper headline shouted, "Aged 3,000, But She Has Traces of Beauty." (In the years that followed, scholarly opinion held that the mummy dated from around 1200 A.D.)

In 1923 the first complete X-ray photograph was made

of the body, and it was discovered that no bones were broken. Junius Bird theorized that the weight of the ceiling pinned the miner and forced blood into the extremities, accounting for the remarkably lifelike preservation of the body. If the skin had dried and hardened while in a distended condition, the normal shrinkage that takes place during mummification would not have occurred. ("When an entomologist wishes to preserve certain larvae," Bird wrote by way of comparison, "he will inflate the skin and dry it quickly in a heated oven.") The Atacama Desert of Chile, where the miner was found, is one of the driest and hottest places on earth.

In 1953 two scientists drilled out cores from the body for study, and discovered that the copper oxides, which gave the body its greenish cast, hadn't penetrated any deeper than the skin. The mummy itself was hollow, apparently another result of rapid dessication.

In the late 1970s, various parts of the body were carbon-dated to determine its age, and to everyone's surprise the Copper Man turned out to be much older than had been thought—having died around 484 A.D., about the time of the fall of the Roman Empire.

The Copper Man was removed from public view in 1967, when the old South American Hall closed. There is sure to be a spirited debate about whether or not he should go back on display when the new hall opens. But perhaps this author's views on the matter are best mirrored by a statement Bird himself made, just before he died. "Mining," he said, "has always been a hazardous occupation. This poor fellow was killed while working with the most primitive tools under extremely difficult conditions. I feel that if he had anything to say about it he would prefer that people see him as he is so they may better understand what was involved in the making of tools, weapons, ornaments, and other metal products before Europeans came to the Americas."

# SIXTEEN

# Harry Shapiro and Peking Man

Not all that goes on in the Anthropology Department is straight anthropology. As in many of the scientific departments, the dozen curators of anthropology often find themselves answering unusual questions and helping various people solve very unusual problems.

One of the "invisible" services the Museum performs is answering all these questions. Robert Carneiro, for example—an expert on South American peoples—finds himself examining a half-dozen "shrunken heads" every year, brought in by hopeful collectors. "They're all fakes," he says. An assistant in the Invertebrates Department helped the police solve a major theft by identifying the source of rocks that had been used to fill crates that were supposed to hold electronic equipment. (He helped solve a similar case by identifying where a load of sand came from.) The insect department, as we've seen, routinely assists people (and restaurants) in eradicating cockroach infestations. And, of course, there is an endless stream of other requests to identify one thing or another—so many, in fact, that the Museum hosts an annual "Identification Day" on which people bring in all sorts of items for Museum curators to identify. The Museum has a policy of answering every letter it receives, no matter how offbeat. (Rest assured that some are indeed *quite* strange.)

One Museum curator has spent much of his sixty-year career at the Museum doing just such *pro bono* work. Some, in fact, credit his early work with laying the foundation of forensic anthropology, which has since become a highly refined science studied by medical examiners all over the country.

This curator, Harry Shapiro, joined the Museum's staff as a physical anthropologist in 1926. He had previously studied physical anthropology under Earnest Hooton at Harvard, where he learned how to extract a great deal of information from human bones. By examining a skeleton, Shapiro is able to deduce such things as height, weight, sex, age, and race, as well as certain kinds of diseases that affect the bones. His research at the Museum focuses on the genetics of various groups and the physical differences between races. (His lifelong research project involves the European mutineers of the *Bounty*, who took Tahitian wives and settled on Pitcairn Island, where their descendants live today. It presented Shapiro with what almost amounted to a laboratory for studying the mixing of races.)

Shapiro had been at the Museum only a few years when he received his first fateful call from a desperate medical examiner. The case involved a complete skeleton, and Shapiro identified the individual's characteristics with ease.

"That started it," Shapiro recalls. "Whenever they ran into human material, they would call me up." In this way, almost by accident, Shapiro became involved in the practice of forensic anthropology. During World War II, the U.S. government asked him to draw up guidelines for the identification of the unknown dead. The government had recently passed a law that all U.S. servicemen who had been buried overseas must be brought home. Many of the bodies were unidentified, and Shapiro devised a set of procedures for identifying these remains. They asked Shapiro himself to examine particularly difficult cases. For these, the body would be shipped to the Brooklyn Navy Yard and a limousine would be dispatched to Shapiro's house early in the morning. He would then spend the pre-noon hours examining the remains, looking for telltale clues that might aid in identification. "It was a hideous, hideous job," Shapiro says. "But I feel strongly that a scientist should be available to help people with his expertise."

Perhaps Shapiro's most famous case occurred in a highly publicized murder of the early 1950s. One day he received a telephone call from the New York City medical examiner's office. They were working on a difficult missing-person case, and needed the benefit of his skill. This particular case, however, turned out to be one of the most difficult he had ever worked on. It concerned the disappearance and suspected murder of a little girl in the Bronx. The police had very little to go on, since no body had been found, but they had reason to suspect the apartment building's janitor of having raped and murdered her. The police had one clue: for three days after the girl's disappearance, residents in the building had noticed and complained about excessive heat coming from the coal-burning furnace in the basement. So the police shut down the furnace and sifted through the ashes for bones—human bones. Because all of the building's garbage was burned in the furnace, they came up with five large ashcans full of tiny, charred bone fragments—but bones of *what*?

The medical examiner's office was called in. They in turn contacted Shapiro, and asked him to go through the garbage cans and identify any human bones that might be there. Shapiro spent days and days examining bone fragments, and finally discovered three unmistakably human bones: a fragment of eye socket, a finger bone, and a tiny piece of pelvis. From those he was able to deduce that the bones were from a girl perhaps ten years of age. It was enough to convict the janitor of murder.

Shapiro has been called upon for help in another area as well—the so-called ashcan babies. This work began over thirty years ago, when he received a call from a lawyer representing a black woman who had had several children by a Chinese man. The man had abandoned her, claiming the children weren't his, and she was suing him for child support. The lawyer wanted to know if Shapiro could provide legal evidence of paternity. Shapiro testified on behalf of the woman, and she won her case. The lawyer asked Shapiro to testify in a second, similar case, which also concluded successfully. Since two cases established this new type of testimony as a legal precedent, the lawyer published the procedure in a law journal. Immediately afterwards, Shapiro was deluged with calls about paternity problems all over the country, and he was forced to restrict such work to New York City alone.

One of his most striking cases occurred in the early 1960s. He was approached by a Jewish couple who had lived with their small son in Poland in the years before World War II. When the Nazis came to power, the couple fled Poland, but because of their fear of capture they left their baby with a nurse who took him to the country, where they hoped the child would be safe. When the war ended the parents could find no trace of the nurse or their child, and they eventually settled in the United States. After the war they had a second child, this one born in the United States. This boy was about sixteen years old when Shapiro saw the family for the first time.

The couple explained their problem to Shapiro. A close relative of theirs had gone to Poland and had seen a young man on the street who bore an uncanny resemblance to the couple's second son. The relative stopped the man on the street and asked him who he was. The man explained that he had been one of the "forest children" who were found wandering in the Polish woods at the end of the war, many of whom were children of Jews who had been sent to concentration camps. The young man was about the same age as the couple's missing older son. They gave Shapiro a picture of the man, and the only picture they had of their young baby, and asked if he could tell whether they were one and the same person.

"I told them if would be very difficult to make a judgment from the picture because of the age differences involved," says Shapiro. "But the wife was so emotional that I said I would try."

He looked at the pictures for several days, and at last—just when he was about to give up hope of solving the mystery—he noticed the ears of both individuals. "Some people have attached earlobes and some don't," Shapiro explains, "a characteristic that does not change from birth to death." In one picture the earlobe was detached, and in the other it was clearly attached. There could be no question—these could only be two different people.

"I told the wife and she was devastated," he recalls. "She refused to believe it. So she sent money to the young man and brought him to the States, and all three of them came to the Museum. We had a long emotional meeting in my office where I explained that the man could not be their son, and they finally accepted it.

"'But,' I said to the woman, 'since you care so much about this young man, and since he has no family, why *don't* you adopt him as your son?' Which is exactly what they did."

Shapiro's detective work is not confined to solving murder, paternity, and missing-persons cases. Since 1971 he has been on the track of the greatest missing person of all—the lost fossil remains of Peking Man (*Sinanthropus pekinensis*), which disappeared during the Japanese invasion of China at the beginning of World War II. The bones (actually those of about forty individuals, not just one) provided rare evidence of an early stage of human evolution, and their loss was an unparalleled disaster in the study of hominid fossils; even though the Chinese have discovered new *Sinanthropus* bones, they are not nearly as complete as the original ones.

Peking Man belongs to the extinct hominid species

*Homo erectus*. While *Homo erectus* fossils have also been discovered in Java, Africa, and Germany, the Peking Man fossils represent a variant in the species, the study of which is critical to our understanding of this stage of human evolution, intermediate between the Australopithecines and our species, *Homo sapiens*.

Shapiro was a graduate student when the fossils were unearthed in the 1920s. The discovery made quite a sensation, as early hominid fossils have always been extremely rare. Later, in 1931, Shapiro traveled to China and became friendly with Davidson Black, who was the custodian of the fossils at the Peking Union Medical College. Shapiro spent several hours examining the fossils himself.

Black died in 1933, and was succeeded by the famous German anatomist, Franz Weidenreich. By the summer of 1941 the situation in China had become very bad, and, unable to continue his research, Weidenreich left Peking and came to New York, leaving the Peking Man fossils behind. Weidenreich joined the staff of the American Museum, where he and Shapiro became close friends. "I remember one day," Shapiro says, "he came into my office in great despair. The fossils had disappeared."

Aside from a number of unreliable stories, an almost complete lack of information surrounded the disappearance until 1971, when Shapiro was contacted by William T. Foley, a prominent New York heart specialist. Foley had been a doctor in the Marine Corps and was stationed in Tientsin in 1941, and he was able to give Shapiro some new information about the fossils. In November 1971, Shapiro recounted the story in an article in *Natural History* magazine, which made front-page news across the country and reopened the search for the fossils. Six months later, Shapiro got a call from Christopher Janus, a man who had just returned from China. The director of a new museum at Zhou Goudian (Chou Kou Tien) in China, where the fossils had been discovered, had heard about the *Natural History* article, and had entreated Janus to do all he could to recover the fossils.

Janus returned to the States and immediately posted a

$5,000 reward for information leading to the recovery of the fossils. Janus enlisted Shapiro's help, and they followed up on the many leads the offer generated.

"A strange story with an offer of reward," Shapiro says, "is bound to attract, shall we say, imaginative people. There was one story about the bones hidden in a cabin high in the California hills. We had a countess living in New Jersey claiming she had seen the fossils. It was one damn thing after another."

In 1974, Shapiro published *Peking Man*, recounting the story of the fossils and their disappearance. Although so far all leads have turned up nothing, just recently new information about the fossils has surfaced. If the information is correct—and Shapiro believes it is—then he knows where in China the fossils might be buried. "I'm reluctant to talk about this now," he says, "because I'm still discussing it with the Chinese. It may well turn out to be nothing, like so many other leads. I can only investigate it with the complete knowledge and cooperation of the Chinese. After all, the fossils are theirs."

In the basement of the Museum, in a dingy corridor between the metal shop and the carpentry shop, is a curious grouping of six thick steel pillars that pierce the ceiling above and are sunk into the floor below. One floor above, resting on these supports, is the massive Ahnighito meteorite, the largest recovered meteorite in the world—the meteorite that Peary salvaged with such difficulty. Its density and mass are so great that without these pillars anchored into the living rock under the Museum, the Ahnighito would drop right through the floor.

The Ahnighito sits in the middle of the Arthur Ross Hall of Meteorites in the Museum. Surrounding the brown, scarred form of the meteorite, like a crowd of lesser officials, are the dark shapes of irons, stones, tektites, and other extraterrestrial visitors.

Until recently the Museum could claim it owned pieces from over half of all known meteorites. (A group of scientists have recently discovered thousands of new meteorites on the glaciers of Antarctica, which in a few years doubled the number of known meteorites.) Meteorites on display in the hall include an iron studded with tiny diamonds,* a piece from the oldest documented fall, and the meteorite that, after it fell several centuries ago, convinced the scientific world of an extraterrestrial origin for these objects. Also in the hall are several other meteorites discovered by Admiral Peary, as well as a rare stony-iron that was used for years to hold down the cover of a rain barrel, and a meteorite that one enterprising farmer tried to chop in half with his ax (the broken ax blade remains embedded in it to this day).

Meteorites have always fascinated mankind, and their dramatic descents to earth have been reported since Roman times and documented since the fifteenth century.† A document in the town archives of Ensisheim, Germany, records the first fall for which we still have the meteorite (a four-ounce piece of which is in the hall):

> On the sixteenth of November, 1492, a singular miracle happened: for between eleven and twelve in the forenoon, with a loud crash of thunder and a prolonged noise heard afar off, there fell in the town of Ensisheim a stone weighing 260 pounds. It was seen by a child to strike the ground in a field near the canton called Gisgaud, where it made a hole more than five feet deep. It was taken to the church as being a miraculous object.

---

*The diamonds were discovered by a gem expert at Tiffany's when his cutting blade was stopped by a small inclusion while he was slicing the meteorite. He found many such inclusions, and to test whether they were indeed diamonds, he removed one, pulverized it, and cemented the dust to a gem-faceting wheel. He then tried to facet a diamond with the wheel, as diamond dust is the only material that is hard enough to facet a diamond. As he touched the diamond to the wheel, he heard that "peculiar singing sound" which can only be made by a diamond cutting another diamond.

†A meteor is a bit of extraterrestrial material that burns up in the earth's atmosphere. If it reaches the ground it becomes a meteorite. While in outer space, these objects are referred to as meteoroids, or asteroids if they are very large. A meteoroid that explodes while streaking through the earth's atmosphere is called a bolide.

The noise was heard so distinctly at Lucerne, Villing, and many other places, that in each of them it was thought that some houses had fallen. King Maximilian, who was then at Ensisheim, had the stone carried to the castle; after breaking off two pieces, one for the Duke Sigismund of Austria and the other for himself, he forebade further damage, and ordered that the stone be suspended in the parish church.

A much later document, this one written by a farmer named J. K. Freed, reports the descent of another Museum meteorite, called the Modoc after the name of the Kansas town near which it fell:

The meteorite appeared as a ball of fire in the west September 12, 1905, at ten o'clock in the evening, the sky being cloudless and the clear atmosphere of the plains being undisturbed by wind. From Scott City to Syracuse, seventy-five miles to the southwest, it was light enough to read common newspaper print on the street and the explosions rattled doors and windows. The mass exploded, and then the resulting fragments exploded several times in rapid succession. Then came the sounds of the explosions, the whistling like bullets or heavy hail of the smaller fragments and a most intense humming like that of a rapidly revolving cylinder of some heavy machine, evidently caused by the larger mass.* This was followed by fierce cannonading (echoes of the explosions?) like the discharge of a battery of artillery or a rapid-fire machine gun, gradually growing fainter and dying out like rolling thunder in the distance. I heard the largest one drop and hunted for it for over two years.

On May 6, 1908, I was breaking ground on the prairie with a gang plow and a five-horse team that was a little too high-spirited to be controlled easily, but having half-mile furrows as smooth as a lawn before me, I had set the plow a few notches deeper into the ground

---

*This humming or singing noise is often noted by witnesses. It is caused by the irregular fragments spinning rapidly as they descend.

and let them go, thinking nothing of meteorites. While congratulating myself upon our speed we suddenly—very suddenly—struck something hard. It threw me out of my seat and piled my gang plow up in a promiscuous heap against the team, which was too badly surprised to do anything. I commenced stabbing with my jackknife and soon located the cause of the disturbance. It was the largest fragment of the Modoc meteorite and completely buried under the tough buffalo sod (virgin soil) and was pounded in so hard that the force of the blow of my gang plow had not loosened it. So completely was it buried, that I had hunted dozens of times all over that pasture without either finding the rock or the hole in the ground which it had made.

Yet another account tells of the fall of a meteorite called the Rose City, as witnessed by a Mrs. George Hall of Rose City, Michigan:

[On October 17, 1921, at 11:00 P.M.] I saw it very light out of doors and heard a roaring sound and then three loud explosions. I thought it was an airship and it was dropping some bombs or something of that character. I jumped up and ran to the door, and the big light was disappearing in the south. The roaring itself was not so very loud, but the explosions were very loud indeed, and while I stood in the doorway watching the disappearing light, I distinctly heard a sound like fine singing.

Although these accounts are fascinating, nothing can quite compare with the amusing and outrageous story of the Museum's Willamette meteorite, the largest ever found in the United States. The Willamette (pronounced Will-*lam*-ette) is certainly the oddest-looking meteorite in the Museum—or perhaps anywhere. Most meteorites are shapeless lumps, but this sixteen-ton chunk of nickel-iron is pitted with huge cavities; a famous photograph taken in 1911 shows two children sitting inside the meteorite. Contrary to popular belief, the pits were not caused by its fiery descent through the atmosphere, but by centuries of rusting away in a damp Oregonian forest.*

In the fall of 1902, a Welsh immigrant named Ellis Hughes discovered an odd, partly buried rock about three-quarters of a mile from his property in the Willamette Valley in Oregon. The next day, Hughes confided his discovery to a neighbor, William Dale, and showed him the rock. By chance, Dale struck it with a stone, and it gave off, to their astonishment, a ringing sound. Since both men were miners, they immediately recognized it for what it was—an iron meteorite. They hid it under a pile of fir boughs and started discussing how they could secure the meteorite for themselves. The problem was that the land it lay on was owned (ironically) by the Oregon Iron and Steel Company. They decided to keep the discovery secret and buy the land on which it lay. Dale went off to eastern Oregon to sell some property to raise the necessary capital.

For some reason, Dale never returned. After many months, Hughes' wife began nagging him about the meteorite, telling him to do something before someone else found it. Without the necessary money, Hughes' only other option quickly became obvious: he had to steal the meteorite.

Purloining a 32,000-pound chunk of iron is not an easy task. In August 1903, Hughes began excavating the huge meteorite. Working in great secrecy with the crudest of tools, he was assisted only by his teenage son and an old horse. After digging around the sixteen-ton mass, they jacked and levered it out of the hole onto a primitive flatbed cart they had built entirely of logs, using tree-trunk sections for wheels. The resourceful Welshman then rigged up a capstan device for hauling the cart. The capstan consisted of a post sunken into the ground, attached to a steel cable. Hughes harnessed his horse to the capstan so that the horse, by walking around in endless circles, caused the cable to wind up around the post, inching the cart and

---

*Meteorites, like most metallic objects, rust. It takes anywhere from several thousand to a million years for an iron meteorite to rust into a brown pile of shingles. The meteorites that have survived the longest on the earth come from Antarctica, where they have been frozen for 900,000 years.

meteorite forward. Since the ground was spongy, Hughes had to lay down a roadway of wooden planks. After every hundred feet of progress, the capstan had to be dug up and moved another hundred feet forward, a new clearing made for the horse, and the roadway dug up and relaid.

Hughes and his son labored for three backbreaking months to move the iron the three-quarters of a mile to his house. During this time his secrecy had been so effective that his neighbors later said they had no idea that anything out of the ordinary was going on. When it finally arrived, Hughes built a shack around it, announced he had found it—on his property, of course—and started charging twenty-five cents admission to view the heavenly visitor.

One of Hughes' early customers, unfortunately, was the attorney for the Oregon Iron and Steel Company. He had somehow deduced that the meteorite had been stolen from the company—probably by following the conspicuous trail back to the large pit on company property.* The attorney told Hughes he knew damn well the meteorite belonged to his client, but as a matter of courtesy and to avoid a lawsuit, he would graciously offer the miner fifty dollars for it. Hughes threw the man out. The lawyer then filed suit on behalf of the company to get the meteorite back, and the case went to court.

Hughes fought long and bitterly, and he seems to have genuinely believed that the meteorite was rightly his. The miner's lawyer chose a novel defense. First he put several elderly Indians on the witness stand who testified that long ago the meteorite had belonged to their tribe. They said it had fallen from the moon and was a sacred object to the tribe. To ensure success in battle, the Indians testified, they used to dip their arrows in the puddles of rainwater that collected in its cavities. In addition, young braves were sent to the sacred stone in the dead of night to undergo secret initiation rituals. Hughes' lawyer presented this as

*This pit was so large that half a century later a Museum curator visited the site and reported that the hole was still there, sprinkled with rusty iron shingles and flakes.

solid evidence that the Indians—not the company—had the prior claim of ownership.

Then the lawyer tried to cloud the issue of "ownership" of an object that had fallen from the sky. He argued that the meteorite might have fallen somewhere else and been carried to the company's land by the glaciers. Whose was it then? Or the Indians may have transported it from somewhere else. The lawyer concluded that the ownership issue was so tangled that the meteorite could only belong to the discoverer, Ellis Hughes.

The company, on the other hand, simply asserted that Hughes had deliberately and egregiously stolen the meteorite from them. They wanted it back.

The court found for the plaintiff. Immediately after the verdict, the victorious company sent a team of horses to Hughes' property and started hauling away the iron. Hughes frantically appealed the verdict to the state supreme court, and managed to get an injunction just as the meteorite was being hauled away. The company hired a twenty-four-hour guard who sat on top of the meteorite with a loaded gun while the case was being appealed.

Meanwhile, Hughes' next-door neighbor started another lawsuit, this one directed at both Hughes and the company. The neighbor contended that the meteorite had, in fact, been stolen from *his* land. To buttress his case he showed investigators a huge crater on his land, which he claimed had been caused by the meteorite's fall. The case was dismissed when the man's neighbors reported that they had heard a great deal of blasting being done on his property only the week before.

On July 17, 1905, the state supreme court upheld the earlier ruling and awarded the meteorite to the Oregon Iron and Steel Company. The company carted it off to Portland, where it was unveiled with great fanfare at the Lewis and Clark Exposition in a ceremony attended by the governor. It was announced that this—the largest *American* meteorite—would forever remain in Oregon, its home state.

When the exposition closed, however, the Oregon Iron

and Steel Company, unmoved by this patriotic rhetoric, sold it to Mrs. William Dodge for $20,600, who gave it to the American Museum of Natural History. It was the highest price paid up to that time for a single specimen in the Museum's collection. Visitors will find this massive iron on the first floor of the Museum's Hayden Planetarium, where children still climb into its holes.

Meteorites have quaint names; in the Hall we find the Wold Cottage, the Canyon Diablo, the Krasnojarsk, the Guffey, the L'Aigle, and many more. Meteorites are normally named after the place where they fell. One of these, named Allende, is perhaps the most important meteorite fragment in the collection. Ironically, it is by appearance among the least interesting, looking more as if it came from a vacant urban lot than from outer space. It is small, gray, and utterly common. But its lack of distinction hides at least one startling fact: it is the oldest thing on earth. Indeed, it is slightly *older* than the earth, the sun, and all the planets, older than the solar system itself. As a result, one scientist has described this meteorite as possibly being more important scientifically than all the collected moon rocks put together.

In the early morning hours of February 8, 1969, a brilliant bolide flashed across the sky and illuminated almost one million square miles of Mexico and the Southwestern United States. High above the state of Chihuahua, Mexico, the bolide exploded in a series of sonic booms, and thousands of dark gray rocks—just like the one in the hall—rained down on a one-hundred-square-mile area near the Rio del Valle de Allende.

Over the next few days, scientists, local peasants, private collectors, commercial rock dealers, and museum curators all converged on the Allende Valley and began a mad search for the peculiar dark stones. Four tons of the fragments were eventually recovered, making it the largest stony meteorite known at that time. Bits and pieces were dispatched to laboratories and museums all over the world. Large chunks were sliced up like loaves of bread and stud-

ied under microscopes and electron microprobes,* and
with X-ray diffraction machinery, mass spectrometers, and
other equipment. Meteorite scientists had never had it so
good.

As examination of the Allende progressed, it soon became apparent that it was no ordinary meteorite.

Scientists have known since the early 1950s that most
meteorites formed at about the same time as the earth and
other planets. While the earth has melted, cooled, eroded,
and metamorphosed, erasing the evidence of its early history, meteorites have remained virtually unchanged for 4.5
billion years. Thus, by studying meteorites, scientists can
gather information about the earliest history of the solar
system. The Allende, at first, looked like any other meteorite seen under a microscope. Prominent in it were many
white fragments and some spherical droplets (called inclusions and chondrules respectively) embedded in the meteorite's dark matrix. But when the composition of these
inclusions was analyzed, they were found to contain unusual minerals. The scientists theorized that this was a particularly early meteorite—and that the inclusions had once
actually been partly molten droplets floating in the primitive cloud that would eventually form the solar system.
Thus, they had to be a little older than the solar system
itself, which put their age at slightly more than 4.5 billion
years.

In 1973 a University of Chicago scientist, Robert Clayton, made an even more startling discovery. In the frozen
fragments he found some isotopes that had never been seen
in nature. These once-radioactive elements could only have
been formed by an exploding star—a supernova.

Clayton followed his discovery to its logical conclusion.
He decided that the current theory about the formation of
the solar system was inadequate. This theory hypothesized
that a large cloud of gas and dust had slowly contracted,
gradually forming the sun and planets. Instead, Clayton

---

*An electron microprobe is a device that determines the composition of a speci-
men by bombarding it with a beam of electrons.

theorized that the solar system began when a dying star suddenly exploded in a supernova. The expanding shock wave plowed into a nearby dust cloud, heating the cloud and reducing its size. Molten droplets and fragments condensed out of the cloud, gradually coalescing to form the planets. Meanwhile, under gravitational attraction, a large pool of hydrogen gas was forming at the center of the cloud. This cloud would, in time, contract to form the sun. Had it not been for the chance explosion of this nearby supernova (a very rare event), we would still—according to this theory—be a cloud of diffuse gas, floating in empty space.

The Allende, like most other meteorites, comes from the asteroid belt that lies between Mars and Jupiter. For some reason, the planet-forming process failed in this zone. Instead of one planet, a number of tiny planetesimals came into being. Hundreds of these tiny planets melted and cooled, with heavier minerals like metallic iron sinking to the core and lighter compounds like silicates rising to the surface. Many small planets formed, and over millions of years they jostled and bumped into each other, eventually breaking up into thousands of jagged fragments. These fragments continue to orbit the sun as asteroids in the asteroid belt. This explains why some meteorites are iron (because they came from the core of the primitive planetesimals), some are stone (because they came from the surface), and some a mixture, called stony-iron. A few chunks of primitive solar system material never got incorporated into the planetesimals, and were thus entirely unchanged from the beginning. The Allende is such a meteorite.

We know that most meteorites come from the asteroid belt by observing their trajectories as they blaze through the atmosphere—if one extrapolates their orbits back to the farthest point, they almost always originate in the asteroid belt. Scientists believe that from time to time asteroids bump into each other in the belt and knock chunks of material toward the earth. These pieces strike the earth's atmosphere at the rapid clip of up to twenty-five miles per second, and the sudden shock usually causes the missile to explode in a fireball. If the chunk is too small, it merely burns up; if it is too large, it actually punches a hole through the atmosphere and hits the earth with such violence that it blasts a crater and vaporizes. Thus, only intermediate meteorites survive for our collection and study.

# EIGHTEEN

# Minerals and Gems

**B**eyond the meteorite exhibits, a doorway leads us into the Hall of Minerals and Gems. This hall contains what is perhaps the single most famous object in the American Museum: the Star of India, a golfball-sized star sapphire donated by J. P. Morgan around the turn of the century. Its history in Ceylon and India stretches back three centuries, although for unknown reasons the history was concealed by the man who actually procured the gem for Morgan.

According to George Harlow, a curator in the Mineral Sciences Department, the Star of India is probably worth on the order of one million dollars or more today. "But because it's unique," he explains, "it's worth whatever someone will pay. We wouldn't know that unless we tried to sell it, and we're not about to do that."

Besides the Star of India, there are several other unique gems in the Museum: the Padparadscha Sapphire from Sri Lanka, a deep orange stone weighing 100 carats, which

Harlow feels might be worth even more than the Star of India; the DeLong Star Ruby, the most famous star ruby in the world; and the 629-carat Patricia Emerald, one of the finest natural emerald crystals ever found.


## Murph the Surf

Any discussion of the Museum's gem collection must include the single most dramatic event in the collection's history: the great jewel robbery of 1964. At 9:00 A.M. on October 30 of that year, John Hoffman, senior attendant at the American Museum of Natural History, unlocked the heavy metal gate at the entrance to the old Morgan Hall of Gems (since replaced by the present hall). Instead of an orderly row of cases glittering with jewels, he found himself gazing upon a riot of broken glass and empty cases. Worst of all, the heavy glass cases that held the famous Star of India and several other superb gems had jagged holes in them, surrounded by adhesive tape.

When the police arrived and the Museum was able to take inventory, the extent of the loss became clear. In addition to three priceless stars the thieves had stolen an eighty-eight-carat engraved emerald, a huge emerald "easter egg" from seventeenth-century Russia, and a number of smaller emeralds; a 737-carat aquamarine; the fifteen-carat Eagle Diamond, and well over a hundred other rare faceted and natural diamonds. While the newspapers reported the loss at $400,000, Museum officials acknowledged that the true value of the stolen gems was incalculable. The Star of India alone was one of the most extraordinary jewels in the world. A rich blue star sapphire, it weighed 563.35 carats and was the largest such stone in the world. The 116.75-carat Midnight Star was equally remarkable for its deep bluish-purple tint; most star sapphires are a gray-blue or light blue color. The DeLong Star Ruby, weighing 100.32 carats, formed the third member of this priceless trio of gems.

Two men (as it later became known) masterminded the robbery: Jack Roland Murphy—better known as Murph the Surf—and Allan Dale Kuhn; a third man, Roger Frederick Clark, drove the getaway car.

Jack Murphy—who captured popular attention like no burglar since—was born in Los Angeles in 1937. His family moved frequently, and in 1957 he left his family's current home in Pittsburgh and headed for Miami Beach. The late fifties and early sixties were the heyday of Miami Beach, the glittery years before the decline set in. The beaches were lined with expensive hotels frequented by the jet set. There was plenty of work, especially for a seemingly charming, athletic young man like Murphy. Murphy became a beachboy. He worked for various hotels, became an expert surfer, and often found employment in stunt diving and water acrobatic shows. A beachboy's salary might be small, but the right type of person could pull down (in 1960 dollars) fifty to a hundred dollars a day in tips. And, of course, with so much loose money floating around, many of them supplemented their income with petty thefts. From his arrest record, it appears that Murphy specialized in jewels.

Murphy carried around business cards that had printed on them "Who Is Captain Kangaroo?" He was in perfect physical condition, and he always dressed impeccably. Pictures of him at the time reveal a strikingly handsome, deeply tanned young man, sporting sunglasses and slicked-back blond hair. Psychiatrists who later examined Murphy testified that he had an IQ of 139. He played the violin beautifully; one psychiatrist, Dr. Michael Gilbert, recalled in a recent interview that one day Murphy came over to his house for an evaluation. Gilbert had two violins, and Murphy asked if they could play together. They chose the Bach Double Concerto, an extremely difficult piece of music. "He played it just beautifully," Gilbert remembered. "He had perfect pitch, beautiful intonation, and a perfect ear." He was also, unfortunately, a brutal murderer and a psychopath as well as a thief.

In September of 1964, the three men, Murphy, Kuhn,

and Clark—who all lived in Miami Beach—decided to visit New York City to see the World's Fair. According to an account of the robbery written by Kuhn for *True* magazine, entitled "How We Stole the Star of India," they arrived in the city on September 19, 1964, and checked into a sixty-dollar-a-day suite of rooms at the Stanhope Hotel.* During the next few days they attended a movie called *Topkapi*, which had just been released. This film was about a jewel robbery at the Topkapi Palace Museum in Istanbul.

The plot of this movie contains striking similarities to the Museum theft. The prosecutor later alleged that this film had actually inspired the burglary, something the robbers never admitted. Later, by the way, Murphy himself became the subject of a movie, *Murph the Surf*, starring Robert Conrad in the role of Kuhn. They also visited the Guggenheim Museum, the Metropolitan Museum of Art, and—finally—the American Museum of Natural History.

Kuhn wrote in the article:

> From previous burglaries, I knew as soon as I entered the J. P. Morgan Hall of Gems and Minerals the first time on September 30 that it would be fairly simple to rob if there were anything worth taking. Little did I know just how much surrounded us. When we first saw the three big "stars" no one said a word. We just stood and stared. Then, as if it was timed, we all looked at each other as if to say—how much is this worth? Can it be done?

The three men checked out of the Stanhope (after spending about $2,000 there) and rented a large apartment on West 86th Street. Here they began planning the theft. "Jack said it couldn't be done," Kuhn wrote. "I said it

---

*The following description of the theft relies heavily on the *True* magazine article, and it should be pointed out that Kuhn had his own reasons for glamorizing the theft, as he was beginning negotiations with film producers at the time. The actor Robert Conrad helped Kuhn rewrite the article, and it was certainly to their advantage to make it as exciting as possible. There are accounts of what happened that do not agree in all details with the story presented here. In my opinion, however, Kuhn's is the most reliable, since it is a firsthand account written shortly after the robbery.

could and Roger wasn't sure." They decided to case the Museum first. They spent the following week wandering about the Museum, looking for exits and alarms, noting the routines of the guards, and spotting possible escape routes. They usually made two visits a day, one in the morning and another in the afternoon, after the guards had been changed. After ten days, they felt ready for a nighttime reconnaissance of the Museum—a dry run of the burglary.

With Clark driving their white Cadillac, the three men circled the Museum, scanning the structure's granite façade and looking for a route up. After parking and scouting around, they climbed onto a small roof along the 77th Street side of the Museum and edged out onto a ledge that ran along the second floor. On the corner of the building they encountered an area of rough-cut granite, which they were able to scale up as far as the fourth floor—the level of the Gem Hall—and a windowsill. To their surprise, Kuhn wrote, the window was unlocked.

> Inside the Museum, the silence was deafening. It didn't take me long to discover that the window we had used wouldn't do because I was still outside the big iron gate across the entrance to the gem room. Next time, we'd have to use another window. . . .
> While I waited I flashed my small light around through the gate into the gem room. It caught a jewel. It shined. I flashed it over some of the other cases and pretty soon I could barely keep myself from saying the hell with it and smashing the lock on the gate, grabbing what I could and running out.

Kuhn waited, hidden behind a case, and timed two rounds of the guard. The guard came at 9:17 and then again at 9:45—thirty minutes between rounds. As soon as the guard left, Kuhn went back to the window, where Murphy was waiting. Ten minutes later they were back in the Cadillac, on the way to their apartment.

The next day they returned to the Museum (dressed in

suits like young executives) to see if their visit had been discovered. Everything seemed normal. This time they noticed a ledge running along part of the fourth floor inside a Museum courtyard, and—incredibly enough—a steel ladder or fire escape running up to the ledge. They managed to find their way to the courtyard through an employees' exit. "The man in charge," Kuhn wrote, "asked what we were doing there and Jack replied, 'Looking for a way out.' I laughed to myself thinking the correct answer should have been 'Looking for a way in.'"

The setup couldn't have been better. The ladder was on the inside of the Museum, where they could ascend with little fear of discovery. It led to a wide, long ledge running under the fourth-floor windows. The entire area was concealed from the street.

Murphy had scraped and bruised his knees during the reconnaissance climb up the Museum, so they decided the jewels could wait for two weeks while he recovered. They piled into the Cadillac and left for Montreal that afternoon. "Gradually Jack's knees began to heal," Kuhn wrote, "and sure enough in no time we were out dancing and raising hell like our regular selves."

They returned to New York in late October, having worked out their plans and picked their tools. In various stores in the city they bought two small walkie-talkies with earphones, two glass-cutters, two flashlights, two pairs of sneakers (which they smeared with black shoe polish), two pairs of tight, dark pants, dark shirts, black socks, and black leather gloves, a screwdriver, two masks (in case they had to make a run for it past guards and out the building), two rolls of three-quarter-inch adhesive tape, and 125 feet of Manila rope. They also bought several sheets of glass to practice their glass-cutting, and were soon able to cut a hole in a vertical piece of glass nearly every time.

Finally they were ready. All that was necessary now was a rainy night, to cut down on the possibility of being seen (professional cat burglars know that people don't look up when it's raining.) When the morning of Thursday, October 19, came around and the weather report predicted possible showers, they chose that evening for the crime.

At 8:00 P.M., Clark dropped Murphy and Kuhn off near the Museum. The plan was for Clark to circle the Museum periodically while the other two stole the gems. Murphy and Kuhn ducked into some bushes on Museum grounds; when all seemed clear, they climbed an eight-foot fence that surrounded the Museum courtyard and ran, crouching, to the bottom of the ladder. Since the fourth-floor ledge didn't go around as far as the windows of the Gem Hall, they had to ascend to the fifth floor, where they tied a rope to a pillar and swung down to a fourth-floor ledge outside a Gem Hall window. "It was 8:30," wrote Kuhn, "in between the night guard's rounds. I heaved. The window opened six inches. I wanted to yell for joy."

They hid in the darkened hall, waiting for the guard to go by on his rounds. When he had passed, they began work on the cases.

The first cut was made on the corner of the case housing all the diamonds. The glass cutter made a "screeeeeee" noise similar to chalk on a blackboard. It sounded loud. . . . We stopped to listen. No one came running in, we heard no excited voices, so I began to scoop up everything through the hole. I passed everything to Jack and he wrapped each piece individually in tissue so it would not be damaged when they banged against each other in the bag.

Then our first problem. I realized I could reach only so far through the hole in the glass. While Jack continued wrapping I scouted around and in a janitor's cabinet I found a squeegee. It was perfect. With it, I reached into the case to scoop the pieces I could not reach before. Some were old cut diamonds, new cuts, uncut, and a small collection of color diamonds that were fairly rare and lovely.

Checking my watch, it showed 9:07 so we waited until the watchman came again. . . . We started for the case of emeralds. Again there was a wide assortment. . . . [After cutting] I reached into the case and came out with a round, shallow emerald weighing thirty

carats, full of flaws, but sellable. I brought out engraved emeralds that must have been hundreds of years
old. Not too valuable. As fast as I handed them to Jack
he was wrapping them in tissue paper. Now I had all the
emeralds. Two huge aquamarine stones, one weighing
over 800 carats [actually 400 carats] and the other
weighing over 1,000 carats [737 carats], were all that
remained. I took those, too. It had taken only ten minutes for all this so we went to the next case which held
the Star of India, the Midnight Star Sapphire, and the
DeLong Star Ruby. . . .

First I tied a piece of short string to the glass-cutter,
then by holding the other end to the pane of glass I
made the string taut and started to cut. It made a nearly
perfect circle.

While Jack taped the area around the hole with the
adhesive, I cut in the same way on the glass in front of
the Midnight Star. Both holes were about eight inches in
diameter. Jack began taping the glass almost as fast as I
cut the holes and in time they were all cut, taped and
ready to tap, but it was again nearing time for the
watchman again. We sat in silence, trying to hold our
breathing. . . .

The click of the punch clock and the rattling of the
gate echoed through the gem room, then the guard hur-
ried away to punch another clock beyond the door. We
gave him a full five minutes to get away, then we went
to the cases again. I whispered to Jack, "It's going to
make a hell of a noise, but here goes."

I whacked the glass with the steel-handled screwdriver. It sounded like a drum, trembled, but didn't
even crack. I hadn't hit it hard enough. We listened a
second. No noise. Then I took careful aim and clob-
bered it this time. That was the most noise yet. It literally rang through the halls of the Museum. Still, no one
apparently heard it. Jack and I went to the window,
looked out to see if it was still clear. It looked all
right. . . .

Jack's small flashlight was steady on the Star of
India, and it appeared more brilliant and full of fire than
it ever had in the daytime. The star was dead in the
center of the stone and the legs of the star were long and
extended to the bottom of it. Around the base was a

gum substance that the stone sat on. Probably to keep it steady in case someone jarred the case.

I hadn't picked the stone up, yet all of a sudden I experienced a wave of panic. Where was the alarm? I hesitated, then grabbed the Star and pulled it up away from the gum. Then I saw it. A needle. When I [had] lifted the stone the needle came up. There's the alarm. We didn't hear anything so we figured it was a silent alarm. But we both knew we had to get the hell out of there.

What they didn't know was that the alarm battery had gone dead—no alarm went off at all. But Murphy and Kuhn figured they had about five minutes to get clear of the building. While Murphy smashed the cases holding the Midnight Star and the DeLong Ruby, Kuhn grabbed the rope and swung out of the window. Murphy followed immediately after. Kuhn untied the rope and let it drop into the courtyard, and they clambered down a fire escape with their tools, then down the steel ladder. In five minutes they were out on Columbus Avenue, where they split up and took separate cabs.

Back in the apartment on 86th Street, they quickly stripped off their clothes and stuffed them, with their tools, into a pillowcase. Meanwhile, Clark, who had been circling the Museum block in the white Caddy, wondering where they were, arrived back at the apartment. "Where the hell have you two been," Kuhn reported him as saying, "and what are you doing running around naked?" But when he saw the three large stones, unwrapped, on the coffee table, "he let out a howl and we all laughed and began jumping around. Jack yelled, 'You said we could do it, Allan, and here it is!' He jumped on the couch like he was surfing," holding the Star of India to his forehead. They waited several hours, listening to the radio for a news bulletin about the robbery, but when nothing was reported they went to sleep. At seven-thirty the next morning they awoke and eagerly switched on the radio, but still there was no news of the robbery.

At eight o'clock an unnamed "friend" arrived to pick up the gems, according to Kuhn's account. "We shook hands," Kuhn wrote, "and I gave him the package and that was the last I saw of the Star of India. The entire lot would be looked over thoroughly, I knew, and a price would be offered."

As planned, Murphy and Kuhn boarded a flight to Miami that morning. Kuhn took along a girl he had met in New York, Janet Florkiewicz. (While waiting for the plane, they disposed of all their clothes and equipment in various wastebaskets around Kennedy Airport.) In Miami they went to Kuhn's plush apartment. By that time the news wires were humming with reports of the spectacular heist. They turned on the TV and listened to the news. To their great consternation, they learned that the alarm had been dead. "It was all a shock to Jack and me," Kuhn wrote, "for only now we realized that all the jewels we left behind could have been scooped up too."

They spent the evening watching TV. The next day, Kuhn went out for a walk at 10:00 A.M. When he returned, he found the door to his apartment ajar. As he entered, FBI agents grabbed him and he was handcuffed alongside Murphy, while the agents tore apart the apartment looking for the gems. At the same time, Clark had been arrested in New York City. Janet Florkiewicz was also detained as a material witness, because the police thought she might have carried the gems in her handbag on the Miami flight. Apparently someone in their apartment building in New York had overheard an indiscreet comment by one of the two on the elevator, and had tipped off the police.

Of the three, the press latched on to Murphy. His off-hand comments and allegedly glamorous beachboy life-style made for great newspaper copy, and his suave, handsome demeanor and impeccably tailored suits brought a lot of attention from the five-o'clock news.*

---

*Even his release from jail on a later charge in December 1984 — twenty years later — merited front-page news in New York City.

Various hearings and legal maneuverings followed their arrest. Finally, on January 7, Kuhn decided to cooperate with the police in hopes of a reduced sentence, and the two others followed suit. He led them to a locker in a Greyhound bus terminal in Miami. In two waterproof bags they found the Star of India and the Midnight Star, as well as some of the larger emeralds. Still missing were the DeLong Star Ruby and all of the diamonds. On April 6, Murphy, Clark, and Kuhn were sentenced to three years at the Rikers Island Correctional Facility in New York.

The recovery of the ruby proved to be difficult, and much of the details remain secret to this day. Apparently members of the underworld had possession of the ruby, and informed the Museum that it would be returned for ransom. After ten months of involved negotiations between the shadowy people who possessed the gem, a jeweler, and a Florida judge, a ransom price of $25,000 was agreed upon. The billionaire insurance executive John D. MacArthur donated the money to pay the ransom. MacArthur and a photographer and a reporter from the New York *Daily News* were present when the gem was retrieved. Following directions, they arrived at a Miami telephone booth, where, over the phone, they were told to rip a hole in the ceiling of the booth. The voice on the phone directed them to reach into a cavity in the ceiling. There they found the DeLong Ruby. The diamonds, being less unique and able to be fenced and recut, were never recovered, and today they probably decorate many wealthy women's rings and necklaces.

Several years later, the three were released from Rikers Island. Immediately following his release, Murphy was hauled back to Florida to face charges that he pistol-whipped the actress Eva Gabor and made off with her $25,000 diamond ring. (The charges were dropped when Gabor failed to show up for the trial.) Murphy and Kuhn were arrested shortly thereafter for other jewel thefts, but this time the charges were dropped for lack of evidence. In 1968, however, Murphy was caught in a spectacular shoot-out with police while robbing a Miami Beach mansion; he tried unsuccessfully to elude capture by catapulting himself through a plate-glass window. The judge in this trial declared him insane. But then, less than a year later, Murphy was arrested on another charge—double murder. In December 1967, the bludgeoned and mutilated bodies of two Los Angeles secretaries had been discovered in Florida. The two women had stolen nearly half a million dollars in negotiable securities from a brokerage firm, and had turned them over to Murphy to sell. In a dispute over their payment while aboard Murphy's boat, Murphy and an accomplice had murdered them, tied their bodies to cement blocks, and dumped them in a creek. When the tide went out, a boater spotted the foot of one of the women bobbing on the surface.

The judge rejected an insanity defense for Murphy, and he was sentenced to two life terms for the double murder. While in prison, Murphy became a born-again Christian. On December 21, 1984, he was released from prison before a cheering crowd of twenty-five inmates, who held up a sign saying "Goodbye Jack, We'll Miss You." He told reporters, "I'm not the same person that came in here a long time ago." MURPH SURFACES: "MY TAB IS PAID" screamed the headlines of the New York *Daily News* the day after his release. Twenty years after Murphy pocketed the Star of India in the Museum one night, he was still big news. At the time of this writing, he is working at the Christian Prison Ministries, a halfway house in Orlando, where he is enrolled in a work-release program.

## A Cave of Gems

Entering the new Hall of Minerals and Gems is like entering a fabulous cave. The floor and walls are covered with thick brown carpeting. Everything is dark except the specimens themselves, which are set off by brilliant spotlight illumination. It is a far cry from the old Morgan Hall of Murph the Surf's days. One notable difference is that the security system is now as sophisticated as modern technology allows—so sensitive, according to popular rumor, that at night the occasional cockroach used to set off the alarms until they were finally adjusted to be a bit less reactive. Of course, the Museum will not discuss security in the hall except to say that is it virtually impenetrable.

We can see the recovered Star of India and its two legendary companions in the new Morgan Hall of Gems, glowing under a softly focused spotlight, their six-rayed stars seemingly following the viewer's eye. Asterism in sapphires is caused by the needlelike mineral rutile. The rutile inclusions are oriented in three directions parallel to each crystal face of the sapphire. If the stone is cut properly, three rays of white light cross it, producing a six-pointed star.

The histories of many of the Museum's most famous stones are sketchy or unknown. Although we know the Star of India was discovered in Ceylon some three centuries ago, we know nothing about its history until it was given to the Museum. "This isn't an uncommon situation," says Joe Peters, scientific assistant in the Museum's Department of Mineral Sciences. "Most dealers don't want to reveal their sources. Perhaps they just want to avoid competition." Peters guesses the Star of India may have come from an Indian nobleman who sold it anonymously to pay off some debts. The procurer of the Star of India, George Frederick Kunz, merely reports that it "has a historical record of three hundred years." He makes no further mention of how he obtained it or what its history might be.

Peters explains that most valuable minerals and gems are found by miners and smuggled out. "Many of our better specimens," he said, "might have originally been illegally obtained—brought out in some miner's lunch pail, perhaps. While we're not thrilled to acquire stones with no history, so to speak, we do feel it's our duty to preserve them if they are important pieces."

Any museum that acquires minerals and gems must, of necessity, work with dealers, some of whom are keeping their sources secret, and the museum must accept stones without knowing where they came from. "Right now,"

Peters says, "we're getting some extraordinary gem-quality crystals from Pakistan. The dealers may be keeping their sources top secret. It may be because they are worried about competition, or it may be that they are getting their crystals from miners."

The Museum's original mineral and gem collection is the result of a happy marriage between the money of J.P. Morgan and the expertise of George Frederick Kunz, Tiffany's first gem expert. Kunz was an early pioneer of gem and mineral collecting, and by 1889 he had assembled a collection of American gems so fabulous that it won a grand prize at the Paris Exposition. In 1890, Morgan bought the entire collection for the Museum. (This collection included the fine series of American diamonds stolen by Murph the Surf and never recovered.) In 1900, Kunz completed the acquisition of a splendid collection of foreign gems for Morgan, which the millionaire also donated to the Museum. These two collections together included— among much else—2,442 natural pearls, a group of 166 splendid sapphires, a dozen rubies, 13 emeralds, 57 beryls, 30 aquamarines, 92 tourmalines, 70 topazes, 24 diamonds, and hundreds of amethysts, gem quartzes, garnets, opals, ancient carved stones, Babylonian cylinder seals, ambers, spodumenes, jades, turquoises, and moonstones.

In 1901, Morgan bought and donated to the Museum the Bement collection of minerals, which even today is considered one of the finest private mineral collections ever assembled. The collection, which reportedly cost $100,000—in 1901 dollars!—consisted of 12,000 minerals and 580 meteorites. Several railroad cars were required to haul it to the Museum.

Although much of Kunz' collection took place among the backrooms of dealers, he often went into the field himself. He had an uncanny ability to locate extraordinary specimens where others had less success. One of his most impressive pieces is the Great Jade Mass from Jordansmuhl, Silesia (now in Poland), which is on display near the center of the hall, with one side cut and polished.

At the time this specimen was discovered by Kunz in

1890, there existed among German scholars a controversy called the *Nephritfrage*, or "nephrite [jade] question."* For many years, archeologists had been turning up worked and unworked jades of the nephrite type from the refuse heaps and dwellings of the Swiss "Lake Dwellers," a prehistoric European people. Raw jade had also been found scattered about in various areas, but none *in situ*—that is, actually embedded in native rock. The question was, where did the jade come from? The earliest "theory" for the origin of European jade was that these pieces were frozen thunderbolts. Later, standard scholarly opinion held that the jade had been bartered by nomadic Asiatic tribes, and that there was no indigenous scource of jade in Europe. Late in the nineteenth century, however, one heretical scholar, a Dr. Meyer, asserted that the jade *was* indigenous to Europe. The *Nephritfrage* was born, and raged in the pages of obscure journals as only a German academic question could.

In 1890, Kunz was traveling across Germany, assembling a collection of historic jades for the Herber Bishop collection (now at the Metropolitan Museum of Art). Being sympathetic to Meyer's theory, he decided to try his luck at finding a source of the jade *in situ*. Kunz made a side trip to Jordansmuhl, then in Germany, where occasional pieces of loose and unworked jade had been found. With a colleague named Dr. Hintze and two assistants, Kunz took a train to the small village. Once there, he looked up Karl von Kreigsheim, a local landowner on whose land loose pieces of jade had been found. Both Hintze and Kreigsheim thought Kunz was a little mad to expect to find—in one day—an example of *in situ* jade that had eluded fortune seekers and scientists for years. It promised to be a fearsome task—especially since all the rock in that area had a greenish tint that made it almost indistinguishable from raw jade. Kunz wrote later in *The Saturday Evening Post*:

> At eleven o'clock, four hours after we began operations, I came across a peculiar protuberance on one side

*There are two varieties of jade: nephrite and jadeite.

of a ledge of rock—green like the rock, but to me, even at first glance subtly different. . . . I soon realized that I had come upon a piece of jade of incredible dimensions. When it was finally lifted out of the embedding rock it was found to be by far the largest piece of jade ever discovered *in situ* anywhere in the world.*

The giant slab measured eight feet by five feet by one and a half feet, and it weighed 4,700 pounds—nearly two and a half tons. Indeed, there was more jade in this single piece than in all European jade found up to that time. The *Nephritfrage* was settled in one decisive blow, which, Kunz noted with satisfaction, ruined the career of more than one German scholar. Von Kreigsheim insisted that the jade was Kunz's by right of discovery, and gave him the specimen.

Unpolished jade looks like ordinary rock (which is one reason this piece had previously eluded discovery), and the Museum was able to store the stone safely in its backyard, unprotected, for several years before space could be found in the mineral hall. Later, one side of the slab was polished at Tiffany's—no small feat, considering jade's extreme hardness.

Another of Kunz's great coups was procuring some extraordinary Russian amethysts from under the nose of the Czarevitch Nicholas II, who was rumored to want them himself. Before the turn of the century, Kunz made a mineralogical trip through the Ural Mountains. On this trip he met Dr. Clerc, founder of a Russian museum, who invited him on a trip through the steppes to gather gems.

During his trip, Kunz picked up some extremely valuable stones collected by peasants. The area was noted for its gems, and before the planting of the spring crops the peasants would scour the land, looking for occasional gemstones washed out by the spring rains. "As soon as our arrival in a village," Kunz wrote, "the peasants, having heard I was a collector of gems, would come to me with their hoarded treasures. . . . Wrapped in dirty bits of rag,

---

*Since then, a fifty-ton jade boulder has been discovered in Alaska.

stuffed into an old stocking, stowed away in some broken bit of crockery with a lot of worthless odds and ends that their presence in the house might not be suspected, they were brought to me in great secrecy."

In particular, there was one famous old peasant women who possessed a quantity of allegedly "perfect" amethysts found on her property. She had already presented five to the Czarina, and it was rumored that Nicholas II wanted the rest. Kunz wrote:

At last I approached the vicinity where dwelt the woman reputed to possess the famous amethysts and, meeting a peasant on the road, I inquired where she lived. He grinned broadly.

"Akh, the Czarina, you mean?"

"No, she who sent the amethysts to the Czarina."

He waved his hand, still grinning. "Yes, it is the Czarina you want—the Czarina Ujakova. She it is who sent the amethysts to the great Czarina." Then he came closer and with a shrewd wink observed, "You see, she is not stupid, that Ujakova. Her amethysts were fit for an empress, and so she sent them to the Empress of all the Russias. But we know her—that Ujakova. Did she expect nothing in return for those great amethysts, big as bantam's eggs, and purple as the hills at sunset?" He leaned impressively nearer. "She expected a title, no less—a rich gift and a title. That is what she was after. And what did she get?" He slapped his knees, doubled up with mirth. "All she got was a brass samovar, and not a sign of a title! But we are more generous—we, her neighbors. We gave her a title. We call her the Czarina Ujakova." And he almost touched the earth in the extremity of his mirth.

But when the so-called Czarina stood before me, barefoot, red and blown from her bake pans, I had some difficulty in believing that she was worth $100,000, let alone the possessor of some of the finest amethysts in the world.

I had seen beautiful amethysts in my day, but when these gems, dragged from beneath a mattress, were poured out before me from the depths of an old stocking

I gasped. Not one, but a dozen perfect gems, of a color found nowhere else in the world, none less than an inch in diameter, all sparkling on the rough table before me in a little pool of light from the low window.

Kunz tried to hide his excitement from the "sharp-eyed peasant woman, wary as a fox." After a long bargaining session he acquired six of the stones, having paid "every ruble they were worth." One of the finest—a grape-purple gem, one and a half inches in diameter—went to the Morgan collection and is on display in the hall, in the large gem case along the back wall.

One of Kunz' last gifts to the Museum was a huge ten-pound garnet that was discovered during the excavation of a sewer at 35th Street and Broadway. According to Kunz, it was the finest large garnet ever found in the United States and the most valuable mineral to have been found in New York City.

Since Kunz' day, the Museum has continued to acquire extraordinary specimens. One of the most spectacular on display in the hall is in fact a world record. It came from Allan Caplan, a gem dealer in New York City, who has brought in many of the Museum's precious stones. As a young man, Caplan traveled to Brazil as a free-lance collector, and brought out extraordinary museum-quality specimens from the rich mines of the interior. On one of his first trips to the mineralogically unexplored inner fastness of Brazil, he passed through Belo Horizonte, where a local collector offered him a six-pound, colorless topaz crystal. Not knowing much about topazes, he declined to buy it, as the price seemed high. However, when he got back to the States and asked about its value, he was told that such a crystal couldn't exist; no large, clear topaz with crystal faces had ever been found. When Caplan returned to Brazil he purchased the stone, and later resold it to a curator at the Academy of Natural Sciences in Philadelphia.

On his next visit to Brazil, a quartz crystal dealer in Rio astonished Caplan by showing him two giant topaz crystals, one weighing 100 pounds and the other 156 pounds.

Caplan bought them immediately and resold them, one to the Smithsonian and the other to the Cranbrook Institute, near Detroit. News of the finds traveled fast, and several wealthy museums approached Caplan to see if he could get them big topaz crystals as well. The Harvard Mineralogical Museum asked Caplan first, and so it was given first choice of any new specimens. The American Museum of Natural History was given second choice.

Sure enough, on his next trip to Brazil, the quartz dealer—a man named Carmo—showed Caplan photographs of three almost impossibly large topaz crystals he had obtained somewhere in the interior of the country. He explained that they were being shipped to Rio on a freight train, and that it would take weeks for them to arrive. "He told me," Caplan said in an interview in the *Mineralogical Record*, "that he had to wrap them with vines, because he had neither nails or lumber, and it was quite a job to get them to the railroad. The locality was not mentioned, nor did I ask for it." Caplan bought the three on the basis of the photos, and signed the bill of sale, as he had to return to the United States before the crystals would arrive at the Brazilian coast.

"Then I sweated in New York," Caplan recalled, "hoping to hear about those crystals, but it was some months before I even got a letter from Carmo." Carmo explained that he was having trouble exporting them, because the Brazilian government officials felt they were too valuable to be allowed to leave the country. After some maneuverings, permission was granted, and the three stones were shipped to New York.

Finally the crystals arrived, and Caplan hastened down to the customs office for the opening of the crates. They weighed an incredible 225 pounds, 300 pounds, and 596 pounds respectively—all the more remarkable, considering that only a few years earlier a six-pound topaz crystal had been unprecedented. When they pried off the top of the crate holding the biggest crystal, Caplan was horrified to find himself looking on a jagged mass of rough topaz—the crystal had no termination (crystal point). "Well, I really got clipped here," Caplan said; either he had been cheated or the crystal had broken in transit. The three crates were resealed and moved to the Museum. When they were actually uncrated, Caplan realized that the customs officials had opened the big crate upside down, and that he had been looking at the butt end of the crystal. When turning right side up, it had a lovely, symmetrical termination.

Harvard was notified, and a curator came down to New York to make the first choice. "There was no doubt in my mind," Caplan said, "that [Harvard] would pick the biggest one, but to my surprise they preferred the 225-pound crystal because of its slightly better quality." So the American Museum got the 596-pounder, by far the largest topaz crystal in existence and, indeed, one of the largest crystals of any kind. In gem terms, the crystal weighs over 1,350,000 carats.

The Caplan topaz sits in the middle of the Mineral Hall, illuminated from below and through the stone; it gives off a gentle amber glow, tinged with blue. According to George Harlow, curator in the Museum's Mineral Sciences Department, if it were to be cut into gemstones, the resulting gems would be colorless; assuming a 10-percent yield (that is, assuming that only 10 percent of the crystal would yield gem-quality stones), the crystal would result in 135,292 carats of gemstones.

We end our exploration of minerals and gems with a brief look at the Newmont Azurite. This mineral, like the Star of India, is unique. Considered by many to be the finest non-gem mineral specimen in existence, it was appraised some time ago at a quarter of a million dollars. Its perfect crystals sprout from a greenish lump of copper ore. The larger crystals are of the deepest, richest blue—so blue that they look black at first glance. They are also perfect, and arranged in what is considered to be an exceptionally pleasing pattern.

The stone came from Tsumeb, Namibia, in Southwest Africa, home to mines that are owned by the Newmont Mining Corporation. Azurite is usually associated with copper, and it was discovered by one of the miners in a

Newmont copper mine, who managed to sneak it out undiscovered. The miner had run up a rather large bar bill at the local tavern (perhaps five or ten dollars), and he offered the tavernkeeper the stone as payment. A local Newmont official learned of the mineral, and arranged to buy it back from the tavern keeper.

The Newmont Azurite eventually made its way to the Newmont corporate headquarters in New York, where it was casually put on display. About ten years ago the company called in a dealer to appraise the azurite and several other interesting specimens that had come out of their mines. When the dealer told them the rock was worth $250,000, Newmont officials realized it was far too valuable to keep around the office, and they generously donated it to the Museum. Along with the Newmont Azurite came another office specimen, a huge mass of crystallized gold found at a company mine in California in a mud-filled pocket. This specimen was also valued at a quarter-million and is on display in the hall.

## From Siberia, with Love

The Mineral Hall and the Meteorite Hall represent either extreme of the Museum's reach, the terrestrial and the extraterrestrial. Here we have come full circle, from animate to inanimate creation, and our tour is at an end.

This magnificent granite pile, this Museum on the west side of Central Park, between two rivers, in the New World, holds between its walls perhaps the greatest single collection of natural and man-made things ever assembled. The only consistent criterion for including something in this collection has been whether it "meant" something—whether it included the necessary documentation required for future study. Since it is impossible to know exactly what information might be needed at some future time, the Museum has tended to collect and save everything. An isolated piece of rock, or a fish in a jar with no label, is valueless for the Museum's purpose, except perhaps as an object of beauty. Objects discovered in the collection with no associated information are usually thrown out.

It is this massive body of information, this invisible collection, that we have tried to chronicle in this book. Having begun our journey with an obscure production of nature, the beetle *Bambara intricata*, we will end it, rather arbitrarily, in front of an equally obscure production of humanity, exhibited in a case in the Hall of Asian Peoples. It is a small scrap of birchbark tied on one end to a red ribbon, and covered with incised geometrical designs. This scrap is actually a letter—a love letter—written by two girls of the Yukaghir, a now-extinct people who once lived in northeastern Siberia, near the shores of the Arctic Ocean. The letter, which was directed to the anthropologist Waldemar Jochelson, is written in a pictographic language that is similar to an early stage in the development of our own alphabetic system, and that may hold important clues to the development of writing in general. It is believed to be the only genuine Yukaghir love letter in existence, although a number of copies of Yukaghir love letters can be seen in Leningrad.

The letter is an unusual example of the misunderstandings that can sometimes arise between anthropologists and the people they study. The letter had languished in an anthropology storeroom for nearly eighty years before it was "rediscovered" by Cynthia Wilder, an assistant in the Anthropology Department, during the preparations for the Hall of Asian Peoples.

Of all the tribes Jochelson studied in Siberia, he felt a particular fondness for the Yukaghir. Jochelson saw them as a mild-mannered people who believed in honesty, kindness, and hospitality and abhorred rudeness, foul language, and personal violence. These qualities resulted in their being exploited and abused by the cossacks, by Russian settlers, and especially by the local priests, and further contributed, Jochelson felt, to the rapid decline and eventual assimilation of Yukaghir culture.

The love letter is one of thousands of artifacts Jochelson saved from the Yukaghir, some of which are on display in the Siberian section of the Hall of Asian Peoples. The history of the love letter is curious. Jochelson received it during his first stay with the Yukaghir in 1895 and 1896, shortly after he had been exiled to Siberia by the Czarist government for his revolutionary activities. He had two companions on this trip, a Yukaghir interpreter named Alexander Dolganoff and a cossack guide.

While the Yukaghir frowned on immodesty and were very bashful in discussing sexual matters, there was considerable freedom in relations between the sexes. Virginity was not important to the Yukaghir, and most girls set up their own tents at puberty and quietly began receiving lovers. One custom in Yukaghir society was to provide an unmarried girl to any man who was away from his wife. A father would normally offer his daughter's bed to a visiting man as a matter of hospitality. If the man was important, the daughter would consider it an honor to share her bed with him. However, it was completely up to the girl whether she had sex with the man. If she found him objectionable, she was perfectly free to "leave her loincloth on," as the Yukaghir proverb went.

Jochelson spent his first four months among the Yukaghir learning their language in the house of a tribal elder, who lived near the Yassachna River. The elder and his wife had an adopted daughter of about seventeen or eighteen years of age. As soon as Jochelson settled in, he noticed that the usual nightly visits of young men to the girl had ceased. After a while, the wife of the elder seemed puzzled by Jochelson's sexual abstinence. She said, "It seems that among you, men can live without wives." Jochelson explained that where he came from, a married man was supposed to remain faithful to his wife, even when he was away for a long time. The woman replied, "Well, it seems that the Russians here have different customs. They go to other girls and wives, even when they have their own wives with them." Later his interpreter, Dolganoff, told him that the elder's adopted daughter was very offended by the fact that Jochelson had not visited her, as was the custom for a male guest in her parents' house.

That summer, at a camp near the Yassachna River, Jochelson wrote, a similar misunderstanding occurred with the same tribe:

In this village lived the blacksmith Shaluguin, an old Yukaghir, who had a large family, among them several daughters. The youngest was considered to be the prettiest on the river Yassachna. For a long time I intended to take her photograph in holiday dress, and meant to do it before my departure; but, as she was then staying with her relatives in another settlement, I asked the old man to send a boat for her. In spite of the fact that I explained to the old man who I wanted his daughter for, my request was understood in another way. The girl arrived late in the evening, and I put off taking the photograph till the next morning. My canvas tent was standing near the skin tent of Shaluguin. Imagine my astonishment next morning when, stepping out of my tent, I noticed between it and that of Shaguluin a separate small tent, which the girl was just then taking away! She was in a very angry mood, and my photographs were not successful. Afterwards my interpreter told me that the young men laughed at the girl for having uselessly put up a separate tent.

When Jochelson left the Yassachna River, the two spurned Yukaghir girls wrote him the love letter together. It told the story of their frustrated romance with the anthropologist and, according to Jochelson, was given to him with no trace of jealousy or bad feeling.

In the Yukaghir love letter, people are represented by thin decorated lines. Jochelson is depicted standing in front of his house. He occupies a position of status, as evidenced by the tallness of the character. On either side of him appear the two jilted Yukaghir girls. Both send passionate thoughts to him — shown as two faint lines emanating from the tops of their heads. But Jochelson rejects their love, as indicated by the two lines turning back in a series of squiggles. Two figures appearing on the far left and right are Jochelson's interpreter, Dolganoff, and the cossack guide. The two girls point out, using crossed designs, that they achieved more satisfying relationships with them.

Jochelson kept this letter in his personal collection and later was not able to locate any similar examples. By 1901 and 1902, when he returned to the Yukaghir on a trip sponsored by the American Museum, drastic changes had already taken place. The tribe had been decimated by disease and starvation, and Jochelson spent much of his time trying to get medical supplies, food, and assistance to them. In the face of overwhelming change and misfortune, the Yukaghir had abandoned many of their traditional customs, including, it seems, the practice of writing love letters. In his ethnography, *The Yukaghir*, published by the Museum in 1910, Jochelson speculated on the future of the tribe:

> The Yukaghir, who in the past, according to all collected information, were a fairly numerous tribe, at the present time consist...of a few hundred people scattered in small groups over an enormous area, which groups are dying out rapidly....This tribe is therefore on the verge of complete physical and ethnic extinction.
>
> The study of the tribe...insignificant in numbers and having no future—was a difficult and, from a practical point of view, a thankless task. But the science of ethnology recognizes that a knowledge of small tribes is equally as important as that of great peoples. In fact... information about the life and history of a tribe which is becoming extinct is particularly important.

Jochelson's statement can be generalized to embrace all the collections in the Museum. This birchbark love letter may seem to a casual visitor to be like any other obscure thing in the Museum. Its label copy gives little indication of the story behind it. And yet, like the love letter, each object in the Museum—just as in the world at large—carries with it a rich and secret lode of history, of information, and of meaning.

# Conclusion

This is as good a point as any to end our armchair tour of the Museum. Let us now ascend to the fifth floor curatorial offices, where a spiral staircase takes us to the sixth floor and the old Animal Behavior Department. From there, a short stair leads to the Museum's roof—the roof where this book began. From this viewpoint we can look over the Museum's jumble of walls, roofs, and turrets that enclose and protect its fabulous collection. Somewhere below us is *Bambara intricata*, the featherwing beetle; Meshie the chimpanzee; the Copper Man; the great dinosaurs; gold and gems, spears and graveposts—in short, the greatest natural history and anthropology collection ever assembled.

Museum personnel will come and go, papers will be published and debated, new exhibitions will be constructed and old ones closed. New wings will be built, storage areas will be renovated, and data will be entered and retrieved from large computers. Discoveries will be made, new hypotheses will be proposed, and scientists will venture forth to return with even more materials for study. But the collections—the *real* Museum—will remain forever.

# Selected Bibliography

Akeley, Carl E. *The Autobiography of a Taxidermist*. The World's Work. Vol. XLI, No. 2, 1920.

Akeley, Carl E. *In Brightest Africa*. Garden City: Doubleday & Co., 1923.

Akeley, Mary L. Jobe. Unpublished journals. Rare Book Room, American Museum of Natural History.

Akeley, Mary L. Jobe, *Carl Akeley's Africa*. New York: Dodd Mead & Co., 1929.

Allen, Joel Asaph. *Autobiographical Notes and a Bibliography of the Scientific Publications*. New York, 1916.

American Museum Journal, 1900–1918. New York: American Museum of Natural History.

American Museum of Natural History, *Annual Reports*, 1869–. New York: American Museum of Natural History.

American Museum Novitiates, 1923–. New York: American Museum of Natural History.

American Museum of Natural History. *Central Asiatic Expeditions, Preliminary Reports. Vol. 1 1918–1925. Vol. 2 1926–1929*. New York.

American Museum of Natural History. Science Guides, Nos. 1–137, 1901–1958.

Andrews, Roy Chapman. Unpublished field journals, Central Asiatic Expedition, 1919–1930. Rare Book Room, American Museum of Natural History.

Andrews, Roy Chapman. *Ends of the Earth*. New York: G.P. Putnam's Sons, 1929.

Andrews, Roy Chapman. *On the Trail of Ancient Man*. New York: G.P Putnam's Sons, 1929.

Andrews, Roy Chapman, et. al. *The New Conquest of Central Asia*. New York, American Museum of Natural History, 1932.

Anthropological Papers of the American Museum of Natural History, 1907–. New York.

Barber, Lynn. *The Heyday of Natural History, 1820–1870*. Garden City: Doubleday & Co., 1980.

Bickmore, Albert S. *An Autobiography with a Historical Sketch of the Founding and Early Development of the American Museum of Natural History*. Unpublished MS, Rare Book Room, American Museum of Natural History.

Bird, Junius B. *The "Copper Man": A Prehistoric Miner and His Tools from Northern Chile*. Washington, D.C.: Dumbarton Oaks Conference on Pre-Columbian Metallurgy of South America, 1975.

Boas, Franz. *Kwakiutl Culture as Reflected in Mythology*. Memoirs of the Folk-Lore Society, Vol. 28, 1935.

Boas, Franz. *Race, Language and Culture*. New York: MacMillan, 1940.

Boas, Franz. *Arctic Exploration and Its Object*. Unbound octavo pamphlet, n.d. American Museum of Natural History.

Burden, W. Douglas. *Dragon Lizards of Komodo*. New York: G.P. Putnam's Sons, 1927.

Brown, Barnum. *Collected Papers*. Volume 1 & 2. (Collections of papers published in many journals, magazines, and monographs. New York: Assembled by the American Museum of Natural History. 1897–1944.)

Brown, William Adams. *Morris Ketchum Jesup, A Character Sketch*. New York: Privately printed, 1910.

Bulletin of the American Museum of Natural History. New York: American Museum of Natural History, 1881–.

Chapman, Frank M. *Biographical Memoir Joel Asaph Allen.* Memoirs of the National Academy of Sciences, Vol. XXI, Washington, D.C.: 1927.

Chapman, Frank M. *Autobiography of a Bird Lover.* New York: D. Appleton–Century Co., 1933.

Curator Quarterly. New York: American Museum of Natural History, 1958–.

Dybas, Henry S. *Two New Genera of Feather-Wing Beetles from the Eastern United States.* Chicago: Field Museum of Natural History, 1961.

Gratacap, Louis P. *The History of the American Museum of Natural History.* Unpublished MS, Rare Book Room, American Museum of Natural History, n.d.

Green, Fitzhugh. Field journal 1913–1915. Crocker Land Expedition. Unpublished, Rare Book Room, American Museum of Natural History.

Green, Fitzhugh. *Arctic Duty with the Crocker Land Expedition.* Proceedings of the United States Naval Institute, Vol. 43, Nos. 175–178; Vol. 44, No. 179. Washington, D.C.: 1914–1918.

Hellman, Geoffrey. *Bankers, Bones and Beetles: The First Century of the American Museum of Natural History.* Garden City: The Natural History Press, 1968.

Henson, Matthew A. *A Negro Explorer at the North Pole.* New York: Frederick A. Stokes, n.d.

Jochelson, Waldemar. *Peoples of Asiatic Russia.* New York: American Museum of Natural History, 1928.

Jochelson, Waldemar. *The Yukaghir and the Yukaghirized Tungus.* New York: American Museum of Natural History, 1910.

Kennedy, John Michael. *Philanthropy and Science in New York City: The American Museum of Natural History.* New Haven: Unpublished Dissertation from Yale University, 1968.

Kinsey, Alfred C. *The Origin of the Higher Category in Cynips.* Bloomington: Indiana University Publications, Science Series No. 4, 1936.

Kuhn, Allen Dale. "How We Stole the Star of India." *True* magazine, 1965.

*Lapidary Journal.* Los Angeles: 1947–.

MacMillan, Donald B. Field journal and geographical reports.

Unpublished, Rare Book Room, American Museum of Natural History, 1914–1919.

MacMillan, Donald B. *Four Years in the White North.* New York: Harper and Bros., 1918.

MacMillan, Donald B. "In Search of a New Land." *Harper's Magazine*, Vol. CXXXI, Nos. 785–786, 1915.

Memoirs of the American Museum of Natural History. New York, 1893–1930.

*Mineralogical Record.* Bowie, MD: 1970–.

Morden, William James. *Across Asia's Snows and Deserts.* New York: G.P. Putnam's Sons, 1927.

*Natural History* magazine, 1919–. New York: American Museum of Natural History.

Osborn, Henry Fairfield. *Collected Papers*, 1877–1933. (Assembled from various sources, bound by the American Museum of Natural History.)

Osborn, Henry Fairfield. *Cope: Master Naturalist.* Princeton: Princeton University Press, 1931.

Ostrom, John H. and John S. McIntosh. *Marsh's Dinosaurs: The Collections from Como Bluff.* New Haven and London: Yale University Press, 1966.

Peary, Josephine Diebitsch. *My Arctic Journal.* New York: Contemporary Publishing Co., 1893.

Peary, Robert E. Log book on board the S.S. *Hope* from St. Johns to Greenland commanded by Capt. John Bartlett, commencing July 10, 1896, on unsuccessful voyage by Robert E. Peary to secure the meteorite Ahnighito. Rare Book Room, American Museum of Natural History, 1896.

Peary, Robert E. *Northward Over the Great Ice.* New York: Frederick A. Stokes, 1896.

Peary, Robert E. "The Value of Arctic Exploration." *National Geographic* magazine, 1903.

Perkins, John. *To the Ends of the Earth.* New York: Pantheon Books, 1981.

Rothschild, Miriam. *Dear Lord Rothschild.* Balaban, 1983.

Shapiro, Harry L. *Peking Man.* New York: Simon and Schuster, 1975.

Shor, Elizabeth Noble. *The Fossil Feud.* Hicksville, N.Y.: Exposition Press, 1974.

Sternberg, Charles H. *The Life of a Fossil Hunter.* New York: Henry Holt and Company, 1909.

Sternberg, Charles H. *Hunting Dinosaurs on Red Deer River, Alberta, Canada*. Lawrence, Kansas: The World Company Press, 1917.

Sternberg, Charles H. *Collected Papers* 1902–1928. Sternberg, George F. *Collected Papers*, 1930–1958. (From many sources, assembled and bound by the American Museum of Natural History.)

Sternberg, Charles M. and R.M. Sternberg. *Collected Papers*. (Collection of papers from many sources. New York: assembled by the American Museum of Natural History, 1937–1966.)

Sternberg, Charles M. *Collected Papers*. (Collection of papers from many sources. New York: assembled by the American Museum of Natural History, 1921–1938).

Sternberg, Charles M. *The Story of the Past*. Boston: Sherman, French & Company, 1911.

Ternes, Alan., ed. *Ants, Indians, and Little Dinosaurs*. New York: Charles Scribner's Sons, 1975.

# Index

295

# About the Author

Douglas J. Preston worked at the American Museum of Natural History for seven years, most recently as Manager of Publications. He was author of a monthly column on the Museum in *Natural History* magazine, as well as managing editor of *Curator* magazine. Mr. Preston resides in New York City, where he continues to work in publishing.

# FACT
## *is stranger than*
# FICTION

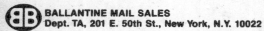